The Art of For

The Art of Forgetting

Edited by
Adrian Forty and Susanne Küchler

Oxford • New York

First published in 1999 by
Berg
Editorial offices:
150 Cowley Road, Oxford OX4 1JJ, UK
838 Broadway, Third Floor, New York, NY 10003-4812, USA

Paperback edition reprinted in 2001

Berg is the imprint of Oxford International Publishers Ltd.

Library of Congress Cataloging-in-Publication Data

A catalogue record for this book is available from the Library of Congress.

British Library Cataloguing-in-Publication Data

A catalogue record for this book is available from the British Library.

ISBN 1 85973 286 0 (Cloth)
1 85973 291 7 (Paper)

Typeset by JS Typesetting, Wellingborough, Northants.
Printed in the United Kingdom by Hackman Print Group, Caerphilly.

Contents

Illustrations vii

Contributors ix

Preface
David Lowenthal xi

Introduction
Adrian Forty 1

Part I: Ephemeral Monuments 19

1 Ephemeral Monuments, Memory and Royal Sempiternity in a Grassfields Kingdom
Nicolas Argenti 21

2 The Place of Memory
Susanne Küchler 53

Part II: Remembering and Forgetting in Images Past 73

3 Girodet's *Portrait of Citizen Belley, Ex-Representative of the Colonies:* In Remembrance of 'Things Sublime'
Helen Weston 75

4 Bribing the Vote of Fame: Eighteenth Century Monuments and the Futility of Commemoration
David Bindman 93

5 Forgetting Rome and the Voice of Piranesi's 'Speaking Ruins'
Tarnya Cooper 107

Part III: War Memorials 127

6 Remembering to Forget: Sublimation as Sacrifice in War Memorials
Michael Rowlands 129

7 Remembering and Forgetting in the Public Memorials of the Great War
Alex King 147

8 Commemorating 1916, Celebrating Difference: Parading and Painting in Belfast
Neil Jarman 171

Bibliography 197

Index 211

Illustrations

1. Jasper Johns, *Memory piece (Frank O'Hara)*, 1961–70 3
2. Moscow, pedestal of statue of Kalinin, removed August 1991 11
3. Rachel Whiteread, maquette for Memorial to Austrian Jews for Judenplatz, Vienna, 1995 12
4. Leaping from the ground: the *ndavos* under construction 25
5. The *ndavos* in January 1997, with its roof beginning to deteriorate 28
6. The *kebambo fon* 30
7. House *Malanggan*, Panamafei village, 1984 56
8. *Malanggan* for sale, Medina village, 1984 58
9. A.-L. Girodet-Trioson, *Portrait of Citizen Belley, ex-Representative of the Colonies*, 1797 76
10. Anonymous, *Equality accorded to Blacks*, coloured etching, *c* 1791 83
11. Anonymous, *Egalité des Couleurs*, playing card, *c* 1794 84
12. L. F. Roubiliac, Monument to Field Marshall George Wade, 1750 95
13. L. F. Roubiliac, Monument to the Duke of Montagu, 1754 98
14. L. F. Roubiliac, Monument to the Duchess of Montagu, 1754 100
15. G.-B. Piranesi, *View of the Bridge and Castello Sant'Angelo*, *c* 1748–1778 108
16. G.-B. Piranesi, *Plan of the drainage outlet at Lake Albano*, 1762 116
17. G.-B. Piranesi, *View of the tomb of L. Arrunzio* (detail), 1756 118
18. Girolami Rossi, after Antonio Buonamici, *Tomb of the Household of Augustus*, 1727 120
19. G.-B. Piranesi, *The Pyramid of Cestius*, *c* 1748 121
20. Rejected design for war memorial, Sydney 135
21. Vietnam Memorial, Washington 140
22. Vietnam Veterans' Memorial, Washington 142
23. Sir Aston Webb and Alfred Drury, Memorial to London Troops (detail), 1920 153

24. Sir William Goscombe John, Lever Brothers' War Memorial (detail), Port Sunlight, 1921 154
25. Walter Williamson and H. S. Wright, Bradford City War Memorial (detail), 1922 155
26. Orange Order banner depicting the start of the Battle of the Somme 177
27. Ulster Volunteer Force bannerette of Monkstown YCV Flute Band 181
28. Mural to the 1916 Easter Rising, Whiterock Road, West Belfast, 1991 186

Contributors

Nicolas Argenti is a lecturer in social anthropology and material culture at the Department of World Art Studies and Museology at the University of East Anglia. He has carried out research on performance and politics in North West Province, Cameroon, and in southern Sri Lanka.

David Bindman is Professor of the History of Art at University College London. His recent publications include *Hogarth and his Times* and, with Malcolm Baker, *Roubiliac and the Eighteenth Century Monument: Sculpture as Theatre*.

Tarnya Cooper studied at Camberwell School of Art and the Courtauld Institute of Art, University of London. She is currently completing her PhD at the University of Sussex on *vanitas* representations in early modern England. She is Assistant Curator of the College Art Collections, University College London, and teaches the history of prints and drawings.

Adrian Forty is senior lecturer in the history of architecture at the Bartlett, University College London, where he directs the Graduate programme in the history of architecture. He is the author of *Objects of Desire*, and of a forthcoming book on the vocabulary of architectural criticism and debate.

Neil Jarman has studied the culture of parading in Northern Ireland for a number of years and has published *Material Conflicts: Parades and Visual Displays in Northern Ireland*. He is currently researching sectarian and political violence and community policing strategies with the Community Development Centre, North Belfast.

Alex King is a cultural historian working in London and Cambridge and author of *Memorials of the Great War in Britain: the Symbolism and Politics of Remembrance*.

Suzanne Küchler is a lecturer in social anthropology at University College London, specializing in the ethnography of Oceania and the anthropology of art. She has published widely on art and memory and is currently conducting research into the ethnography of mathematics.

Michael Rowlands is Professor of Anthropology at University College London. His recent publications include *Shopping, Space and Identity* and *Social Transformations in Archeology*.

Helen Weston is senior lecturer in the history of art at University College London. She has written extensively on the art of the period of the French Revolution and on the image of the Black in eighteenth century French art. She is preparing a book on portraits of Black and mixed-race men and women from France's colonies during the period of the slave rebellion in Saint Domingue (Haïti).

Preface

David Lowenthal

'Come home, my boy', the Alzheimer-ridden father implores his prodigal son, 'all is forgotten'. His confusion of forgiving with forgetting underscores the close etymological connection of amnesia with amnesty. Hobbes termed forgetting the basis of a just state, amnesia the cornerstone of the social contract. Remedial oblivion was a common tool of 17th-century English statecraft, with 'Acts of Oblivion' exempting from punishment men who had borne arms against Charles II or had opposed William III.[1]

The prodigal parent's plea also reminds us that forgetting is often, if not usually, involuntary. Erasure of memory is a haunting collective malady in Gabriel García Márquez's *One Hundred Years of Solitude*. His Macondo villagers struggle in vain, by means of written signs and other artifices, to fend off final oblivion. But the affliction is not confined to a few unfortunates; partial if not total oblivion is the inescapable human lot, especially during early childhood and old age, and it is episodically endemic in every society. Contrary to common belief, most of what is consciously experienced is soon forgotten. We are unaware of how many things we forget, explains the psychologist Marigold Linton, precisely because we have forgotten them.[2]

Yet much forgetting turns out to be more benefit than bereavement, a mercy rather than a malady. To forget is as essential as to keep things in mind, for no individual or collectivity can afford to remember everything. Total recall would leave us unable to discriminate or to generalize. We would be idiot savants, like Jorge Luis Borges's 'Funes, the Memorious', the sheer burden of whose disjoined and unselective recollections in the end proves lethal.

Individual forgetting is largely involuntary, though suspected felons are credited with special expertise in this craft. Collective oblivion, on the other hand, is mainly deliberate, purposeful and regulated. Therein lies the art of forgetting – art as opposed to ailment, choice rather than compulsion or obligation. The art is a high and delicate enterprise, demanding astute judgment about what to keep and what to let go, to salvage or to shred or shelve, to memorialize or to anathematize.

Artfully selective oblivion is necessary to all societies. Collective well-being requires sanitizing what time renders unspeakable, unpalatable, even just inconveniently outdated. Thus medieval prelates expunged the memory of monastic founders when subsequent times demanded new dynastic alliances and hence patrons.[3] Mere unfamiliarity often dooms public memorials, as when classical motifs no longer convey their allegorical intent. Thus Frederick MacMonnies's 1922 statue of *Civic Virtue* triumphing over the Siren of Temptation was banished from New York's City Hall to the boondocks, when viewers ignorant of mythology took umbrage at a man trampling a woman.[4] Language change consigns much to oblivion. Thus it is no longer the stomach but the heart that is the accepted organ of emotion. We still 'stomach' things and speak of 'gut feelings', but Wesley's great hymn, 'How blest the man whose bowels move', is today unsingable and hence forgotten.

This book explicates the myriad artful modes of expelling things and thoughts that distress us or have become redundant or obsolete. Every culture, each epoch, crafts and accredits particular conventions for selecting what and how to forget: by ritual destruction of emblems of generational exchange, as among tribal New Guineans; by funerary monuments that highlight material decay, as in the double-decker tombs of early-modern Europe and Roubiliac's 18th-century sculptural allegories; by the protracted submergence into invisibility of anti-fascist memorials, as in several German cities.

The essays in this book properly raise more questions than they answer. If organized oblivion is as widespread as they suggest, should we conclude that every society consciously forgets? Are there historical moments when forgetting is especially favoured? Are phrases like 'Forget Columbus' and 'Forget the Millennium' symptoms of such a moment, a backlash against current obsessions with memory, or simply a modish figure of speech? Is the stress between memory and oblivion periodic in character, and if so, are cycles of forgetting diurnal, seasonal, annual, generational or dynastic? Are there appointed agents of oblivion as there are of memory, official erasers like official scribes? What is the fate of individuals who, like Winston Smith in Orwell's *Nineteen Eighty-Four*, fail or refuse the command to forget? What happens to memory when hegemonic agencies enjoin a dissident minority to forget?

Common to the acts of forgetting discussed in this book is the sense, even the insistence, that they are part and parcel of a larger project of remembering. Their perpetrators disclaim any aim of general oblivion. Yet many do strive to expunge memory wholesale, especially that of despised enemies. Against the infection of idolatry, Reformation Protestants sought to make 'utterly extinct and destroy all shrines', in the 1547 Tudor injunction,'so that there remain no memory of the same.'[5] Pequot Indians vanquished by 17th-century English settlers were required to forget the very name of Pequot. Old Warsaw was eradicated by Nazi iconoclasts so that Poles would forget their glorious past. The library at Sarajevo and the bridge at Mostar were destroyed precisely in order to force those who treasured them to forget their heritage.

Blanket oblivion may seem indefensible, but being forced to remember may be still worse, above all when the memories are lies, fabrications of what might be termed a collective false memory syndrome. Far from wanting to expunge all memory of the Holocaust, the Nazis in fact planned a museum of former Jewish life in Prague which was intended to celebrate the Final Solution. 'The Jews were not to be annihilated and then forgotten, but annihilated and then remembered forever', in Elisabeth Domansky's phrase; their 'eternal death was not to be oblivion, but the torture of being eternally remembered by the[ir] persecutors.'[6]

This book shows that forgetting is often a merciful as well as a mandatory art.

Notes

1. S. S. Wolin, *The Presence of the Past: Essays on the State and the Constitution*, Baltimore, The John Hopkins University Press, 1989, pp. 37–38, 142.
2. M. Linton, 'Transformations of Memory in Everyday Life', in U. Neisser (ed.) *Memory Observed: Remembering in Natural Contexts*, San Francisco, Freeman, 1982, p. 86.
3. P. J. Geary, *Phantoms of Remembrance: Memory and Oblivion at the End of the First Millennium*, Princeton, Princeton University Press, 1995, pp. 135–46.
4. D. Glassberg, 'Monuments and Memories', *American Quarterly,* 43 (1991), p. 46.
5. M. Aston, *England's Iconoclasts: Laws against Images*, Oxford, Oxford University Press, 1988, p. 256.
6. E. Domansky, '"Kristallnacht," the Holocaust and German Unity', *History & Memory*, 4:1 (1992), p. 60.

Introduction

Adrian Forty

Photography 'is an eye which records in order to forget'

J. Berger, 'Ways of Remembering'[1]

'Remembering is a malady for which forgetting is the cure'

Georges Perec, 'Think/Classify'[2]

In his book *The Mind of a Mnemonist*, the Russian psychologist Alexander Luria described the case of a man with an exceptional ability to remember everything and anything he wanted. Taking advantage of his extraordinary memory, the man became a professional mnemonist and gave performances at which he would recall with complete accuracy prose, poetry, or random lists of words and numbers presented to him by the audience. With his capacity to remember everything, his greatest difficulty became the chaotic congestion of his mind with unwanted memories: he had to learn to forget what he no longer needed to remember. Experimenting with various techniques, he first tried writing things down, on the assumption that if this method enabled other people to remember what they did not want to forget, it might help him to forget what he no longer wanted to remember. 'Writing something down', he said, 'means I know I won't have to remember it.' Finding that simply writing things down was not sufficient to forget them, he took to throwing the pieces of paper away. Finally, when even this failed, he tried burning them.[3]

The mnemonist's efforts to forget illustrate something of the problem with which the essays in this book are concerned – how does forgetting occur, and what do material objects have to do with it? The mnemonist's experiences make clear the need to be able to forget for normal, healthy life. In his attempts to forget, he made use of two well-tried and familiar techniques: first of all the making of an artefact – in this case writing on a piece of paper; and secondly its destruction – iconoclasm. The mnemonist's concern was with personal forgetting, however, and the issue with which we are concerned here is social, collective forgetting; for just as individuals are obliged to forget, so too are societies – but we should not assume that the processes involved are necessarily the same. Ever since Durkheim identified the concept of 'collective memory', there has been a tendency to confuse the memory of individuals with the memory of societies, and to attempt to explain the one through the other. This confusion has to be challenged – and one person who has done so recently is Paul Connerton in his interesting book *How Societies Remember*, where he argues that as far as societies are concerned, material objects have less significance in perpetuating memory than embodied acts, rituals and normative social behaviour. The question of how societies *forget* remains uninvestigated, however, and here one may ask how much object making has to do with the process. This is the theme that underlies *The Art of Forgetting*. While the topic of social memory has generated a vast literature since the late 1980s, the relationship between objects and memory continues to be uncertain – and relatively little has been written about forgetting.[4] This book should be regarded as an early adventure into a subject where there are few guides. With so little work – either theoretical or empirical – on forgetting, the essays in the book are to be read as preliminary and provisional suggestions as to how one might start to think about the relationship between material objects and collective forgetting.

The Western tradition of memory since the Renaissance has been founded upon an assumption that material objects, whether natural or artificial, can act as the analogues of human memory. It has been generally taken for granted that memories, formed in the mind, can be transferred to solid material objects, which can come to stand for memories and, by virtue of their durability, either prolong or preserve them indefinitely beyond their purely mental existence. Much Western artefact making (and this would include products as diverse as funerary sculpture on the one hand and information technology on the other) has been dedicated to the creation of material substitutes for the fragile world of human memory. It would appear that this Western tradition owes a great deal to the concept of memory put forward by Aristotle, according to whom memory 'is like the imprint or drawing in us of things felt';[5] in this scheme, forgetting is the decay of the imprint. The American artist Jasper Johns in his work 'Memory Piece (Frank O'Hara)'(Figure 1) presents an ironic simulation of this process: a box with three drawers, each filled with sand, has a hinged lid on the underside of which is the positive cast of a human foot. Close the lid, and the top tray of sand receives the imprint of the foot, which survives as long as the box remains undisturbed, but shake it about, and the imprint is lost. Western civilization has developed various

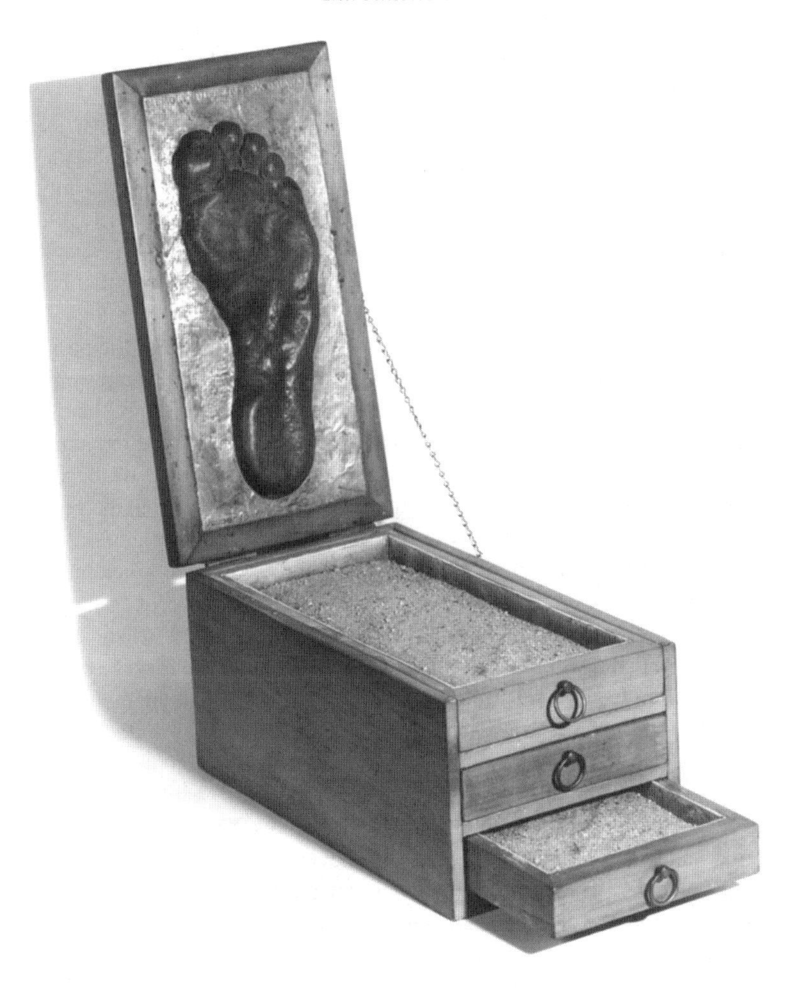

Figure 1 Jasper Johns, *Memory piece (Frank O'Hara)*, 1961–70. Collection of the artist. (Copyright Jasper Johns / VAGA, New York / DACS, London)

technologies that are realizations of the Aristotelian model of memory and forgetting: these include the 'magic slate' (the subject of Freud's 1925 essay 'A Note Upon the Mystic Writing Pad') and, above all, photography, a medium whose technique would appear to be the most complete fulfilment of Aristotle's theory. The transfer of an object seen in life to a plate or film is preserved for as long as the image so created can be fixed;

the faded Daguerreotype, the result of an inadequate fixing process, is the perfect metaphor for forgetting within this scheme.

In general, within the Aristotelian tradition, if objects are made to stand for memory, their decay or destruction (as in the act of iconoclasm) is taken to imply forgetting. A particularly explicit application of this model occurs in the well-known, often-quoted essay 'On the Modern Cult of Monuments', written in 1903 by the Austrian art-historian Alois Riegl. In his essay, Riegl warned that, at the time he was writing, the quality for which monuments were most venerated was what he described as their 'age value', their emotional evocation of a general sense of the passage of time, rather than for any specific historical knowledge they might contain. When a monument is considered by this criterion, its being an object, explained Riegl, 'has shrunk to a necessary evil. These monuments are nothing more than indispensable catalysts which trigger in the beholder a sense of the life cycle, of the emergence of the particular from the general and its gradual but inevitable dissolution back into the general'.[6] A monument displaying age value, distinguished by 'its incompleteness, its lack of wholeness, its tendency to dissolve form and colour',[7] signified memory of no particular historical person or event, nor the artistic quality of a particular age, but simply a generalized sense of the passage of time. The difficulty that age value presented to the guardians of monuments was that any attempt to arrest or reverse the natural process of decay would at once detract from their age value; indeed, Riegl recommended that ultimately acceptance of age value was 'the only viable strategy . . . because natural forces are ultimately more powerful than all the wit of man, and man himself is destined to inevitable decay'.[8] The appeal of age value lay in its acknowledgement of natural decay; in the tendency of monuments to reduce themselves to dust, they became material enactments of the mental decay of images supposed to constitute the process of forgetting and, ultimately, oblivion.

For a variety of reasons, there is cause to doubt the general assumption that material objects can take the place of the mental form of memory. Among the grounds for scepticism, we might consider three in particular. The first are the phenomena usually known as ephemeral monuments. A feature of non-Western societies, these are artefacts with apparently memorial purposes, but which are made only to be abandoned immediately to decay – a practice that simply cannot be explained within the Western memorial tradition. Ephemeral monuments are the subject of two of the essays in this collection. Nicolas Argenti's description of the rituals forming part of the succession of the king in a West African tribe recounts the creation of structures that were destroyed almost at once, and of an effigy that was studiously ignored by the inhabitants and left to decay, as soon as it had been put in place on the edge of the village (Figure 6). In the case of the Melanesian society described by Suzanne Küchler, the death of an individual is followed by the carving and painting in great secrecy of an elaborate device, a *malangann*, which at a certain moment is publicly revealed to the assembled villagers who crowd around to see it (Figure 8) – but once seen, they show no further interest and abandon it to the forest, or, conveniently, dispose of it by selling it to Western collectors who ensure its removal. In neither of these cases is the object's permanence a necessary feature of its existence – indeed, quite the opposite – making it hard to explain within the Western conventions for thinking about memorials. These objects may be interpreted as the means by which the members of the society get rid of what they no longer need or wish to remember – like the mnemonist burning his pieces of paper. Or, as Susanne Küchler argues, their brief exposure acts as a momentary confirmation of what everybody within the culture already knows, but of which otherwise they have no need to be reminded. If, as the ephemeral monuments suggest, collective memory does not dwell in material objects, the central problem in understanding both memory and forgetting is to know how to describe wherever it is that memory does reside – and this is the issue with which Küchler's essay is concerned.

The second reason to doubt the assumption that objects are the analogues of memory is Sigmund Freud's theory of mental processes, a theory that effectively inverted the Aristotelian model of memory. In Freud's view it was axiomatic that 'in mental life nothing that has once been formed can perish – that everything is somehow preserved and in suitable circumstances . . . can once more be brought to light'.[9] What passed for forgetting was in reality the repression of the Ego, which obscured the impressions received by the mind from consciousness; within the life of the individual, forgetting was an impossibility, and oblivion non-existent. Rather than memory loss taking place through the passive attrition of time, as in the Aristotelian model, Freud posited it as the active force; rather than being natural and involuntary, Freud stressed that 'forgetting is often intentional and desired'.[10] In a sense, the purpose of psychoanalysis was not a memory cure, but rather to provide the patient with the means to truly forget the repressed material of which they were otherwise the victim. As Freud once remarked, the aim was to give patients the '*freedom* to decide one way or the other', whether to remember or forget.[11]

If Freud's theory inverted the Aristotelian model, it also called into question the relationship between objects and memory that had grown up as a result of the Aristotelian tradition. For Freud, physical artefacts could no longer be regarded as analogues of memory, because mental material was not subject to the same processes of decay as objects in the phenomenal world. Although Freud was fond of describing psychoanalysis as akin to archaeology, and a number of times referred to the city of Rome as a metaphor of mental processes, he was also careful to insist that this image is ultimately unsatisfactory as an account of the workings of the mind.[12] Were a city to truly represent the mind, it would have to contain simultaneously all the structures that had ever been built within it, with many sites occupied at once by the successive buildings of different ages. While Freud's psychology refers to the life of individuals rather than that of societies, it has nonetheless helped to weaken the previously assumed relationship between objects and memory.

A third reason to doubt the assumed relationship of objects and memory has been brought about by the difficulties of the remembrance of the Holocaust, and the realization that conventional memorial practices were inadequate and inappropriate to the task. As the greatest atrocity of modern times, the natural reaction to its unbearable memory was to forget – which is exactly what many of the survivors themselves did, or attempted to do. Yet, as they and everyone else knew, to forget it was to risk its repetition. The difficulty was to know how to remember the atrocity without lessening its horror, without somehow sanitizing it by making it tolerable to remember. In a sense, only those who survived, *can* remember it: as the Spanish writer Jorge Lemprun has said, they alone know the smell of burning flesh, and 'a day is coming when no one will actually remember this smell; it will be nothing more than a phrase, a literary reference, an idea of an odour. Odourless, therefore'.[13] Against the inevitability of the Holocaust being forgotten, attempts to preserve its memory look futile, and if they take the form of artefact making, probably counter-productive. When the French Jewish artist Christian Boltanski was asked if he would make a Holocaust memorial, he replied 'If one were to make such a memorial, one would have to remake it every day'.[14] The peculiar problems presented by the Holocaust have created a genre of anti-memorials, some of which are described in James Young's comprehensive book, *The Texture of Memory: Holocaust Memorials and Meaning* (1993). Among the most vivid of these anti-memorials are those by the German artist Jochen Gerz. The Hamburg memorial against fascism, unveiled in 1986, consisted of a 12 m high square column sheathed in lead, which over the course of several years was gradually lowered into the ground, until only its top was visible. On the lead surface, of which a new portion was progressively brought within reach, people scratched graffiti, which were in time interred below ground. In another memorial, the square in front of the palace at Saarbrucken was paved with stone sets, on the underside of each of which Gerz carved the name of one of the 2146 Jewish cemeteries existing in Germany before 1933. To the visitor, the paving is indistinguishable from any other paved area; the memorial is invisible, only known about.[15]

For these reasons – the ephemeral monuments, Freud, the holocaust memorials – it is clear that the relationship between objects and memory is less straightforward than Western thinking has been in the habit of assuming. We cannot take it for granted that artefacts act as the agents of collective memory, nor can they be relied upon to prolong it. The French philosopher Michel de Certeau writes suggestively that 'memory is a sort of an anti-museum: it is not localizable'.[16] For de Certeau, the principal feature of memory is 'that it comes from somewhere else, it is outside of itself, it moves things about',[17] and that when it ceases to be capable of this alteration, when it becomes fixed to particular objects, then it is in decay. Seen in these terms, objects are the enemy of memory, they are what tie it down and lead to forgetfulness. If there is any sense in these suggestive remarks, how then are we to talk about the relationship between objects, memory and forgetting? How does a non-localizable phenomenon make itself known in the world? What would an 'anti-museum' be like?

Before we start to consider these questions, it is worth stressing that forgetting has, in a manner of speaking, been *the* problem of the twentieth century. Although the present century has been obsessed with memory in a way that no other ever was before – witness its colossal investment in museums, in heritage, in memorials to the dead of its many wars, in information technology, and its passion for ever-larger and expanding archives – nonetheless forgetting has been one of its greatest difficulties. This is not a new situation. The very word 'amnesty' speaks of a public forgetting, and most of the social contract theories of the state upon which modern democracies are founded assume their members are prepared to forget the more divisive differences existing between them.[18] As the French nineteenth century writer Ernest Renan wrote, 'the essence of a nation is that all the individuals share a great many things in common and also that they have forgotten some things. Every French citizen should have forgotten the Bartholomew massacre'.[19] In post-war Europe, the ability to forget has been put to the most severe test. The relative stability of Western Europe since 1945 has in part been due to a colossal act of collective, consensual forgetting – of the divisions between wartime partisans and collaborators, which whatever may be said in private, have in public been forgotten. As a *New York Times* reporter commented,

'Europe's apparent amnesia about the war is a largely willed phenomenon. Europeans old enough to remember those years have not forgotten the past, but often remember it all too well, and they deeply resent being reminded of it'.[20] The outbreak of violence in the former Yugoslavia may in part be seen as the result of a refusal to forget past events. Similarly, the Northern Irish troubles are distinguished by an extraordinary reluctance by both political and religious groups to forget events from the time of the First World War that other people might no longer feel the need to remember. Neil Jarman's essay in this book, on the banners and murals commemorating 1916, shows how selective commemoration can be. From these and other examples, it is clear how necessary to stable political life, as to healthy individual life, a degree of amnesia may be.

The central problem that the essays in this book have in common is how artefacts constitute part of the process of social forgetting. Might it be possible to construct a history not of memorials, but of amnesiacs? The first task in doing so would be to try to identify the principal categories through which objects have been agents of forgetting. Such a scheme might include the four following themes, set out here.

Separation The double-decker tombs of the late Middle Ages and early Renaissance are among the more intriguing of memorials. Incorporating an effigy of the deceased in his or her garments of office above, they carried below a second effigy of the deceased as a corpse. Ernst Kantorowicz's interpretation of these tombs commemorating kings, queens and clerics in his classic study *The King's Two Bodies* (1957) was to present them in terms of the doctrines of mediaeval kingship, central to which was the axiom that 'the king's Dignity never dies'. According to Kantorowicz, the double effigies allowed the king's two bodies – his natural mortal body, and the body politic, the king's 'Dignity' – normally united in his living flesh, to separate at death; they made visible the normally invisible, but immortal body politic, while the king's normally visible mortal body was left to decay and oblivion.[21] The same principle applied to the tombs of bishops, like that of Bishop Beckington at Wells, while the most spectacular examples were the tombs of the sixteenth century French kings at St Denis, where the dual effigies became an artistic conceit. In these double effigies, we see an explicit representation of a feature common to most memorial artefacts, of performing a separation between what is to be remembered, and what can be forgotten.

Tension between remembering and forgetting The funerary sculptures executed in eighteenth century England by Louis Francois Roubiliac, discussed by David Bindman in his essay, provide a particularly vivid enactment of the tension existing between forgetting and remembering. In the monument to the Duke of Argyll in Westminster Abbey, the Duke reclines on his sarcophagus, while Fame writes his name on the obelisk above – but she has written only the first two letters of the last part of his title before the action is frozen, leaving it in the balance as to whether his name will be remembered or not. In the Wade memorial nearby (Figure 12), General Wade is commemorated not by an effigy, but by a column bearing the soldierly attributes of armour, banners and weapons, with a portrait medallion at its base. The main drama of the memorial takes place around the column: the figure of Time steals up to it, intending to push it over and consign the General to oblivion, but Fame rushes forward to push him back, so for the time being at least, his memory is preserved. Roubiliac's allegories of the fragility of memory against the force of forgetfulness, were as David Bindman shows, exploited to the full by the sculptor; part of their interest is that they dramatize a tension present in all effective works of commemoration.

Exclusion War memorials are the objects most closely connected in modern consciousness with memory. The commemorative activity brought about by the First World War and repeated after subsequent wars had no equivalent in previous centuries. Yet, as both Alex King and Michael Rowlands argue in their essays here, what purpose those memorials served, and what exactly they commemorated is far from certain. In the memorials of the First World War, the choice of certain conventions for the figurative representation of the soldier – a figure at rest, showing no aggression (Figure 23) – was a highly selective, and in some people's view, a most misleading view of the war that had just been fought. But it is surely an inevitable feature of memorials – and this is true not only of war memorials, but of all commemorative artefacts – that they permit only certain things to be remembered, and by exclusion cause others to be forgotten.

A particularly striking case of the process of exclusion is provided by the story of the Frauenkirche in Dresden. This great domed eighteenth century baroque church had been one of the splendours of pre-war Dresden until, along with most of the rest of the city, it was destroyed in the air raid of 13 February 1945. While most of the rest of Dresden was gradually rebuilt in the succeeding forty years, including the other great architectural monuments, the Zwinger palace and the Opera, the Frauenkirche was left a weed-infested pile of rubble dominating the city centre. By default, if not by intention, it became one of the most potent memorials anywhere of the Second World War. During the 1980s, the ruins became the site of silent protests against the GDR, when on the anniversary of the air raid, they were covered with candles. Following the collapse of communism and the reunification of Germany, when the numerous monuments of the Soviet occupation and the East German regime were mostly pulled down, this particular monument underwent the reverse. The citizens of Dresden actively set about its reconstruction. This was clearly an attempt to erase the memory of the GDR, but at the same time it deprived the city of its best memorial to the other cataclysmic event of the century. In this bizarre piece of counter-iconoclasm – remaking something in order to forget what its absence signified – the result is to suppress one memory (the GDR) and at the same time to exclude another (the Second World War). An even more remarkable case of counter-iconoclasm is the rebuilding of the church of Christ the Saviour in Moscow, originally built in the nineteenth century by public subscription to commemorate the victory against Napoleon, then blown up in the 1930s to create the site for the Palace of the Soviets, which was not built. It was then made into the Moscow open-air swimming pool. After 1991, the reconstruction of the church has been a major project in Moscow, whose purpose is to suppress the memory of Soviet communism. The lesson of both the Dresden and the Moscow projects is that the filling of a void, whose emptiness had exercised diverse collective memories, ends by excluding all but a single dominant one.

Iconoclasm The destruction of buildings and monuments – iconoclasm – must be the most conventional way of hoping to achieve forgetting. Yet are its results always what is intended? The overthrowing of statues of Lenin, Marx and other heroes of Soviet communism that took place throughout Eastern Europe and the Soviet Union following 1989 was one of the most demonstrative signs, to the outside world as well as to the citizens of those countries, of the collapse of the old regime. As a Russian art critic, Viktor Misiano, remarks in Laura Mulvey and Mark Lewis's film *Disgraced Monuments*, 'All successful revolutions end with statues coming down'.[22] As this film about the destruction of monuments in the Soviet Union after 1989 showed so vividly, however, the effect of removing fifty of the sixty monuments to Lenin in the streets and squares of Moscow was to leave fifty empty plinths, above which the voids were as noticeable as the sculptures that stood on them previously had been invisible (Figure 2). The empty pedestals, far from erasing the memory of the communist regime, became memorable in a way that they had never been when topped by statues. These acts of iconoclasm must be put in context. To refer to another country formerly under Soviet control,

Figure 2 Moscow, pedastal of statue of Kalinin, removed August 1991. Still from *Disgraced Monuments*.

Czechoslovakia, the proliferation of Lenin memorials was perceived there as part of a programme of suppressing the memory of Czech culture. As the exiled Czech writer, Milan Kundera, says in *The Book of Laughter and Forgetting* (written 1976–8) 'statues of Lenin are nowadays springing up in Bohemia by the thousands, springing up like weeds among ruins, like melancholy flowers of forgetting'. He perceived the state, under Gustav Husak, whom Kundera named the 'President of Forgetting', as actively creating a world without memory. In the words of one of Kundera's characters, 'You begin to liquidate a people by taking away its memory' – under which circumstances a necessary act of resistance was the active exercise of memory.[23] Part of the liquidation of memory was the superimposition of Lenin monuments on sites where other statues had previously stood. Seen in these terms, the pulling down of these statues was not so much an act of hoped-for forgetting, but rather a reclaiming of a memory attaching to these places that the installation of the Lenin monuments had caused to be forgotten. In the Soviet Union, and elsewhere, the Russian critic Mikhail Yampolsky has written: 'Destruction and construction can be understood, in a certain context, as two equally valid features of immortalisation . . . A tradition has developed historically to build a new monument precisely on the site of the old one, as though accumulating in one place two commemorative gestures: vandalism and the erection of a new idol'.[24] Seen in these terms, the lessons of iconoclasm are largely negative – rather than shortening memory, it is just as likely, whether intentionally or not, to prolong it.

'Remembering is only possible on the basis of forgetting'

Bringing together the previous themes, we might consider a single work, the English sculptor Rachel Whiteread's design for a memorial to the exterminated Austrian Jews for the Judenplatz in Vienna[25] (Figure 3). This project, the result of a competition held in 1995, is due to be completed early in 1999. The scheme consists of the cast of the interior of a room, a room of the same dimensions as those in the buildings around the Judenplatz, a small square in central Vienna. It is a library, a room of books, the repositories of memory, and as such it points to recollection – although it is a library whose space and books are permanently inaccessible

Figure 3 Rachel Whiteread, maquette for Memorial to Austrian Jews for Judenplatz, Vienna, 1995. (Photo: Mike Bruce; Anthony D'Offay Gallery, London)

to us. There is a contradiction, however, for the casts of the books are not of their spines, as would be the case if the piece were truly the negative cast of the interior of a library, but instead the casts show their backs: the books themselves are positives, implying that the library represented is one from which the books were absent, whose shelves were empty, carrying only the negative voids left by the books. The library and its contents are thus doubly inaccessible to us. Whatever is being remembered here has already previously been removed, forgotten: we can only speculate on what it is that we are supposed to remember. One might see this work as bringing about in our minds what Martin Heidegger wrote in *Being and Time*, that only what has been forgotten can be remembered: 'Just as expecting is possible only on the basis of awaiting, *remembering* is possible only on that of forgetting, *and not vice versa*'.[26] As in Roubiliac's allegories, there is recognition that memory is dependent upon its counterpart, forgetting – but in this case forgetfulness has been there first, and memory struggles to retrieve what it can.

Whiteread's Judenplatz memorial clearly belongs within the genre of Holocaust anti-memorials that have attempted to deal with the risk that a monument may contribute less to memory than to forgetting. However, compared to the examples of the genre discussed earlier, the Vienna memorial is an exceptionally positive object – it might be seen as akin to the solid blocks of minimalist sculpture. Or, alternatively, it may be seen as an empty plinth – like the empty plinths of Moscow – an effect that is reinforced by the imprint of the ceiling rose on the top, suggesting the previous presence of some now removed object. This effect is further suggested by the presence its neighbour in the Judenplatz, the statue of the eighteenth century poet G. E. Lessing, who stands in conventional manner upon a stone pedestal. In a variety of ways therefore, Whiteread's memorial is not merely – in common with much of her other work – about absences, but it draws its effect from causing us to try to remember what remains permanently out of reach, and inaccessible to us.

If these various modes – separation, exclusion, destruction and the tension between memory and forgetfulness – are some of the characteristics through which one might explore the manner in which any given object exercises the art of forgetting, how might one consider their application within any given art practice? Here we might look briefly at the case of architecture and urbanism, practices where 'memory' was taken up enthusiastically in the 1970s and 1980s. In architecture and urbanism, we find a particularly striking case of a persisting and almost wholly uncritical attachment to the traditional Western belief that material objects – in this case buildings – provide a complete and satisfactory analogue for the mental world of memory. If the hope that 'memory' might have turned architecture from a blank and silent art into one that was popularly meaningful has not been realized, it may have something to do with architects' lack of attention to the uncertainties that have emerged in the relationship between objects and memory during the twentieth century.

As a work often regarded as one of the more successful representations of 'memory' in architecture, we might take the Staatsgalerie in Stuttgart, designed by the British architects James Stirling and Michael Wilford in 1977 and completed in 1983. This building, a museum of modern art, shocked many people in Germany at the time it was finished because it employed a variety of neo-classical features – rotunda, columns with simplified capitals, heavy cornices, travertine cladding – last seen in use in Germany during the Third Reich. A whole range of motifs that had been carefully avoided by German architects in the post-war era in the interests of a 'democratic' modern architecture now made their appearance. Some of the features were derived from surviving nineteenth century buildings around the new gallery, but much exaggerated; the new building provided a core, which while being modern, at the same time seemed to heighten and intensify the properties of this otherwise unremarkable area of Stuttgart. At the same time, the semi-ruined appearance of parts of the building, and elements partially submerged underground, gave it the air of a survival from a now remote past – even if this impression was at once contradicted by the newness of the constructive methods, and evident modernity of other parts of the building. In the Staatsgalerie a number of themes originally developed for a slightly earlier, but unbuilt, competition design by the same architects for a museum at Dusseldorf were reworked; in this scheme, the evocation of a past, now vanished city, within a new building had been even more explicit. Here, the representation of memory had relied on a series of forms – rotunda, arcaded loggia with hall above, and so on – that were seemingly archetypal elements of urban architecture, though they were treated unconventionally. The 'memory' evoked in both schemes was of an older, primarily Italianate tradition of urban culture, and of architecture's own history.

The Staatsgalerie created surprise and interest because it had been a long-standing axiom that 'memory' should have no part in modern architecture, or in its perception. While eighteenth and nineteenth century architecture had valued 'memory' highly, one of the most distinctive features of early twentieth-century modernism, not only in architecture but in all visual arts, was to deny 'memory' any place, and indeed to negate it altogether. The sudden reappropriation by architects of memory in the 1970s may be understood as a reaction to so much 'unmemorable' architecture in the period after 1945, but the results did not necessarily restore architecture to the position of a popular art that it had once, supposedly, enjoyed. Questions remain as to what exactly the new memory-laden work of the 1970s and 1980s caused to be remembered – was it simply the generalized 'age value', consciousness of the passage of time, of which Riegl had written, or could architecture succeed in some more specific recall? And what was the process by which it was hoped architecture might achieve these results?

Throughout the various attempts to create through architecture and urbanism a consciousness of collective memory – or, perhaps, as seems more likely, to fill the emptiness that comes from having no memories – what was remarkable was the unquestioned assumption that the objects created would come to stand for memory. In every respect, architecture most perfectly reproduced the old, Aristotelian-based assumption that to transfer memories to objects would preserve them from mental decay. Looking at the works with claims to reconstitute the memory of cities, they reveal no misgivings about the capacity of objects to take the place of memory – buildings and memory seem to have been treated as exchangeable currencies. The impression the works themselves give of confidence in the transferability of memory to things, and vice versa, is confirmed by the architectural writings about memory. Of those, by far the most influential and widely read have been the writings of the Italian architect Aldo Rossi, in particular his book *The Architecture of the City* (1966) where, as part of his critique of orthodox modernism, he suggested that the way to develop new forms of urban architecture was by studying those already existing. Not only did the buildings of every existing city reveal a pattern of *permanences* specific to it, but at a deeper level, these characterized its 'collective memory'. As Rossi put it, 'the city itself is the collective memory of its people, and like memory it is associated with objects and places. The city is the *locus* of the collective memory'. And summarizing his argument, he wrote 'Memory . . . is the consciousness of the city'.[27] The lesson drawn from Rossi's very widely read book was that whoever undertook to build in the city would effect not merely a physical transformation, but more audaciously, a transformation of the collective mental life of its inhabitants.

With hindsight it is indeed surprising that Rossi and the many architects who adopted his ideas should have so readily accepted that notion that buildings might stand for memories. There was no shortage of warnings against this assumption in the literature and philosophy of the twentieth century – we have mentioned Freud's, and we might add a book widely read by architects, the French philosopher Gaston Bachelard's *The Poetics of Space*, in which he argued that while memory might be described in terms of buildings, he warned that memory did not lend itself to physical description, let alone construction.[28] Similarly, in the source from whom Bachelard certainly drew some of his ideas, Marcel Proust's great novel *A la Recherche du Temps Perdu*, the whole project was to recall what lay just beyond memory, with what cannot quite be recalled – Walter Benjamin described Proust's book as 'a work of forgetting', 'in which remembrance is the woof and forgetting is the warp'.[29] Proust was the first among a succession of modernist writers to be interested in the power of objects to trigger memory – yet Proust was careful to stress that this process was always haphazard, that objects could never be relied upon to deliver memories to consciousness. It is the impossibility of memory that fascinated Proust, and in turn Bachelard, and Michel de Certeau.

Had architects paid more attention to these warnings and acknowledged more readily that perhaps, after all, architecture is and always has been above all an art of forgetting, their experiments with 'memory' might have proved more successful. Had they recognized that whatever mnemonic potential buildings may have, 'memory' only becomes interesting through its struggle with forgetfulness, then the representation of collective memory might have become more meaningful. A rare case of a building in which there is some recognition of these tensions is the Jewish Museum extension to the Berlin Museum by Daniel Libeskind, opened in 1998. This building is not a memorial: as the architect has said, 'the building is not a metaphor' – it does not 'stand for' memory of the Berlin Jews – but rather its disturbing and disorientating interiors invite one 'to explore a single name which remains forgotten . . . a single piece of music that remains unwritten'.[30]

The lesson of the example of architecture – and of this book as a whole – is that any art practice aspiring to deal with memory can only do so by taking into account what memory struggles in vain to resist. An art cannot deal with memory without also confronting forgetting. Not for nothing did the ancient Greeks locate the springs of Lethe (Forgetfulness) and of Mnemosyne (Memory) nearby, and make those who came to consult the oracle at Trophonios drink the waters of first one and then the other.[31]

Notes

1. J. Berger, 'Ways of Remembering', *Camerawork* 10 (1978); reprinted in J. Evans (ed.) *The Camerawork Essays*, London, Rivers Oram Press, 1997, p. 48.

2. G. Perec, *Species of Spaces and Other Pieces*, trans. J. Sturrock, London, Penguin Books, 1997, p. 199.
3. A. R. Luria, *The Mind of a Mnemonist*, Cambridge MA, Harvard University Press, 1987, p. 70.
4. Two of the most useful works on forgetting are: D. Lowenthal, 'Memory and Oblivion', *Museum Management and Curatorship* 12 (1993), pp. 171–82; and E. S. Casey, *Remembering: a Phenomenological Study*, Bloomington and Indianapolis, Indiana University Press, 1987.
5. Aristotle, *De Memoria et Reminiscentia*, 450b11, trans. R. Sorabji, *Aristotle on Memory*, London, Duckworth, 1972, p. 51.
6. A. Riegl, 'The Modern Cult of Monuments: Its Character and Its Origin', trans. K. Forster and D. Ghirardo, *Oppositions* 25 (1982), p. 24.
7. Riegl, 'Modern Cult of Monuments', p. 31.
8. Riegl, 'Modern Cult of Monuments', p. 37.
9. S. Freud, *Civilization and its Discontents*, trans. J. Riviere, London, Hogarth Press, 1969, p. 6.
10. S. Freud, *Case Histories*: 'Lucy R.', *Standard Edition*, trans. J. Strachey, vol. 2, London, Hogarth Press, 1960, p. 111. See also chapter VII of Freud, *The Psychopathology of Everyday Life*, *Standard Edition*, vol 6, London, Hogarth Press, 1960.
11. Casey, *Remembering*, p. 300; Freud, *Standard Edition*, vol. 19, p. 50n.
12. Freud, *Civilization and Its Discontents*, p. 8.
13. J. Lemprun, *Literature or Life*, London, Viking, 1998.
14. Speaking on a BBC television programme, May 1994.
15. See M. Steinhauser, 'Works of Memory: On Jochen Gerz's Memorials', *Daidalos* 49 (1993), pp. 104–13.
16. M. de Certeau, *The Practice of Everyday Life*, Los Angeles, Berkeley, University of California Press, 1984, p. 108.
17. De Certeau, *Practice of Everyday Life*, p. 87.
18. See S. S. Wolin (1989), 'Injustice and Collective Memory', in Wolin, *The Presence of the Past*, Baltimore, Johns Hopkins University Press, 1989.
19. Quoted in Wolin, *The Presence of the Past*, p. 37.
20. Quoted in C. S. Maier, *The Unmasterable Past: History, Holocaust and German National Identity*, Cambridge MA, Harvard University Press, 1988, p. 161.
21. E. H. Kantorowicz, *The King's Two Bodies, A Study in Mediaeval Political Theology*, Princeton, Princeton University Press, 1957, pp. 419–37.

22. *Disgraced Monuments* (1992), directed by M. Lewis and L. Mulvey. Script published in *Pix* 2 (1997), pp. 102-11. For some of the thinking behind this film, see M. Lewis, 'What is to be Done', in A. and M. Kroker (eds), *Ideology and Power in the Age of Lenin in Ruins*, New York, St Martins Press, 1991, pp. 1–18.
23. M. Kundera, *The Book of Laughter and Forgetting*, trans. A. Asher, New York, Harper Perennial, 1996, pp. 217–8.
24. M. Yampolsky, 'In the Shadow of Monuments', in N. Condee (ed.), *Soviet Hieroglyphics*, London, British Film Institute, 1995.
25. On this project, see *Judenplatz Wien 1996. Competition Monument and Memorial Site dedicated to the Jewish victims of the Nazi Regime in Austria 1938–1945*, Vienna, Folio, Stadt Wien, Kunsthalle Wien, 1996; and R. Comay, 'Memory Block: Rachel Whiteread's Proposal for a Holocaust Memorial in Vienna', *Art and Design Profile* 55 (1997), pp. 64–75.
26. M. Heidegger, *Being and Time*, trans. J. Macquarrie and E. Robinson, New York, Harper & Row, 1962, pp. 388–9.
27. A. Rossi, *The Architecture of the City*, trans. D. Ghirardo and J. Ockman, Cambridge MA and London, MIT Press, 1982, pp. 130–1.
28. G. Bachelard, *The Poetics of Space*, trans. M. Jolas, Boston, Beacon Press, 1969, p. 13.
29. W. Benjamin, 'The Image of Proust', in Benjamin, *Illuminations*, London, Fontana, 1973, p. 204.
30. D. Libeskind lecture at the Bartlett, University College London, February 1998.
31. Pausanius, *Guide to Greece*, vol. 1, trans. P. Levi, Harmondsworth, Penguin Books, 1971, p. 394.

Part I
Ephemeral Monuments

Ephemeral monuments, made only to be left to decay, are an inexplicable contradiction within the Western memorial tradition. Yet such objects are regularly produced in non-Western societies – and even if they end up in Western ethnographic museums, that itself is, as far as their makers are concerned, only another means of disposing of them.

The chapters by Nicolas Argenti and Susanne Küchler describe two different cultures in which ephemeral monuments appear. Nicolas Argenti's account of the royal succession in Oku, Cameroon, shows how the destruction of the objects produced in connection with the event serves to legitimate the transfer of power following the king's death.

Susanne Küchler's discussion of the ephemeral memorials created by a Melanesian people, speculates upon Western assumptions about the location of memory, and suggests that the Western identification of memory with physical objects may be a relatively short-lived phenomenon, soon to be superseded.

–1–

Ephemeral Monuments, Memory and Royal Sempiternity in a Grassfields Kingdom[1]

Nicolas Argenti

> *Years later, he would remember that terror also has its enchantment and its uses. It was the terror of what he saw that probably woke him up to the last moment of his old life.*
>
> Okri, *Astonishing the Gods*[2]

The Bodily Memory of Royal Appearances

The lineage masquerades performed regularly in the villages of the kingdom of Oku in the mountains of the North West Province of Cameroon are occasions treated with exteme ambivalence by the people. To shed some light on the potency of these masquerades, and on the ambivalence shown towards them, I refer to a series of events following the 'loss' of the king (*fon*) and the installation of his successor that took place during the first stages of my field work in June 1992. Briefly, the events during the interregnum involved the appearance, disappearance, and the falling-into-decay of several highly ambiguous objects: a small building was erected in the palace and then left to decompose; a carved effigy of the king was placed in a small sacred forest close to the palace; a pair of 'twins' – two neophytes from the palace regulatory society – were rubbed in kaolin and briefly exposed in the palace court yard; and a man representing a deity known as the 'God of the Market' crouched in the undergrowth on the edge of the palace compound before the new king's first sortie.

The Oku language has no collective term for these events, and I shall call them 'appearances', to suggest the variety of simultaneous experiences that they presented to the beholder. Of the striking features common to these disparate phenomena, the first was the suddenness of their materialization in or around the palace grounds and the brevity of their presence there. This momentariness did much to contribute to the sense of arrest and surprise that the phenomena elicited. The second feature shared by all of them was the ambiguity of their identities. What might have been considered the objective condition of each object or persona's invention, construction or genesis was systematically denied, and replaced instead with a myth of origin or a blurring of messages about the phenomenon's exact provenance, nature or 'significance'. This ambiguity was paralleled by the manner in which the rites of royal installation mark an attempt to place the king within a cosmological order of the polity – not an objective structure, but a phantasmal one as perceived only by the king and the members of his court. Furthermore, the ambiguous identity of the appearances in and around the palace had a parallel with the lineage masquerades, as did their suddenness and the sensation of arrest and surprise.

Both the palace appearances and the lineage masquerades assist in the conversion of the deceased into an ancestor. Both partake of the element of *surprise*; with their sudden, unannounced appearances and disappearances, their silence, and their seeming lack of meaning or referent. Both operate upon a suspension of disbelief which refuses *a priori* human agency in the appearances, both around the palace and on the dancing ground. Both allude to metamorphosis (*finte*). Both refer to concepts of the wild and of Europe as the 'other'. Both contain life force, as do masks, and make multifarious and layered allusions to or represent metaphors of the ancestors, status and power.

Metamorphosis lies at the heart of these relationships, and is central to the exercise of power in Oku. The king's particular ability to metamorphosise is acquired by medicinal applications during the enthronement ceremony, which allows him to become a leopard at night, a form in which he is able to travel invisibly (the coat of the leopard, through an effect known as *warle*, is considered to have the magical potential to render it invisible) and to gain knowledge of all that passes in his kingdom. This power is also a power of bi-location, since, during his nocturnal journeys, he does not leave his bed. Though it is widely believed to be the basis for the omniscience of the king, metamorphosis – *finte* – is nevertheless not exclusive to him. Masqueraders (those who enter the masquerade costume, and who are never referred to verbally in Oku) also engage in a transformation from person to a type of wild creature which also is said to come from the forest, and to have close contacts with the world of the dead. Masqueraders thus gain access to the other world when they use the powers of the masquerade to metamorphose (*finte*). Finally, certain infants and children, known as 'children of the gods' do not acquire, but are born with this ability: often referred to as 'single twins', they are never completely in this world, but have kept a foot in that of the ancestors who perpetually tempt them back. In addition, or as another dimension of, this tendency to hover between two worlds, children of the gods also transform themselves into lizards or snakes and climb into their mothers' baskets as they set out to the farm in the morning. The various forms of metamorphosis are thus closely related to each other, and the metamorphosis of the king is by no means a discrete privilege. In one notable homology between the king and the children of the gods, it is said that Mkong Mote, one of the first and most glorified kings of Oku, was resurrected as a snake after his burial in the palace, emerging from the king's grave and setting forth upon a journey deep into the forest where he pointed out the site for a new, twin palace to be built.[3] In another homology, this one between the king and masquerades, myths of origin of the early kings of Oku depict them as hunters who spent most of their time in the forest, whereas those concerning masquerades often emphasize the sylvan origin of the creatures, and the fact that they were roaming amongst the ancestors in the most inaccessible, secret spaces of the forest before they were lured into the compound. In other words, to possess a masquerade house in one's compound is to have direct access (access not mediated by the palace) to the other world.[4]

The significance of the rites surrounding the installation of a new king in Oku can be approached from two different theoretical directions. On the one hand, one could adopt a cognitive approach that would focus on the symbolic content of the appearances and their 'meaning'. On the other hand, one could focus on the emotive impact of the appearances, on the sense of surprise and danger associated with them, and the way this form of embodied reaction to the palace appearances might create structuring memories which help to define the experience of danger associated with lineage masquerades. In preferring the second, embodied approach, I agree with Schieffelin that:

> Symbols are effective less because they communicate meaning (though this is also important) than because, through performance, meanings are formulated in a social rather than cognitive space, and the participants are engaged with the symbols in the interactional creation of a performance reality, rather than merely being informed by them as knowers.[5]

Cognitive memory is self-conscious and reflective; as such it is easily verbalized. Performative or habit memory, on the other hand, is not easily verbalized and is 'as nearly as possible without reflection'.[6] Such pre-reflective bodily memories materialize only through enactment. Furthermore, habitual bodily memory informs present bodily actions.[7] Though not often explicitly said, habit memory has nonetheless been assumed to be governed by rules. Bourdieu takes this position to an extreme; in his analysis, habit memory is not only governed, but governing.[8] It may however be possible to accept the importance of bodily memory without resorting to the determinism of Bourdieu, and that is what I attempt to do here.

While the form and choreography of the palace appearances have an immediate contemporary significance, a 'meaning' which the subject can verbalise and consciously reflect upon, they may also be considered in relation to the vintage masquerades in outlying villages. By juxtaposing the quotidian masquerades with the memories of the historical moment of the appearances surrounding the loss of the king, we can explore the hegemonic consequences of bodily memory. Yet while bodily memory has been seen as highly rule governed, it may also be possible for it to be a malleable, plastic space open to re-interpretation through re-experience over time. The potential for the reshaping of bodily memory suggests that a memorial dialectic of power may obtain in Oku – that the bodily experience that the village masquerades elicit can allow one to relive and thereby to call into question one's memories of the palace appearances.

A timetable of events leading to the coming out by the new *king*

- 1 June 1992; Construction of the *ndavos* building going on (*cf.* Figures 4 and 5).
- 21 June 1992; The *kebambo fon* statue installed (Figure 6).
- 22 June 1992; cloth stretched across the *ndavos*.
- 24 June 1992; The 'twins' appear.
- 26 June 1992; The procession takes place, display of the palace treasury, during which the king appears wearing the white feather headdress.
- 29 June 1992; The 'God of the Market' appears in the old market, followed by the king with his wives and the 'things of the palace': the palace collection.
- 29 June 1992; The *ndavos* building shot through with spears by the princes. Appearance and 'regicide' of the leopard (*ba'*) in the palace court yard.

Loss and Eternity: A Royal Installation

The death of the palace

In early June 1992, while the new king was still in internment inside the palace in Elak, the building of a structure known as the *ndavos* (Figures 4 and 5) was undertaken by members of the *ngele* royal society in the western end of the palace courtyard on the edge of the road. The word *ndavos* is a composite of *nda* – house – and *ebves*, meaning fire, but also, by association with this original meaning, having come to signify 'dane gun' as well. Dane guns, once used in hunting and warfare, are still a very important element of death celebrations throughout the Grassfields region[9] being fired on the day of the burial by groups of relatives and the societies to which the deceased belonged. The building of the *ndavos* is undertaken every time a king is 'lost' in Oku, the last time being in 1956. Although most of the dwelling houses (as opposed to houses erected for ceremonial purposes) are now built of mud blocks and roofed with corrugated aluminium sheets known as 'zinc' or 'Star' in Pidjin, the *ndavos*, like the central building of the palace compound, is built of bamboo and daub walls with a pyramidal thatched roof. Though only a single-room building measuring no more than 2.5 m by 2.5 m, it is metonymically representative of the palace as a whole. This is evident not only because of its anachronistic style, but also because it was built with two doors – a privilege once reserved exclusively for palace buildings – and cross-hatched bamboo ribs as opposed to parallel vertical ribs, another prerogative of royal architecture.

'Traditional' buildings involve group coordination and activity to construct. The first stage occurs in the higher altitudes of the montane forest, where mature bamboo is cut to build the framework of the walls

Figure 4 Leaping from the ground: the *ndavos* under construction. (Photo: N. Argenti)

and roof, and younger shoots are cut and skinned to produce flexible strips with which to tie the structure together. Being able to build a traditional house in Oku necessitated the status and affiliations necessary to delegate a large enough group of men to collect the materials and erect them, and of women and children to prepare food and accomplish peripheral tasks on the work site, and as such was seemingly a natural statement of the new owner's fitness for his position as the head of a household.[10] A man's power, both physical and economical, is referred to as his *kediar'*. It is a man's *kediar'*, for instance, which determines how many wives he is able to marry.[11] One says of a powerful or influential man in Oku 'he has many people.' The building of the traditional house at the palace therefore brought with it connotations of potency, maturity and control or influence over many people by the *banda*, or 'father of the house', who is related metaphorically to the patron of a masquerade (who also needs a large progeniture to found a masquerade), as a man of power and influence.

Both young and old men of the royal lineage joined together in all stages of the work on the *ndavos*, some of the older men taking it upon themselves to show the younger ones how to go about the intricacies of the task, tying the bamboo poles together in the crosshatched manner reserved as a prerogative of royal family members. Certain days were set aside for work to go on, such that the house might stand in a semi-finished state for some time without change, then proceed by fits and starts to a more completed stage. The walls and roof for 'traditional' houses are all assembled on the ground before being lifted and tied together all at once, so the house seemed one day suddenly to leap from the ground in a nearly finished, though skeletal state; still lacking its grass roof and red mud plastering.[12] Then, as the king continued his internment in the palace, which is known as a 'fattening' period and during which he is treated like a child, being washed and fed by others, so too the house gained its own 'flesh' of red mud and its coiffure of thatch. I use the term 'coiffure' advisedly. The Oku term for the roof of the house, *ketu nda* means 'head of the house', in keeping with a general anthropomorphization of the parts of the house, such as *ebtshuo nda*, meaning 'mouth of the house' for the door, and *eshã nda* 'rump of the house', for its foundations.[13]

Similarly, in the case of the *ndavos* not only is the king the *banda,* or 'father of the house', but the *ndavos* is itself the king. This was made evident in stages: first by the sudden erection of the house close to the moment of the emergence of the king from the palace for the first time; second by the fact that the house is not just built by the community as a whole, the way the rest of the palace is, but by the 'children of the leopard bed' as young royal eligibles (in other words the king's brothers and half

Brothers) are called; and thirdly by the fact that, once built, the house is left to fall into decay, never to be repaired again. As the king grows old in his palace, so too the house will fold in upon itself and crumble into the ground. One of the first signs of deterioration evident on the building when I returned to Oku in early 1997 was the decay of the thatched roof (Figure 5). As one *ndavos* inevitably retreats back into the ground, however, a new one eventually rises nearby on the palace grounds; and already the *ndavos* of the last king is all but invisible, barely guessed from the mound of rotten debris which used to form its structure. In a parallel manner to the cycle of descent into the ground and re-emergence of the *ndavos*, one does not refer to the death of the king explicitly in Oku, but mentions euphemistically that 'the sun has set' or that the king is temporarily 'lost', only to be found again at the culmination of the events described here. Thus is the cyclical perpetuity, or sempiternity[14] of the king's 'body politic' made a part of Oku experience: though each individual king is forgotten as the *ndavos* with which he was associated decays, the office of Fonship endures.

In keeping with these homologies between the king and the *ndavos*, soon after the building had been completed it was wrapped all round with a sheet of *kelanglang* cloth. This is a type of cloth made of resist dyed indigo which is reserved for use as clothing by the king. The cloth is worn only rarely even by the king himself though, and, notably, the last time he does wear it is for his burial, at which stage it is used as a shroud in which to wrap him. As I shall describe below, this funerary use of the cloth prefigures the demise of the *ndavos* which is wrapped in it. It is worth noting that, until the early 1960s, it was rare for ordinary people in Oku to wear any clothes, thus wearing any clothes at all, let alone the *kelanglang* cloth, was in itself a royal marker. In this sense, in the past (including the last installation in 1956) the berobed *ndavos* would have been even more obviously representative of the king. Two days after the clothing of the *ndavos*, and with the king still interned inside the palace, some members of the *ngele* society which built the house entered it in a procession to begin a dance. Standing inside the building as if in the body of the king, they played a drum and a clapperless double bell, and sung '*O nda me kongse we ma jie kemuy e we ndu ko!*' ('Oh! *mekongse* house, When you've eaten 'till all is finished, go back to the forest!')

It is not by chance that this song is sung only in the *ndavos*.[15] Already, within the single artefact we see the concatenation of two elements – the forest and the foreign – which the people of Oku keep returning to, both literally and conceptually, for everything that sustains them: water, food, clothing, work, riches, knowledge and power, both in the form of medical

Figure 5 The *ndavos* in January 1997, with its roof beginning to deteriorate. (Photo: N. Argenti)

or spiritual powers and in the form of political connections. All of these come either from the forest or from *ebey*; a word literally meaning 'outside' but with multi-layered references to other chiefdoms in the Grassfields, to the South West Province where many young men go to find work in the palm plantations, and to the nation-state or to foreign nations. Just as the song refers explicitly to the forest, so the *kelanglang* cloth refers implicitly to 'outside', where it is produced in a highly peripatetic manner, being woven in one part of the country, transported for its wax-resist painting to another, and finally dyed indigo blue in a third, which makes it both rare and expensive, and a highly charged symbol of the many forms of *ebey* condensed in the single artefact.

On 26 June, four days after the 'clothing' of the *ndavos* and two days after the dance by the princes, the new king made his first exit from the palace in front of a crowd of thousands. Before describing this event though, let me tell of one more event involving the *ndavos*, which was not to take place for a further three days after this event. On that day, three royal eligibles from the *ngele* society were chosen to approach the *ndavos* and shoot through the cloth with their spears, which were left bristling from the building for the gathered crowd to see.[16] Later the same day, echoing this symbolic act of internecine regicide, a number of palace retainers emerged from the palace *kwifon* compound to hand out blades of the plant called *jzie*, but which in this case could not be referred to as such, and was called by all present *eghong* – spears. Men eagerly crowded round to get their own and formed a long human corridor stretching the length of the outer palace courtyard. After a few highly charged moments, from somewhere inside the palace a retainer – bent over and with a leopard skin tied to his back – came sprinting through the narrow passage. As he rushed past, the assembled men threw their 'spears' at the hide on his back, shouting triumphantly and shaking their right fists as they did so, in a gesture often made after firing a dane gun or when dancing with a gun or a spear.[17] The person wearing the hide and the event are both referred to as *ba'* – leopard. As I mentioned earlier, eligible princes are known as 'children of the leopard bed'. It is sometimes said that there is a leopard skin on the king's bed, and that a child must be conceived on this bed in order to be eligible for the throne (the child should not have been conceived before his father was himself the king) but there is an even more direct connection between the leopard and the king in the expression *ghon ghe ebkun eba'*: and that is that *ebkun eba'* can mean both 'leopard bed' or 'leopard's bed', because the possessive is not sounded in *eblam ebkwo* the way it is in English. According to this latter, possessive meaning, the expression translates as children of the *leopard's* bed, not the leopard bed. The bed's owner, the king, *is* the leopard.

In keeping with this reading, in the times when there were still leopards in the Oku forest (as late as the 1960s) they were considered royal game, and never intentionally killed. When caught in a trap by mistake, they had to be taken to the palace by the warrior's society members of the nearest village, and the owner of the trap had to be cleansed of his crime with medicines. The king would then appropriate his metamorphosed self, for it is well known that the kings of Oku walked in the forest at night in the form of leopards. Thus, on that single day, not one, but two separate regicides occurred, the killing of the *ndavos* repeated by the killing of the *ba'*. If the building of the *ndavos* had been the first outward sign that the king was 'missing', the symbolic double killing of the king marked the last of the sudden appearances around the palace. Those I shall discuss now therefore occurred within what one might call the 'lifespan' of the *ndavos*.

The royal effigy

On the night of 20 to 21 June, two nights before the *kelanglang* cloth was stretched over the outer walls of the *ndavos*, a statue appeared in a small forest on the northern side of the palace (Figure 6). It was c. 2 ft. high and rubbed in camwood. The statue was carved in the semi-realist style typical of human and animal representations in the kingdom, with a proportionately large head and abdomen and shortened legs. It was known as the *kebambo fon,* and the forest it is placed in, the *kebambo ko*, is named

Figure 6 The *kebambo fon*. (Photo: N. Argenti)

after it. For weeks it had been expected by everyone in the kingdom. People often spoke to me about it before it had appeared, especially the young, who could never have seen one themselves before. No one knew precisely when it would appear though, and when it finally did, the news was spread by word of mouth throughout the kingdom remarkably fast. In spite of its predicted arrival by the people of Oku, there was nevertheless an air of muted awe and surprise when it did finally appear one night. Unlike the *ba'* or the *ndavos*, it was more explicitly seen as a representation of the 'lost' king. As Fai Ndintonen once put it in an interview I had with him, 'He [the *kebambo*] cannot talk to people again, he has gone'. This silence of the statue is an important aspect of it. (Sulking children are sometimes chided by their mothers with the question, 'What are you, a *kebambo*?'). It is both literally and mythically true that the *statue* comes from the forest. I was never able to discuss it with my informants as anything but an apparition which catches everyone unawares during the time when a king is 'lost', but some *kwifon* society members did tell me it is placed in that forest by them. Most of them were in agreement that it used to be left to decay where it stood, like the *ndavos*, but this time it would be taken away back to the *kwifon* compound after some time, for fear of theft.

Like the king in life, the statue stood in the forest with a small basket of kola nuts next to it, ready to 'give' to those who came to see it. There were also four single clapperless bells standing next to it in a row, which Fai Ndintonen likened to the king's palace guard, a few of whom always stand next to the king when he appears in public. It is a fact that the musical instruments of the *kwifon* society are traded as gifts between chiefdoms during the course of royal visits, and that they are normally hidden from public view. When they are brought from one palace to another, they are always hidden from view in ceremonial bags, and given by a messenger directly to the king, who opens the bag in private, putting something from his palace back into it before returning it to the messenger. The instruments are only ever played from behind the palace walls since seeing them while they were being played, like seeing a mask without its full costume in a dance, would be harmful to the non-initiated. Thus, in the statue as in the *ndavos*, we find the two elements of forest – as the literal and mythical provenance of the object, the clapperless bells and as the outside or foreign represented by concatenated into a single appearance. The camwood with which the statue is anointed nicely unifies these two symbols in itself since it has to be obtained from the lower altitude chiefdoms of the south-west, and is thus a thing from 'outside', but it is also a forest product, not a manufactured artefact. The forest king and his musical guard were a symbol of royal potency as much as they were a memorial to a deceased man,[18] and they appeared in a manner seemingly as benign and innocuous as it was surprising.

The display of the 'twins'

On 24 June, three days after the installation of the *kbambo fon* and still five days before the double act of regicide in the palace court yard, came one of the most puzzling of the appearances; the *mboke, nokan* 'twins'. These are never seen bar once during the time of the loss of a king. And yet, like the statue of the king, the twins were eagerly anticipated before their sudden appearance, by people who had little idea what to expect or exactly what would happen when they did appear. All that was known by most people in Elak was that they were a sort of *nokan* or palace jester. A less unusual occurrence around the palace compound, the ordinary *nokan* appears for the death celebration of any *kwifon* or royal death, which includes not only kings, but also any one of the kings' mothers, or fathers. They only come out carrying the statues they call their 'children', however, at a royal death. These behave like palace jesters who appear stripped to the waist, their faces rubbed with kaolin, and carrying oversized twisted sticks in their rough state, as if just pulled out of the forest. They also sometimes carry statuettes, not unlike the statue of the king, but rubbed in white kaolin rather than red camwood. These figures are often referred to as their 'children' and used by them for making suggestive jokes. What few clothes they wear are always in complete tatters, and much of their behaviour is intended as a mimicry of madness.

There is a flip-side to their merriment, however. They are, after all – like a masquerade – metamorphosed from their human state in spite of the transparency of their 'disguise', which does not hide their identity. Finally, in the pouring rain, people crowded in the main courtyard started to shout that the twins were approaching. Suddenly, to everyone's consternation and in the midst of cries of hilarity, two men (who were not referred to as men but only as *mbska nokan*) rubbed from head to foot in (white) kaolin and naked but for a leaf covering their genitals, were forcibly led down to the front of the palace. The interest of the gathered crowd exceeded anything I have witnessed either before or afterwards in the kingdom. The two were prodded and pulled along by the lone jester who led them by a cord attached to their wrists down to the centre of the main court yard, where they were made to sit as hundreds of people crowded round in spite of the driving rain and the interdiction on using umbrellas round the palace. The guardian jester kept the curious from getting too close by waving his long, ungainly stick about, and elicited yet more gales of laughter by beating down all the umbrellas he could get at. The two twins, meanwhile, sat in silence (like the *kebambo fon*), their heads down, looking dejected. After some time, all of the palace retainers, appearing in the guise of ordinary palace jesters, came down in single file, to perform the dance known by the verb *senar'*,[19] at which point the two 'twins' were allowed to leave by their tormentor, and set off running back into the palace compound.

It turned out that those chosen to be the 'twins' were new members of the society, recruited (the Oku word is *ghal*, to hold in the sense of catching something and holding it fast) as part of the ceremonies, though the great bulk of the new recruits were not to be 'held' until over a year later. In an interview with one of the new recruits who had himself been chosen to be a 'twin' (and whose name I consequently cannot disclose) I discovered that the lack of exegesis went much further than the youthful crowd gathered at the palace. In fact, the new recruit told me that he himself had had no idea of the existence of the 'twins' before he was asked to be one himself. He refused, but was told he had no choice, being one of the only ones suitable because of his membership to both *kwifon* and *mbeley*, a masquerade group. His colleague and he were then put in a room alone with one *ntshinda* who undressed them (here again, as with the king during this period, treating them like children) and rubbed their whole bodies with the kaolin. The colour white in Oku is associated with sickness and disease. It is thus opposed to red, such as camwood or *red people*, as Europeans are called, and to black, the colour of the healthy body. Those who are unwashed and covered in dust (such as children or the insane) and those who are ill or dying are referred to with an active form of the colour: '*eb fefe fefe*'; which can be glossed as he/she *is whiting* rather than the passive form *is white*. These three colours are the only ones explicitly named. White is associated not only with pallor, but also with dullness, while red (such as camwood and palm oil both used to rub the body) and black are shiny, glossy, and suggest health and vigour. The two 'twins' therefore suggest caricatures of children, or madmen (like the *nokan* themselves) or walking corpses once they have been rubbed with kaolin. After being rubbed, the left hand of each one was tied with a creeper picked inside the traditional forest of the *kwifon* compound. These creepers were later used as leads with which they were dragged into the centre of the compound. Again, my informant told me that most of the other *kwifon* society members were 'very surprised' when they suddenly saw them appear, for most of them had had no forewarning of the event, whereas the ones pulling them on were senior members who had seen this before during the celebrations in 1956.

After their double humiliation in the *kwifon* compound itself then outside it in the public arena of the palace court yard, the two 'twins' were made to wash (they were not washed by another) and put their clothes on before being offered a luxurious meal. At this stage they had regained their autonomy and were no longer treated as children. The food they were offered was not prepared in the *kwifon* compound however, but in the king's side of the palace, and the person who prepared it for them was the king's private cook. Are the 'twins' then to be seen as embodiments of the *lost* king? At this point in the events, the previously described regicide around the *ndavos* has not yet happened, and the old king is therefore still symbolically alive. We can now turn our attention to Fai Ndintonen again. He has lived long enough to see the 'twins' appear three times, and says it is the same each time, just as the other appearances are also very similar. His answer to my question was 'yes', not only, he went on, do the 'twins' stand for the lost king, but the new king is *himself* transformed into the lost one (who has not been announced as lost at that stage) when he first enters the palace. At that time, he stays for two days without being washed or rubbed with oil or camwood. This results, the Fai explained, in his skin going 'white' or *'whiting'* in the active form of the word, just like that of the lost king, and just like that of the 'twins'. '*Mboke nokan* is for the old one' he stated, referring to the lost king. 'They are made to show he has been sitting just like that, and he has died'.[20] The king is always buried in a sitting position. I asked, if it was really such a symbol of royalty, why the members of the crowd were laughing and jeering rather than showing respect.

'The young ones laugh, even the last time, only small children were laughing; those who don't know . . . even the way they see you now, they will be laughing at you, how you are white, but they will respect you. You saw that no one can touch it'.

Over and above the single vision of symbolic correspondence between the white 'twins' and the king then, the 'twins' represent a layered and plastic nexus for signification, taking on different forms of relevance at different times and in different places, or even in the same place over a short period of time, such as with the process of metamorphosis described for the cassowary/tree dancer for the Umeda of New Guinea by Gell.[21] The distinction between the separate kings is blurred in the apparition of the twin figures, hence their very doubleness. Turner has described this situation already with respect to rites of passage, including those of the *mwadi*, or chief-designate among the Ndembu:

> The symbolism . . . surrounding the liminal persona is complex and bizarre . . . The structural invisibility of liminal personae has a twofold character. They are at once no longer classified and not yet classified. In so far as they are no longer classified, the symbols that represent them are . . . drawn from the biology of death, decomposition, [and] catabolism . . . The metaphor of dissolution is often applied to neophytes; they are allowed to go filthy and identified with the earth . . . [They] are neither living nor dead from one aspect, and both living and dead from another. Their condition is one of ambiguity and paradox, a confusion of all the customary categories.[22]

Ambiguity about the origins of the appearances as 'inside' or 'outside', local or foreign, is echoed in other ambiguities relating to the 'twins' status as human or masquerade, white or black, healthy or sick, alive or dead, and it is echoed in the most puzzling ambiguity of all, is it singular or plural? Why do we see two 'twins' when there is only one king? As Turner has argued, the twin figures mark the momentary co-existence of the no-longer with the not-yet: there is no king, and yet there are two coexisting (the former as yet not symbolically assassinated).[23] In a way, this is the problem all the appearances set about solving; they are a means of sending the old king to the land of the ancestors.[24] But there is another reason for the representation of the king in two bodies. The answer lies in the notion of *koyui*; breath or life force. The *mboke nokan* appear like twins, and it is well known that twins are travesties of nature because, although they have two separate bodies, they share only one life force. The means by which twins manage to appear in two places, two bodies, when they have only one life force, is because they are capable of metamorphosis. They can transform themselves at will into a variety of animals and have the power to be in two places at once, as anyone who has ever seen identical twins can attest to. Thus two individual kings of Oku, as represented in the appearance of the 'twins', are revealed to share a single life force, and by this principle to rule according to the same right. The 'twins'' appearance marks their unity; and though it emphasizes the descent into the earth of the *whiting* ruler, it emphasizes in the same stroke the rebirth into the world of that same ruler. This tendency is demonstrated with respect to twins and 'single twins' (children born through breach birth, with clenched fists, or with their umbilical cord wrapped across their chest – mimetic of the king's protective bands of medicine, *waf*, worn across his chest)[25] with respect to their widely acknowledged proneness to die and reappear in their mother's womb at her subsequent pregnancy, a tendency which has given rise in Oku to the practice of naming such returning children 'Ghost' (*Kvosay*).

The king' s first public appearance

26 June, 1992. It was after the remarkable appearance of the *twins* but before the symbolic regicide already discussed that the new king came out of the palace for the first time. This involved a ceremony on a grand scale (although the audience, large as it was, was not quite what it had been for the appearance of the 'twins') which, like the appearance of the 'twins', was remarkable for the unpredictability of its timing and for its brevity as much as anything else. Again, the audience at the palace was speculating for days about when it might happen, with rumours and counter-rumours running wild as to the appointed day. On the morning of 26 June, however, the xylophone from Pa Yundji's compound in Ichim, which only plays outside its own compound for royal death celebrations at the palace, was playing at the palace. From that moment it was certain that, barring rain, the ceremony would occur that day. After the xylophone had been played for hours on end, during a brief lull in the rain, the procession suddenly burst forth from the main door of the palace.

The surprise was overwhelming. The vast majority of those present had never witnessed the event before and had little idea what to expect. During the brief minutes of the procession itself, in the midst of the music and the noise, the rush to get closer and the rush not to be pushed too close, there was time to do nothing but to look, to see, to witness. At the head of the procession came the *fon* of Sawe, a chiefdom to the north of Oku.[26] Directly behind the *fon* of Sawe came Fai Nsaanen, the second in command in the royal family after the king, and directly behind him the new king of Oku followed by his wives (all inherited from the last king) who carried the 'things of the palace'. On his head, only on this single occasion in his life-span, the new king wears a cap of white feathers known as the *fenen mbong*. This cap is associated with the second king of Oku, Mkong Mote, who is reputed to have had greater *finte* powers than any other of the kings of Oku, and to have obtained the cap at the bottom of the sacred lake Mawes, which he entered along with a rival chief to have the god Mawes decide herself/himself who the rightful ruler of the lake and the lands around it should be.[27] In the end, the rival chief was killed, or in other versions of the myth was condemned to roam indefinitely at the bottom of the lake, and Mkong Mote arose from Mawes triumphantly bearing the cap of white feathers on his head.

In other myths about Mawes a whole town is said to exist at the bottom of the lake, and we can thus see Mawes as a Sawe-like inversion of the kingdom of Oku. Like the 'twins', the cap of white feathers is a symbol at the essence of the kingdom itself. It springs from within the kingdom, from a time when the kingdom is seen to have been in the midst of its own formation, and reveals itself as an ambiguous collage of the natural reorganized in a man-made mythical bird. As a gift from Mawes, it sanctions the origins of the kingdom through supernatural agencies grounded in the landscape, and it gives a sense of continuity to the royal line exclusive of any outside influence. It is not surprising then that one *kwifon* member I spoke to about it likened the pure whiteness of the cap to that of the 'twins'.

Just as the cap of white feathers the king wears alludes to notions of an exclusively 'inside' Oku, hermetically sealed in its autonomy from the influences of outside sources of power and influence, and tracing descent back to the most *finte* of all the kings through an artefact associated not only with the ground, but with a god who resides deep inside a submerged crater of the landscape, so the 'things of the palace' that his newly acquired wives carried behind him represent a creolized version[28] of all the sources of power in the Oku cosmology which lie beyond the borders of the kingdom. The women who carried the objects seemed to want to efface themselves, to disclaim any rights to the objects for which they simply acted as the impersonal vehicles. The objects, most of them from outside the kingdom, portray human faces, such as the European Toby jug or the Bamoum brass drinking horns from Foumban. Others bear exotic motifs not usually seen in Oku, such as bats' heads, and they are carved and decorated in styles that look distinctly foreign. Beaded calabashes and whisks allude to contact with the palm oil producing regions to the south, beyond the borders of the Grassfields culture area. Although foreign, the items in the collection have evidently been chosen according to a truly local aesthetic: the faces on the ceramic Toby jugs are seen as homologous to carvings of faces made in the kingdom, which are always reserved for use by the king. Only the palace can have representations of human beings on its lintels and posts. Only the king can sit on a stool with human caryatids, or use bowls of wood or clay with human faces incised into them. This aesthetic prerogative is simply transposed to the European artefacts in the collection. Objects of European (or perceived European) provenance have been included in palace collections in the Grassfields at least since first contact with Europeans, and probably before. See, for example, Geary, *Things of the Palace*,[29] on the Bamoum palace collection, and Ankermann, *Völkerkundliche Aufzeichnungen*,[30] who described Fon Tam of Bum's grave house thus: 'On the grave, a large porcelain vase, a pith helmet and a broken earthenware dish. At the head of the grave . . . was a bench, and on and below it was a carved wooden stool of spider design and an old phonograph'. Sally Chilver[31] wrote likewise 'I examined some of the Bali treasure and found Toby jugs (English, Staffordshire), red Bohemian glass carafes with gilt stoppers, and some perfectly awful German (allegedly) Art Deco jardinières. The fon of Big Babanki (Kedjom Kegu) showed me some very pretty blue-banded lustreware (English?) jugs "worth plenty slave". At Bamali palm wine was being poured out of a very large brown-glazed teapot, lid missing'.[32]

Just as the inside or local appearances that reveal the highest essence of the chiefdom relate the king back to the foundational myths of Oku as a locus set in opposition to the outside, so the appropriation, the reinterpretation, the dissimulation and the selective revealing of the foreign or outside through the palace, like the representations of the wild in the *ndavos* and the *kebambo fon*, reveal the palace as the essential nexus whereby the unmanageable, the untamed, the unknown, the unpossessed, are transformed into the knowable, the civilized, the cultured, the contained. The container here is not only the palace as a structure that houses the collection, but the sacred office of kingship.[33] Indeed, the *finte* powers of metamorphosis attributed to the king are not innate in the individual chosen for the office, but are fed to him in the form of medicines from the forest by the king-makers inside the palace. The office thus transcends the individual who fills it at any one time, and king and palace are simply two facets of the ongoing metamorphosis of the wild or the foreign into the civilized and the local. The power of kingship in the time of the loss of the king and the installation of the new one is revealed in the appearances at the palace as an ambivalent juxtaposition of the risible with the dangerous, the approachable with the forbidden, the benign with the deadly and of the foreign with the local. These are not discrete oppositions; together they form an organic continuum of power and its negotiation between Oku, its neighbouring polities, and the nation state.

The God of the Market

29 June 1992. Nowhere is this more true than in the case of the final appearance I want to discuss; that of the God of the Market, so called after the site on which he appears; the old market place by the roadside on the northern edge of the palace. The site, long since overgrown, had been cleared with cutlasses on the night before the God's appearance. Thus on the morning of 29 June, what had always looked like a part of the *kwifon* sacred forest which surrounds the palace suddenly appeared like a rough clearing. I walked down to the palace around mid-morning, at which point the God was already present on the site, and had been since before the break of dawn; squatting by a standing stone in the hard,

steady rain. On his head was a bamboo umbrella of a type no longer made or used in the kingdom.[34] The God carried a plant (Dracaena) in his hand. This plant, several species of which can be found growing wild in the forest, is often cultivated around people's houses and considered both decorative and functional. It is used in certain medicines and considered effective in warding off sickness. In its natural state it tends to grow in dark, wet places, so it is associated with coolness. The word *sane* means both cool and wet and has positively valued connotations of fecundity, as opposed to heat and dryness which refer to bareness, unruliness and disorder, chaos or insanity. Fresh, clean cold spring water is described as *sane*. In Pidjin Dracaena is known throughout the Grassfields as a 'peace plant', but the masquerade of *kwifon* uses a large species of it to wield in its dance. In this context the plant has a different name: it is called *fiar'*, meaning cutlass or sword, and the leader or *kam* of the masquerades does in fact dance with a real, Fulani-style sword from the north. Cutlasses and knives are often used in medicine in the kingdom, where they are considered an essential means of warding off the spells of evil-wishers. Perhaps for this reason the plant is associated with kings throughout the Grassfields, often being depicted on the rubber stamps they use to authenticate their official communications. In Oku the king also has the power to grant special dispensations (*bur'ma*) for a masquerade group to gain the right to dance with the plant in the mouths of some of its masks. The plant of the God is therefore both a weapon and a symbol of peace at once; an assertion of medicinal power and of royal authority that links the God, and by extension the king which it is meant to call forth from the palace, with the ambiguous powers of the forest. The apparent paradox of why the God of a market should be intimately linked with the king is apparent in an expression used by Fai Ndintonen, who, in order to placate me, told me that the God comes from the *ebtshuo mj in*. This composite term translates as 'the mouth of the gods', and refers to the house which the kings are buried in. This house is in fact hidden in the forest just a few paces from where the God appears at the path on the way from the *kwifon* compound to the market. His appellation as God of the Market is therefore a complete misnomer.[35] In keeping with the anthropomorphization of buildings discussed above, the word for mouth in Oku is the same as the word for door. The burial house of the kings is therefore known as the 'doorway to the gods', and this God is the God of that house. This God has a duty, Fai Ndintonen went on, 'the duty of the God is to bring the new *fon* to address the public.'

Again, like some of the other appearances, the God's presence had been eagerly anticipated by the people of Elak, but when I went down to the palace to photograph him I was alone. Unlike with the 'twins', the very few people who happened to be passing did not stop and stare or even give any sign that they had seen the God. I do not interpret this apparent lack of attention as disinterest, but rather as the conscious avoidance of something dangerous, much like the correct behaviour relative to secret society houses, which people will contour at a distance rather than walk straight past, or the avoidance of the palace *kwifon* society along a road in daytime. People said of the God of the Market that one never sees him arrive or leave. The informant from *kwifon* I mentioned earlier went on to compare the surprise caused by the 'twins' to that caused by the God of the Market. Both of them were relatively unknown except by the older generation. Both appeared unpredictably in a metamorphosed state, which prohibited inquiry into their personal, social identities, or into their place of origin.

The expression used to refer to what I have called surprise is rendered in 'my mouth dried', a phrase which not only highlights the loss for words which results from amazement or wonder ('dry' or *yume* also alludes to an absence in a more general sense, and connotes emptiness, lack or disappearance – in this case a lack of words) but that also points to the lack of saliva that accompanies fear. Apart from the linguistic exegesis to be drawn from the expression used to refer to the state of surprise, I would add that the experience of 'dry mouth' itself seems often to include the sensation of the presence of the unknown, of that which one has no conventional social norms for assessing. It is at the heart of this sense of surprise or fear-and-attraction[36] that one does not know how the appearances of the palace came into being or where. If people were 'surprised' in spite of the fact that they evidently eagerly expected the appearances, it is because the state people described to me had to do with this proximity to the unfathomable rather than the unexpected.[37]

After associating the 'twins' with the essence of insidedness in Oku, the *kwifon* member went on to relate them to the God of the Market, which in his view was equally essential to the kingdom. The fact that no foreigners are allowed to participate in the 'twins' ceremony he said, was 'Almost just like the *feyin ewey ntok* which just comes out on the cry of the *fon*. It's just like the 'twins'. It used to come out in the night at *ebtshuo mjin* (the Mouth of the Gods)'. My informant then went on to describe how when the king is coming out of the palace for the second time everyone turns to look at him and the God disappears . . . 'People are surprised' he repeated, referring to the sense of wonder created by the sudden absence. Even he, as an official member of the king's entourage, and other young officiates at the ceremony 'were surprised by the God's disappearance'.

Another informant, Pa Ngek, with whom I had had an interview on the subject of the God of the Market declined to entertain a final question about the origin of the statue which until then I had only been able to gather came 'from the forest', like the God. When I asked him about where the statue had come from he replied 'if I knew that I could have told you where the *feyin* came from also!' I got a distinct sense of impropriety when asking such questions. I got the sense that my informants would not by choice ask *themselves* these questions.

The Bodily Re-Experience of Danger as a Form of Collective Memory

How can memories of the palace appearances that have been described in some detail be re-evaluated in the light of people's experience of lineage masquerade performances as they occur in the villages? Although the palace appearances taken as a cognitive memory may seem static, in the sense that they seem ultimately inscrutable – a cultural *étant donné* – I suggest that seeing these memories as not only cognitive but embodied, not only thought but experienced, paves the way toward an affective history of memory in Oku. Such a history would emphasize *not* the supposed doxic, unquestionable nature of embodiment, but rather the fact that 'habitual bodily memories intersect with cultural traditions and are sometimes deeply influenced by such traditions in a complex dialectical interplay'.[38] My interest is in the specific configuration of this dialectic, as memories, *qua* experience, come to be re-experienced and thereby re-evaluated during masquerade performances. The palace hierarchy as it is acted out and lived bodily, and the lineage masquerades as they are performed and experienced, are connected by the tissue of an experiential dialectic. These two sets of experience are not ultimately discrete; each gains its particular salience from the memorial proximity of the other. I suggest in particular that the bodily memories of arrest or 'surprise' – 'dry mouth' – at witnessing the palace appearances are not 'habitual' but particularized, only occasionally elicited, and then only by phenomena giving rise to a similar, though more explicit experience of danger, such as a lineage masquerade performance. Cases such as this may cause us to doubt the deterministic position that embodied or 'habit' memory constrains the subject in a Procrustean structure anchored in the past while leaving the subject to believe himself or herself to be free.[39] Bodily memory is not merely about replication, it also concerns difference: difference on the subjective level in terms of the opening-out to new horizons which the experience of masquerade performances enables, and thereby difference also in terms of the subversion of the hegemony of the memories of the palace appearances through the counter-hegemonic experience of lineage masquerades.

A brief account of the lineage masquerades, of their relationship to the other world of the forest on the one hand, and to the village on the other, will be sufficient to explain this point. Lineage masquerades are owned by lineage elders, the heads of extended families living in large compounds from which subsequent generations of men have gone out to form their own sub-compounds. These lineage elders house the paraphernalia of their masquerades in a building within or close to their compound. The masquerade group as a whole is made up of a set of individual masquerades – by which I mean the dancer (who is never verbally acknowledged to exist) and the costume, made up of a gown, jute face covering, wooden mask or feather head-dress, ankle rattles and spear, whisk or cudgel. Those wearing carved wooden masks must include a minimum set to be complete, including a representation of a military society officer, which leads the group, two representing young women, one a titled elder, a bush cow or elephant, which brings up the rear of the dancing line, and a zoomorphic creature carrying two weighty cudgels, which polices the audience and the other masquerades, keeping the latter in step to the rhythm of the accompanying xylophone and drum ensemble.

All sorts of prohibitions surround masquerade groups and very few of the actors, even when prompted by me, are able or willing to come up with any verbal exegesis or historical information about the groups. Even the stories of origin common in other chiefdoms of the Grassfields are relatively uncommon in Oku, and told very much tongue-in-cheek when they are told at all, with the implication that these have no explanatory value. Many interdictions prevent speaking about masquerades in public at all, and women, as in many parts of the world as well as in Oku, are never meant to admit that they know the secret that men dance the masquerades. Behaviour when in their presence is accordingly reserved and calculated. Even when such behaviour appears natural, it is the result of years of meticulously learned and embodied precautions; not to step on the veranda of the masquerade or secret society house (*ndamkum*), not to go into it without taking one's shirt off, not to sleep with a woman after dancing a masquerade, not to dance too many of them for too long for fear of madness. Indeed the threat of illness is all-pervasive concerning masquerades. A performance can seem like rather an overpowering exercise in which the individual disappears in the face of the authority of the *bamkum*, the father of the masquerade, and his barely restrained creatures. In spite of these precautionary habits, however, (habits mimetic of those regarding proper behaviour in the palace) I believe that Oku notions of metamorphosis (*finte*) and danger, actually lie at the heart of a form of *revealing* of the hegemonic structures in the chiefdom, and that, in the act of revealing, they question, challenge and reformulate as much as they support or perpetuate, the structures of power with which they are juxtaposed.[40] The experiences of danger, radical departure from normality, bi-location and animality to which we may now turn are themselves a form of embodied knowledge.[41]

Those attending a memorial death celebration crowd into the host-compound's courtyard, going about the business of preparing and consuming food and drink, greeting each other and merrily socializing and reminiscing about the deceased compound elder(s) who is being transformed into a *bona fide* ancestor. It is into this packed and teeming environment that the masquerade (belonging to that compound or to another) suddenly bursts forth, producing a breath-taking explosion of sound and movement. Masquerades are known to be medicinally potent and dangerous, and their dance is electrifying in its display of barely contained energy, but they are also felt to be beautiful and attractive, cool and fertile. During the performance the crowd does not merely spectate – it joins into a heady dialectic of pleasure and fear, proximity and avoidance, seduction and revulsion, and it participates in the performance; a man, for example, grabs a masquerades' spear and brandishes it above his head while sprinting around the xylophone. Meanwhile, a group of women dances around the outside of the circle of masquerades as others still throw gifts of small change at their feet as they come crashing past. In to the midst of this complex, multi-centred dance bursts the *bamkum*, the father of the masquerade, with a live cock from which he ostentatiously plucks feathers to stick onto the 'perspiring' mask of the leading masquerade. The rest of the onlookers are not passive either: in the tightly knit circle they have formed round the dance, they actively contain the masquerade, the members of which threaten to burst through the crowd at any moment with the momentum of their gyrations.

If, at the end of the day, memorial rites are celebratory in Oku, it is not only because the passage of the deceased elder to ancestorhood has been marked, but because the appearance of a masquerade signals a sort of triumph for the attendant crowd over the danger it represents. This participatory aesthetic of danger is precisely what is not available during the palace appearances. There is no Manichæan opposition between 'bad' or 'harmful' palace appearances and 'good' or 'harmless' lineage masquerades. Rather, the danger that masquerades represent is physically overcome during a village death celebration, while at the palace the audience never participates with the appearance, no proximity or dialectic ensues between person and appearance, and the explicit sensation of danger is sublimated. The palace appearances juxtapose positive themes of 'the known', of harmlessness, beauty, attraction, playfulness and hilarity with themes of 'the unknown', of death, disease, subjection, violence, danger, absence and disappearance. The emotive effect of all of these themes is collectively summed up at the time in the laconic gloss of 'dry mouth'; a euphemism which emphasizes the lack of verbalization of the experience of witnessing the palace appearances, and discourages conscious reflection upon the themes of subjection which they ultimately refer to. As a result, these experiences are sublimated and, as it were, left dormant. The sense of danger that was sublimated at the palace, furthermore, is later enacted there bodily, through practices that at this stage *are* habitual, experienced simply as respect or as a precaution (such as the embodiment of the attitude of self-effacement practised by those who set foot in the palace, including a myriad of physical minutiae such as bending over, looking at the ground, removing one's shoes, not carrying a bag, stick or umbrella, covering one's mouth when speaking in the presence of the king and avoiding his gaze) such that the actor does not *think* the danger or the structures it refers to so much as act in accordance with its unspoken experience. I suggest, however, that these experiences are memorialized for re-use in the sense of fear-and-pleasure at the appearance of the masquerade in quotidian time.[42]

According to this argument, the implicit sensation of danger at the palace in the time of the loss of the king would be mirrored by the explicit sensation of danger in the face of the masquerade. The explicit revelation of danger is only available at a remove from the palace, in the quotidian time and place of the satellite village.[43] Here, the masquerade performance, recalling the fundamentally ambiguous appearances of the palace in its sudden appearance and disappearance – even for those who have never seen the latter, but have embodied the precautions of subjection in their habitus of deference at the palace – at once both reveals in the experience of danger the true face of the hegemonic sway of the palace over the kingdom while simultaneously presenting itself as a limiting factor to that sway. Masquerades, after all, allude to the same amalgam of themes pertaining to 'inside' and 'outside', forest and imaginal Europe, that the palace and kingly bodies are themselves mythically and practically constituted from. They are subversive, or at least traducing, getting their power to reveal directly from the sources that the palace also has recourse to in constituting itself. The palace is at pains to subjugate the revelatory propensity of the masquerades to its own unidirectional model of power flowing from or through the palace as the single source, in which case the only final referent of the experience of danger would be the memories of the appearances at the palace. The masquerades, however, reveal a more pluralistic access to the forest – 'the place of potential'[44] – in their autonomous practice of *bringing in* that which is outside without initial recourse to the palace.

I suggest that it is only once the memorial link between the sense of surprise or wonder – a form of hegemony – around the palace appearances and the more explicit sense of fear-and-attraction, of danger and fascination, at a village masquerade performance – a counter-hegemony – has been established that one can begin to grasp the dialectic of power in Oku. The alluring danger at the heart of the masquerade, which is memorially inseparable from the danger at the palace, opens hegemonic structures to questioning. At the palace, there is perhaps only once in a lifetime *appearance*, but in the village, the masquerade engenders revelation. The experience by the subject of the explosion of palace-based memories of subjugation by way of the village-based lineage masquerades is at once both a recognition of the power of the palace and a revealing of the constructed nature of that power. This moment of resolution is akin to a moment of self awareness, it is an act of transgression that engenders a re-assessment of the taken for granted.

Notes

1. Special thanks are due to Sally Chilver, Mark Johnson, Susanne Küchler, Alexandra Pillen, Michael Rowlands and Edward Schiefelin for their comments on earlier drafts of this paper, and to the members of the Department of Social Anthropology of St Andrews University, where an early draft of this paper was presented in December 1994. The fieldwork that provided the data for this paper was partly funded by the Dapper Foundation.
2. B. Okri, *Astonishing the Gods*, London, Phoenix House, 1995, p. 21.
3. For details of the myth of the python in Fumban, to the east of Oku, see M. D. W. Jeffreys, 'Serpents = Kings', *Nigerian Field* 12 (1947), pp. 38–40, and Jeffreys 'Snake Stones', *Journal of the Royal African Society*, (Oct. 1942), p. 250. V. Turner, *The Forest of Symbols: Aspects*

of Ndembu Ritual, Ithaca and London, Cornell University Press, 1967, p. 99, argues that the symbolism of the snake in many African myths, thanks to its habit of shedding its old skin and re-appearing in a new one, emphasizes re-birth and immortality.

4. See R. Fardon, *Between God, the Dead and the Wild. Chamba Interpretations of Religion and Ritual*, Edinburgh, Edinburgh University Press, 1990, pp. 148–69, on this theme among the Chamba. As he puts it (p. 159):

   > When humanity, the dead and the wild are envisaged as spatially discrete forms of life – within, below and surrounding the village – the mask has the sense of a man-made anomaly that enters the village from the bush and combines the features of the dead and the wild . . . The mask is the exemplary crosser of boundaries.

5. E. Schieffelin, 'Performance and the Cultural Construction of Reality', *American Ethnologist* 12 (1985), p. 707.
6. M. Oakeshott, *Rationalism in Politics*, London, Methuen, 1962, quoted in P. Connerton, *How Societies Remember*, Cambridge, Cambridge University Press, 1989, p. 30.
7. E. S. Casey, *Remembering: A Phenomenological Study*, Bloomington and Indianapolis, Indiana University Press, 1987, p. 149; Connerton, *How Societies Remember*, pp. 21–2.
8. P. Bourdieu, *Outline of a Theory of Practice*, Cambridge, Cambridge University Press, 1977, p. 77.
9. J.-P. Warnier, 'Trade Guns in the Grassfields of Cameroon.' in *Paideuma: Mitteilungen zur Kulturkunde* 26 (1980), pp. 79–92.
10. E. Shanklin, 'The Path to Laikom: Kom Royal Court Architecture', in *Paideuma Mitteilungen zur Kulturkunde* 31 (1985), p. 123.
11. N. J. Bah, 'Marriage in Oku', Baesseler Archiv, Basle, in press, p. 2.
12. For a detailed description (with illustrations) of this process for the Kom palace in 1937, including this stage of the procedure, see P. Gebauer, 'Architecture of Cameroon', in *African Arts*, 5 (1971), p. 46.
13. Shanklin ('Path to Laikom', p. 146) has also noted the 'pun' in the neighbouring kingdom of Kom, where she translates *esaindo* as both 'clan' and 'buttocks of the house'.

    F. Ferretti, *Afo-A-Kom: Sacred Art of Cameroon*, New York, Third Press, 1975, p. 34, likewise noted that this is also the case for the Kom palace, the many buildings of which he argues are laid out anthropomorphically to represent the parts of the human body. Further afield among the Fali of Northern Cameroon, J.-P. Lebeuf (*L'Habitation des Fali*, Paris, Librairie Hachette, 1961, p. 118) has noted that the process of house construction parallels the process of gestation and birth, and S. P. Blier (*The Anatomy of Architecture: Ontology and Metaphor in Batammaliba Architectural Expression*, New York, Cambridge University Press, 1987, p. 119) argues that the Batammaliba of Togo

> suggest that their houses are human, that they represent men and women. The fabric of the house . . . complements that of the human body; the earthen core is its flesh . . . the water used in moistening the earth is its blood, the numerous pebbles are its bones, and the smooth, clay-plaster surface is its skin.

She also notes that the words for house and family — *takieta* — are one and the same (*ibid.*, p. 131), and that the body parts of the human are transposed onto the architectural features of the house; here as in Oku, the door stands for a mouth, the windows for eyes, and so on (*ibid.*, pp. 121-4). Furthermore, she argues, the very act of building a house is itself mimetically evocative of the actions of the ancestors, who model infants from a ball of earth in their mother's womb (*ibid.*, p. 119).

14. E. Kantorowicz (*The King's Two Bodies: a Study in Medieval Political Theology*, Princeton, Princeton University Press, 1957, p. 385) points out that in medieval and early-modern Europe it was said of kings, as Danasus put it in 1215, that *Dignitas nunquam perit, individua vero quotidie pereunt* – 'The Dignity never perishes, although individuals die every day.' This is the core of the notion of sempiternity, according to which kings were not said to have died, as ordinary people, but to have met their 'demise', by which was meant the separation of their body natural from their body politic (*ibid.*, pp. 7 and 13). While the king's body natural perished, his body politic lived on. Thus Bracton could state in the twelfth century that *nullum tempus currit contra regem*; time runneth not against the king (*ibid.*, pp. 164–5).
15. Another verse of the same song goes *we jie ngal-o, Ba ebka, we jie ngal-o* – 'you will eat fire, Ba Ebka, you will eat fire' (*gal* here is synonymous with *vos* – fire/gun).
16. The clothing and piercing with spears of the *ndavos* is remarkably similar to the case among the Batammaliba, who drape clothes on the house of a deceased elder and shoot it with poisoned arrows to ensure that the soul of the deceased will depart in earnest. As S. P. Blier

(*The Anatomy of Architecture: Ontology and Metaphor in Batammaliba Architectural Expression*, New York, Cambridge University Press, p. 125) puts it, 'throughout the funeral drama, the house serves as a surrogate for the recently deceased man or woman', and becomes the locus of symbolic forms of aggression against the deceased elder. In addition to 'killing' the house with poisoned arrows, the elder's ritual adversary calls his secret birth-name, thus denuding him of his former social status in preparation for devolving his position onto another family member.

17. Warnier ('Trade Guns') has recorded this gesture in other chiefdoms of the Grassfields and related it to the act of throwing the spear, or of feigning a throw, a tactic that may have been used a lot in ceremonial forms of warfare in which the death toll seems to have been minimal, even for extended wars.
18. Kantorowicz (*The King's Two Bodies*, p. 420) emphasizes that the effigies produced of kings and placed on top of their coffins in the regalia of State during the burial ceremonies, while their real bodies lay naked or wrapped in a coarse and simple cloth inside the coffin, did not represent the body of the deceased king, but the body politic. '[The king's] normally invisible body politic was . . . visibly displayed by the effigy in its pompous regalia: a *persona ficta* – the effigy – impersonating a *persona ficta* – the *Dignitas*.' Similarly in Oku, though overt statements associate the statue to the deceased *fon*, there is an ambiguity about its identity that has a similar effect to that of the effigies of Early Modern Europe. The oxymoron of representing precisely the *fon* who is 'lost' suggests simultaneously that it is fonship, and not this or that particular *fon* who is represented.
19. This dance does not occur like a normal masquerade dance, but rather like a parody of one played out by a host of fools. For one thing there is no xylophone played, and the *nokan* simply beat their twisted sticks together for any rhythmic accompaniment to their 'dance', which is actually more of a pathetically disordered shuffle. As they proceed slowly round the palace courtyard, their leader call out phrases of gibberish in a high-pitched voice, and the others all answer in a similarly emasculated giggle: 'Hi! Hi! Hi! Ho! Ho! Ho!'
20. Note the similarity of this statement to that above (recorded on a separate occasion) regarding the *kbambo* fon: 'He cannot talk to people again, he has gone.'
21. A. Gell, *Metamorphosis of the Cassowaries: Umeda Society, Language and Ritual*, University of London Monographs on Social Anthropology, London, Athlone Press, 1975, pp. 236–7.

22. Turner, *Forest of Symbols*, pp. 96–7.
23. In a recent article, P. Petit ('Les Charmes du Roi Sont les Esprits des Morts: Les Fondements Religieux de la Royauté Sacrée Chez les Luba du Zaïre', *Africa* 66 (1996), pp. 349–366) has quoted an excerpt of an incantation used during the enthronement of the Luba king in Zaïre (from J. A. Theuws, 'Naître et Mourir dans le Rituel Luba', *Zaïre* 14 (1960), pp. 115–73) which also emphasizes the ambiguity of the king;

    The chief has no preference
    The chief has no good or bad
    The stranger is his, the villager his
    The good is his, and the bad is his
    The sane is his and the insane is his

    My translation. (On Central African kings and otherness, *cf.* also L. de Heusch, *The Drunken King, or the Origin of the State*, Bloomington, Indiana University Press, 1982.)
24. Tardits has described an obviously related event that supports this claim. Accounts remembered by some of his older informants in the Kingdom (now Sultanate) of Foumban to the East of Oku would have it that two slaves used to be emasculated and buried alive with the king:

    > Tradition relates that in the past a pair of twins, amongst whom the chief of the palace twins, were buried at the same time as the king after having been emasculated: The deed cannot but be very ancient, associated as it is with the death of King Mbuambua.

    (C. Tardits, *Le Royaume Bamoum*, Paris, Librarie Armand Colin, 1980, p. 707, my translation.)
25. *cf.* Diduk, 'Twins, Ancestors and Socio-Economic Change in Kedjom Society', in *Man* (n.s.) 28 (1993), pp. 551–71, for a description of the 'single twins' of the nearby kingdom of Kedjom Keku. Diduk argues that there was a growing propensity to diagnose children as 'single twins' throughout the economic crisis of the 1980s.
26. The *fon* of Sawe had been sitting in public on the throne in the palace at Elak for days on end, and is the king *ex-officio* during the period in Oku when the *fon* is lost, and before he is found again. Sawe has historically been the place to where those exiled from the kingdom of Oku have fled, and even the original king there is said to have arrived as the result of a miraculous accident. He had been sentenced to death in Oku and was being executed in the customary way – that is, he was

carried, with his hands and legs bound, and left to stand on a stone precariously balanced in the middle of a rushing torrent that flows over the edge of a cliff just inches to the front of the stone. Somehow, once he fell, he failed to die, but was carried by the river to the place he founded as his kingdom. This myth fits in with another one that equates Sawe with the land of the dead, for surely the king did die, and it is his spirit (*keyus*) or his ghost (*kvosay*) which went on to found the kingdom. In any case many people in Oku today still refer to Sawe as the place they will go to once they are dead. Speaking of Sawe is a euphemism for speaking of death, and those now living in Sawe are seen as the souls (*keyus*) of those who once lived in Oku. Sawe, like the lake Mawes, is an inversion of Oku, and its king, when the one in Oku is lost, *is* the king of Oku, he is the soul of the lost one, for it follows from the logic of the myth that the king, once lost, should find himself as the king in Sawe.

27. N. Argenti, 'The Material Culture of Power in Oku: North West Province, Cameroon', PhD. thesis, University of London, 1996, pp. 18–19.
28. M. Rowlands, 'The Creolization of West-African culture', *Museums Journal* 91 (1991).
29. C. Geary, *Things of the Palace a catalogue of the Bamum Palace Museum in Fumban (Cameroon)* Studien zur Kulturkunde 60, Wiesbaden, Franz Steiner Verlag, 1983.
30. B. Ankermann, *Völkerkundliche Aufzeichnungen im Grassland von Kamerun 1907–1909*, eds H. Baumann and L. Vajda, Basle, Baesseler Archiv, NF, Bd. VII/2, 1959.
31. S. Chilver, private communication.
32. F. Kramer, (*The Red Fez*, London, Verso, 1993, pp. 46–9, 73, 130) points out that palace collections dating from as early as the eleventh century have been found at Zimbabwe, including, from the thirteenth century onward, Persian faiences and Chinese plates traded across the Indian Ocean. He sees such collections in sub-Saharan Africa in terms of *being possessed by* the foreign as much as possessing it through its material culture. He interprets possession, whether in objects of foreign material culture, masquerades or possession cults, as statements about power, hegemony and centre-periphery relations, and suggests that rituals reproducing the foreign represent a political dimension to cult possession. Members of a Mami Wata cult in Mina, Togo, sit down to a 'five-course, French-style meal' including such dishes as raw vegetables and salad – the predilection of Europeans – which they eat at a table covered in a white linen table cloth set with

knives, forks, spoons, plates and glasses (H. J. Drewal, 'Performing the Other: Mami Wata worship in West Africa', in *Drama Review* 32 (1988), pp. 179–80). In keeping with the theme of European provenance of this goddess, Mami Wata figures placed in shrines are often adorned with the trappings of Western fashion such as sunglasses, hand-mirrors, jewellery, clothing and the gifts offered are often of Western origin.

33. Warnier, 'Trade Guns'; and Warnier, *L'Esprit de L'Entreprise au Cameroun*, Paris, Karthala, 1993.
34. These umbrellas were gendered, the womens' one, which is still produced and used, being long enough to cover the back while bending to work the fields. The male one is smaller and square, very similar in shape to the shield once made for warriors.
35. A fact which recalls the habit of people in Oku not to refer directly by name to certain feared masquerades, but to use elliptical euphemisms to refer to them.
36. Shock or fear would perhaps be better glosses, but I have avoided these terms because of their predominantly negative connotations of unpleasantness and disorder. *Btshuo byumene* is more pluralistic in its connotations, alluding to fascination, admiration and attraction as well as to shock, fear or apprehension. My use of the gloss 'surprise' (the translation used by Oku people) for the sensation of 'dry mouth' should then be interpreted as a compound of fear and attraction.
37. The Pidjin term used is 'wonders', for example 'We don see wonders today!'
38. Casey, *Remembering*, p. 150n17.
39. For example H. Bergson, *Matter and Memory*, New York, Doubleday, 1959, pp. 70*ff*; Bourdieu, *Outline of a Theory of Practice*, p. 77.
40. Casey (*Remembering*, p. 164) speaking not of traumatic but of erotic memory, highlights the revelatory nature of bodily memory when he points to its open-endedness: such memories are 'projective of the still-to-come . . . the ahead-of-ourselves where certain possibilities might be realised.' M. Heidegger ('The Question Concerning Technology' in Heidegger, *The Question Concerning Technology and Other Essays*, New York, Harper & Row, 1977, p. 32) used the term itself, also emphasizing its quality of 'opening out':

> The granting that sends in one way or another into revealing is as such the saving power. For the saving power lets man see and enter into the highest dignity of his essence. This dignity lies in keeping watch over the unconcealment – and with it, from the first, the concealment – of all coming to presence on this earth.

41. Similar to Schneider's 'sociological understanding' (S. Schneider, 'Rumpelstiltskin's Bargain', in A. Weiner and S. Schneider (eds), *Cloth and Human Experience*, Washington D.C., Smithsonian Institution Press, 1989, pp. 177–213).
42. We are speaking here perhaps not of memory so much as 'antimemory' (G. Deleuze and F. Guattari, *A Thousand Plateaux: Capitalism and Schizophrenia*, London, Athlone Press, 1992, p. 294) whereby the remembering agent is not passively submitting to a previous experience, but actively reconstituting that experience within the parameters of her or his life-world.
43. C. Tilley (*A Phenomenology of Landscape: Places, Paths and Monuments*, Oxford, Berg, 1994, pp. 27 and 31) has pointed out that places sediment memories only in relation to other places the subject has previously experienced. These place or landscape memories are not uniform, however, but re-negotiable (S. Küchler, 'Landscape as Memory: The Mapping Process and its Representation in a Melanesian Society', in B. Bender (ed.), *Landscape: Politics and Perspectives*, Oxford, Berg, 1993).
44. R. Fardon, *Between God, the Dead and the Wild*, p. 149.

–2–

The Place of Memory

Susanne Küchler

The commemorative function of the monument appears self evidently universal; made to enshrine the knowledge of the cultural past for the sake of future generations, a culture without monuments appears to us like a ship lost to the sea – unable to navigate and correct mistaken judgment.[1] Only hunter gatherer societies, lacking institutionalized authority, are genuinely bereft of the need to memorialize the lives of their dead. Within the remaining grey zone of cultures that clearly invest time and energy in memorializing their dead, yet divest themselves of the products of memorywork in a more or less dramatic manner, this practice is generally accounted for as 'iconoclasm'. Such riddance of monuments appears tantamount to acts of 'finishing' memory that mark moments of transition from one political era to another by withdrawing representations that could serve as vehicles for popular recollection. Conversely, the perceived end of culture that marked the close of the nineteenth century propelled a Western fascination with and need for monuments without previous parallel.[2] To stem the tide of sweeping cultural amnesia about to beset the modern world, monumental culture was both salvaged and its endurance protected by new laws that have come to form the foundation of a 'heritage crusade'.[3]

We are ill at ease about the phenomenon of monument destruction as it appears to us to effect the erasure of representations that serve as anchor points for remembrance. Where else should be the place of memory, if not in the 'loci' made visible in the figures of cultural monuments such as Giotto's Virtues and Vices in the Arena Capella in Padua? The importance we conventionally assign to the lasting memory image is grounded in an assumption that Frances Yates has famously traced back to the age of Scholasticism and Medieval memory where *memoria*, the conscious elicitation of past experience through visual imagery, served to facilitate the spreading of devotional forms of learning to laymen.[4] From medieval times onwards, the destruction of such visual imagery appeared to be tantamount to forgetting.

Yet, while we might still cling to the object as the place of memory, the re-discovery of *memoria* by Frances Yates for the humanities coincided with the ending of its cultural relevance. As collective, unconscious memory stored in visual representation, *memoria* had been of merely practical interest: it was recommended for the reckoning with the past, as educational tool, as programme for museums, as legitimization for archives. Reserved as 'black box' for brain physiology and belittled as 'hobby horse' for historians, *memoria* became of broader interest only with the rise of artificial intelligence and the use of computers for the storage of data – when the accessibility of the memory store and thus the individual connection to collective memory came into question.[5] The assumption essential to the conception of *memoria,* that things of the mental world have a necessary correspondence to things belonging to the moral and temporal world, appeared suddenly no longer tenable.

This paper investigates the consequences of abandoning *memoria* for a new understanding of the place of memory not in objects, but in the space created by rendering absent the products of memorywork – a place that is evoked and rather substituted by objects. In the humanities, the context within which such an exploration takes place is based upon the rediscovery of Aby Warburg's unpublished *Mnemosyne Atlas* that visually expounds on *mneme*, Aristotle's long-neglected counterpart to *memoria*, which describes the ability to remember by chance something previously experienced.[6] A well-known description of a mnemic recollection is Proust's[7] account of childhood memories incited by a madeleine cake. Here, the cake does not stand in for, and thus assist in the recollection of, forgotten events, but effects a synaesthetic experience of remembering. *Mneme* enables the most direct experience of the forgotten, an experience that may be sustained like a dream long after the object inciting it has ceased to exist.

Ginzburg[8] recently reminded us of this other, forgotten, sense of recollection through representations that are not substitutes of what one wishes to remember, but recall what has been rendered absent in a momentous, involuntary and yet conscious manner. To describe this kind of representation and its memorial intent, Ginzburg draws on the classic study by Kantorowitcz, *The Kings Two Bodies*, which describes the fourteenth- and fifteenth-century celebration of the death of French and English kings. Here, wooden effigies made to replace the body of the dead king were treated like the king's body in life before being symbolically sacrificed. The symbolic death of the king's effigy and its subsequent destruction has been famously argued by Kantorowitcz to effect a separation of the body natural and the body politic, the mortal body and the body that is unchangeable in time.[9]

The memorial world of the medieval body politic was thus immortalized through acts of finishing and of displacing memory from the temporal world of things. Resonances of such acts of finishing pervade also the writings on contemporary Western war memorials, in particular the essays by Mike Rowlands and Alex King in this volume. The memorials of war are shown to preserve not a single memory, but rather allow a variety of different memories, often conflicting, to co-exist. This dialogical space of the monument implies a looser connection between memory and objects than previously assumed – a relation that, I argue, can only be understood when questioning the memorial intentions of monuments.[10]

The memorial form of the contemporary war monument, and the changes it may reflect in memorial practice, may further be illuminated by drawing on examples of so-called 'ethnographic' collections. Their potential to present comparative evidence on the relation between monument and mourning has long remained obscured due to the assumption that all 'non-Western' artworks reached the West in the same manner, that is as 'salvaged' artworks symptomatic of colonial history.[11] In fact, however, the size of certain collections may not reflect Western interest alone, but of acts of 'finishing' of the work for the dead that rendered its figural 'remains' into eminently collectable things. Such artworks, it will be contended in this paper, are embedded in cultural acts of sacrifice marking the transcending powers of a body politic, a process described by Kantorowitcz in relation to the memorials to medieval kings. We may fail to recognize such objects as monuments, as their perishability and fleeting presence in culture conflict with our assumption that commemorative works should provide a lasting visual referent for acts of remembrance, yet it is their ephemerality that allows us to understand the place of memory in modern culture, best exemplified by the war memorial.

A Land without Monuments

The artworks that I examine in this paper have been collected over the last 120 years from the northernmost island of the Bismark Archipelago, north-west of Papua New Guinea. Far from being the remnants of a tradition phased out under the impact of acculturation, the figures that have reached our museums represent a thriving mortuary tradition. Issues of identity and relations of loyalty and labour are comprehensible only with reference to what is colloquially known on the island as the practice of *malanggan* which marks the finishing of the work for the dead. Saying this, the visitor to the island will not be aware of the existence of monuments, unless he or she arrives during the month in the year when up and down the coast the dead make their final appearance in shrouds that recall the collectivity of the dead and thereby surrender those who died to the ancestral domain.

Carved from wood or woven from vines, *malanggan* mark the finishing of the work for the dead (*haisok ine mamat*) who are buried in the grounds of a village. Often several metres in lengths or width, the spectacularly carved or woven and painted monuments form the annual appearance of the ancestral 'body' (*bung*), which is brought to life as it is placed on the grave of those who died since the occurrence of the last *malanggan*.

Visually and conceptually, *malanggan* recall a body wrapped in images that draw attention to bodily folds, contours and shape. Incised to the point of breakage, the emerging fretwork takes the forms of instantly recognizable motifs found in abundance in the physical and animate environment of the island culture that produces them. We can recognize carved and painted planes birds, pigs, fish and seashells, which are depicted with such an accuracy and attention to detail that they appear almost lifelike; the same can be said for the figure set within the fretwork that appears to stare at the beholder with eyes that could hardly be more

Figure 7 House *Malanggan*, Panamafei village, 1984. (Photo: S. Küchler)

vivid. Surrealist artists, from well-known figures such as Giacometti to others such as Brignioni, were attracted to these figures, however, not because of their lifelike character but because of the apparently ornamental and yet not quite self-evident nature of the shape given to the figures. Motifs appear enchained as figures stand inside the mouth of rock-cods, framed by many different kinds of fish that bite into limbs and chins, birds that bite into snakes and snakes into birds, and the skulls of pigs that appear to metamorphose into birds. Inner shapes appear enclosed by outer frames in ways that contest the apparent reality of what is depicted like a vision in a dream.

Each shroud, or 'skin' (tak), as the memorial to the dead is called, is identified with one of six named 'sources' (*wune*) that are associated with ancestrally derived, generative and reproductive powers. Standing on the grave for only one night, hidden behind a thick fence of coconut leaves, the memorial to the deceased is then publicly unveiled before the spectators, often numbering several hundred. As the fence falls, pushed out from inside by the mourners, the spectators rush forward to throw money at the shroud's base. As the money is passed to the mourners who sponsored the carving of the *malanggan*, the 'skin' of the figure changes hands. Like all living things that lose their skin, *malanggan* dies. This 'killing' of *malanggan* (*luluk a malanggan*) finishes a period of mourning that in some cases may extend over twenty years. The spirit of the dead returns in a 'soul canoe' (*bul musung*) to the island of the dead .

The death of malanggan abandons the figure-corpse to a process of decomposition that mirrors the ritual disaggregation of the social body after death. While figures woven for the female dead and the young are burned, their wooden counterparts made for male dead and the elders are taken to certain places where rain and the spray of the sea soon efface all traces of carving and colouration. Left thus to rot, the wooden remains are turned to the fertile 'smell' (*ngusung*) of the sea, which is annually recalled from the land of the dead to replenish the gardens of the living.

The decomposition of the remains of mourning thus concludes the sacrifice of the dead and marks the triumph over death by turning the finality of death into a process of eternal return. Sacrifice achieves immortality as it effects a form of exchange between the invisible world of the ancestors and the visible world of the living, an exchange that, in New Ireland, is of a peculiar olfactory nature. Unwittingly, yet predictably as part of a millenarian scenario common through Melanesia, we have come to fill the void of the ancestral domain by becoming the site for the deposition of such sacrificial remains. Instead of being abandoned at the edge of the sea, the majority of the carvings are thus taken to purpose-

Figure 8 *Malanggan* for sale, Medina village, 1984. (Photo: S. Küchler)

built houses or the local mission to be eventually sold to the visiting tourist and collector.

As the figure-corpse leaves, so do the people who lived with the dead. Dwellings and their burial places are abandoned, soon to be submerged by forest, which leaves no visible trace of the commemorative work that once provided the common focus for a community. Not remembrance, but forgetting through the literal burying of memories thus effects the finishing of the work for the dead in this culture. As elsewhere in the Pacific,[12] monument destruction or disposal served to send away the dead and shield the living from the potentially harmful intentions of the gods, while at the same time creating a resource from which all future commemorative work could draw. This displacement of remembrance from the object to an intellectual resource is, however, peculiar not just to the little island cultures in the Pacific that will figure prominently in these pages.

We have recently been reminded of the significance of such an imaginary space, being at once the product of 'forgetting' as well as the resource for memory work, within the tradition of epic poetry from Virgil to Dante and Milton.[13] According to this view, the received language of the poet was itself a 'burial place,' the Land of the Dead or an the underworld where all pasts were made equally present – 'an arena where the poet can contemplate the past as past, where, to use Freud's terminology, he can remember the past without being obliged to repeat it'.[14] Similarly, Kantorowitcz's account of Renaissance funeral effigies showed how an absent identity could be made visible, by replacing it with an image whose momentary coming to life allowed a glimpse of the immortal powers of the king that were renewed with the impending 'death' of the effigy.[15]

Memorial representations of this kind do not effect recall by symbolizing matter already known or experienced from the phenomenal world, but by visualizing access to what exists 'out there' in a world entirely made up of 'freed' or 'forgotten' memories. A comparable world 'outside' memory may be that of cyberspace where knowledge that does not exist in time or space may nonetheless be accessed. No one has more beautifully captured the rootedness of memory in an imaginary space than De Certeau[16] for whom 'memory comes always from somewhere else.' He managed to foreshadow memory's contemporary problematic – of a memory that as an unmoored, mobile force has shed its material trappings on which we so long have relied. In the face of the ending of industrial economy with its object-based notions of knowledge and recollection we are led with De Certeau to reappraise the paradoxical – that recollection does not cease when there are no longer any traces of what is to be remembered, but draws its force from this absence.[17]

Burial-Places of Memory

That things, or their pictorial or literary representation should be assumed to lead to an imaginary space of forgotten memory is the result of an obsession with recollection that has beset the West since the death of Milton. The model of *memoria*, the conscious recollection of past experience, has dominated the post-Renaissance art world to such an extent that we find it difficult to conceive of representations in any other way. How, we may ask, are we to distinguish memorial representations conceived to aide remembering in the tradition of the classical art of memory from those that aimed to 'bury' memory and thereby create reproductive and generative resources in which 'all pasts are equally present'?[18]

In a recent essay on cultural memory Aleida Assmann[19] offers in a comparison between modes of remembering a poignant insight into the forgotten domain of displacement and forgetting: the first mode is a temporal metaphor, referred to as eschatological memory, which assigns to remembering a political and messianic force capable of bridging across a lost present to a desired future that is envisioned in the image of the past; the second mode is a spatial metaphor, referred to as animatorical remembering, which initiates a momentary collapse of past and present by forcing past and present, distance and proximity into a single point that is exploded out of a linear and narrative time construction.

In these modes, memory is consigned to an experience of 'awakening', in one case passive and in the other active, whose distinctive characteristics are not apparent in the English language, for the German word *erwachen* denotes the temporal mode of awakening from a dream at which moment one intuitively grasps a separation from the past without having fully left it. Involuntarily awoken, the daydreamer longs to return to a world forcibly left. Michael Roth[20] has recently elaborated on the popularity of this notion of 'eschatological' awakening and its concomitant symptom of nostalgia in nineteenth-century France.

In contrast to this passive mode of awakening there is the active sense of 'animatorical' *erwecken*. In the active mode of awakening is captured the momentous sensation of past, present and future collapsing in a single point. What above all distinguishes this sensation is the fact that while it can be repeated, it can never be recollected.

While both modes certainly coexist in the potentiality of remembering, it is always one or the other that is singled out as the forum for the fashioning of a collective memory to legitimize political and cultural identity at particular points in time. The first mode of eschatological remembering has been the one best known to Western culture at least since the sixteenth century, when ruins began to be seen as articulating a sense of a cultural heritage from which visions of the future could be construed. On the threshold of the modern age, the contemplation of death and decay carried a curiosity as to what might be learned from it about the future;[21] Piranesi's 'narrations' of ruins, described by Tarnya Cooper in this volume, is a famous example of the emergence of an increasingly temporal definition of cultural memory through his contrast of the ancient monuments and their present condition.

The second mode, animatorical remembering or the collapse of past, present and future in the space of a single moment, appears at odds with Western post-Renaissance memorial culture. It describes the coming to life of the past as a performative experience with its own distinct temporal dimension; momentary and point-like in nature, the enlivened past has a beginning, middle and ending symptomatic of the experience of ritual. Vinograd[22] recently described the collective viewing of Chinese literati scroll paintings as an example of this process. Every act of unrolling and viewing scroll paintings of the scholar-amateur period was in itself a 'site of commemoration'; the viewing created an identity as intangible, momentary and yet affirmative as the brush-stroke techniques whose recognition brought to life the painting as the secret asset of the community. To emphasize the representation fundamental to Chinese literati culture, Vinograd compares the inherent temporality of the viewing of scroll-painting to the inscription of temporality as 'witnessed event' in Renaissance painting. Whereas in Italian Renaissance paintings knowledge of the past is recalled in a symbolic manner, the Chinese literati scroll affirms the scroll as the source of knowledge itself.

Many comparable examples come to mind that reinforce the cross-cultural significance of an atemporal, point-like and spatial, mode of recollection which at once anticipates and arises out of the disappearance of the memorial object; such as the Aboriginal barkpainting seen from the corner of the eye[23] before its destruction at the height of funerary and initiation rituals, or the ritual work of re-fencing surrounding the royal tombs in Madagascar.[24] The example to be described here is, like these, a memorial representation that derives its ritual efficacy from acts of finishing. There is nothing to be recalled, but much to be forgotten, figuratively 'buried' in 'sites' periodically opened up for the reanimation of the past.

Yet why should we be interested in the representation of animatorical memory? Just as, in the *Story-Teller*, Walter Benjamin[25] described how phenomena take on a new sense of importance and beauty when they are ending. So what may now be coming to an end is the notion of *memoria*, of conscious apprehension of past experience through material remains and *memoria's* displacement by new electronic means of reproduction, which involve the at least figurative burning of the object.[26] Computer-designed prototypes, for example, are comprised of digitized codes which are 'found' by dissecting an object into its constituent parts. We may be generally unaware of any change in our capacity to recollect by means of an object, and yet one cannot ignore a new aestheticization of 'rubbish' which has gripped the art world in the 1980s. In our response to 'recyclia,' remains are about to become the imagistic vehicles in processes of transmission not of material, but mental resources.[27]

Not long ago the monument was conceived as a surviving remainder of a culture's experience against whose loss it provided some protection; present perceptions of the monument blur the distinction between the 'left-over' of experience and what is found as rubbish.[28] Whereas a fascination with remains as rubbish has a history prior to the twentieth century, originating in the German romantics' aesthetic validation of the 'fragment', the artistic practice of collage and assemblage has, among other things, given a momentum to a new appreciation of remains.

The earliest sculptural use of industrial manufactured objects date from Picasso's works from 1910, followed by Marcel Duchamp's Ready Made's and Klee's method of utilizing old cut-up drawings as basis for his collages.[29] Since the early 1980s, however, that category of sculpted objects defined by the newly coined term 'recyclia' was no longer made simply of reused material, but from materials that Euro-Americans consider waste – empty tin cans and bottles, old cigarette ends, used tyres, and other household or industrial fragments and debris.[30]

Originating from remains, such contemporary sculpture calls into question remains as site of remembering and therefore alters the significance of the monument.[31] It is perhaps for this reason that monuments erected today may allude to their own disappearance or to the accidental fashion in which memories are grafted on them.[32] The monument, as argued by Young[33] is fast becoming a 'dialogical space' that facilitates the 'finding' of memories that are personal and contextual. The monument is experienced thus in a primarily non-temporal manner as the monument's memorial value has been replaced by something that, extending Riegl's categories, one may call 'viewing' value.[34] Comparable to a tourist 'site', the momentous experience of a monument is possessed through photographs or other mementoes such as pieces of its fabric. We cling to a tangible reminder of a site that was brought to life for the brevity of our encounter with it. In this way, we are now possibly closer to an animatorical reading of monuments that appears to have governed medieval church art and certain non-Western artefact traditions than we have been at any point since the Renaissance.[35] Yet, whereas we now can possess the experience offered by the monument intellectually and have the means to reproduce this experience, we still customarily conceptualize the memorial's value as residing in the object or parts of the object, rather than in a mental resource created through the object's disappearance.

Contractual forms: Monuments as intellectual property

In a recent study, Simon Harrison[36] distinguishes between the widespread existence of 'information societies', which emphasize mental resources and assets as the target of proprietary rights, and the societies in the modern industrial economy with their emphasis on material resources and productive capacity. We should consider the possibility that, rather than being the norm, the modern industrial economy with its attachment to material, rather than mental resources, may be the odd one out.

Foregrounded in both systems is the notion of 'intellectual property', which, according to Harrison, refers to rights asserted in the products of the mind: 'in Western economies, these may include diverse products as inventions, industrial designs, works of literature or art, trade secrets, commercial brand names . . . and . . . any sorts of mental products that are, or can be, owned as values, assets or resources.'[37] In the industrial economy, the reproduction of such mental products and the right to innovate is restricted through the incorporation of intellectual property into matter over which property rights can be established; in so called 'information societies' such innovation in reproduction is the norm as a shared knowledge technology assures the continuing generative and reproductive capacity of its intangible resources.

Melanesia is a particularly clear example of a culture within which intellectual property is not an analogue of material property. The information-based economies of Melanesia are embedded in rituals whose performance only every ten or even twenty years gives them a particularly long-term transmission span.[38] Typically, rituals are centred around the construction of visually and conceptually complex architectural structures which form the temporary abode of ephemeral commemorative artefacts. Famously among the inhabitants of Sepik River villages in North-east New Guinea, entire cult complexes including cult houses, figures, paintings, fences, dances and songs are fabricated for ritual occasions which climax in the transfer from one village to another of rights to the cult-complex. With the deliberate ephemerality of the commemorative structures, ownership centres less on the object as material product, than on the right to reproduce an image out of the pool of soon to be 'forgotten' assets; as an absent and temporarily forgotten image, commemorative architecture recalls a mental resource that can be subdivided, shared or even sold.

While the Western monument in the modern era enabled as much a process of forgetting or collective amnesia as it marked a memory, the Melanesian counterpart enables with its erasure, the creation of an inherently recallable image; it thus instigates a process of remembering that is not directed to any particular vision of past or future, but which repeats itself many times over in point-like, momentary and thus 'animatorical' awakening of the past in the present.

In foreshadowing their own displacement, architectural complexes and their contents are capturing the 'alterity' of memory, that is memory's capacity to implant itself in forever new places – and its freedom to make connections between things that otherwise would be disassociated fragments lost forever to life. For De Certeau[39] alterity is one of the most important aspects of practical memory within whose parameters nothing is ever fixed: 'The oddest thing', he writes, 'is no doubt the *mobility* of this memory in which details are never *what* they are: they are not objects, for they are elusive as such; not fragments, for they yield the ensemble they forget; not totalities, since they are not self-sufficient; not stable, since each recall alters them. This "space" of a moving nowhere has the subtlety of a cybernetic world. It restores the unexpected pertinence of time in places where powers are distributed.'[40] He beautifully captures the absent space of memory as constituted by a double alteration 'both of memory, which works when something affects it, and of its object, which is remembered only when it has disappeared.'[41]

With Gillis[42] one may argue that remembering in the everyday today draws more than ever on absence as potent resource for implanting the present with a sense of connectedness. Gillis describes social relationships in the post 1960s as no longer framed by a coherent narrative; multiple work related relocation and multiple families within a single person's life, mean that more is got rid of or left behind that nevertheless inform a person's sense of 'collected' identity.[43] This absent space of memory is less easily embraced within a linear, narrative frame, but demands representations that recall what is absent into the present. The rise in local, rather than national, monuments as pointed out by Gillis or the contemporary collecting mania may be a response to the preoccupation with 'finding' the absent in new things that thereby become animate with a sense of present past.

Returning to Melanesia, one is struck to find the evaluation of absence as resource at the heart of institutions which have a marked economic as well as religious significance.[44] Perhaps the best documented example of an intellectual economy and its concern with the flow of memory mobilized through ritual acts of erasure is known under the generic term *malanggan* which I introduced earlier in this chapter and to which I now will return.

Malanggan, we may recall, designates a ritual performance centred around the construction of architectural structures which become the site for the display of effigies, songs and dances, commemorative vessels for the transposition of life force after death. Often taking months to produce, *malanggan* with all its ritual paraphernalia, is no more than a temporary abode to the soul of the dead. Upon destruction of its container, the soul becomes image and thus a mobile, floating memory.[45] The control over this memory is of paramount importance to the regulation of other forms of ownership in land or titles.

Malanggan is practised to this day in the north of New Ireland, an island situated to the north-east of New Guinea. The northernmost elevation in a chain of volcanic islands, New Ireland was brought under German colonial administration in 1885 and reached independence within the state of Papua New Guinea in 1975. Together with the east coast of New Guinea, New Ireland was discovered and placed on the map in consecutive Dutch and Spanish explorations between 1527 and 1756. The economic viability of coconut-oil production lead to a surge of traders arriving in the islands off New Guinea towards the end of the eighteenth century, with permanent trading posts established around the coastal shore of New Ireland in 1840, some 45 years before colonial rule.

Here, as well as elsewhere in what came to be known as German New Guinea, the colonial administration found in place institutions concerned with the commemoration of the dead and with initiation fostering some kind of contractual relation whose effect was to appease inter-tribal warfare. Because of their apparent political and humanitarian benefits, these institutions, which themselves may have arisen in the form we know today only during the indirect colonial period, were allowed to remain active.

While no one can say for sure whether the contemporary institution of *malanggan* reflects what it may have been like over a century ago when it was first described as commemorative practice, it is the treatment of the monuments to the dead which stands out as a lasting and distinctive trait. Like the effigies of kings in sixteenth century England, which matched or even eclipsed the dead body itself, a *malanggan* is attended as though the figure was the living person himself – being animated and subsequently allowed to die, thus allowing the deceased person's soul to achieve symbolic immortality.[46] As the death of the king's effigy in French and English Renaissance rites effected the separation between the king's mortal body and the immortal body of kingship, the death of *malanggan* concludes mourning by putting in its place the body politic of *malanggan*.

Reading Kantorowitcz's account of *The King's Two Bodies* one cannot help being struck by formal similarities with *malanggan*. In both cases, the figure replacing the dead man's body 'recalls' the soul in ways that transform it into an image of an infinitely renewable kind thus testifying to the possibility of an enchanted, transcendental world. Although none of the king's effigies have survived, for like *malanggan* they are destroyed, we can say for certain of the *malanggan* that the figures are neither portraits of deceased persons, nor are they emblematic in character.

Malanggan, instead, serve as vessels for the transmission of names, which are considered to be the source of an augmentable, regenerative life-force. Names become synonymous with a regenerative resource as the death of the figure effectively separates the name from a person's mortal body. Names of *malanggan* are thus equally shared by the ancestors and the living alike, whereby the possession of a malanggan name and the right to visualize it in materials testifies to the genealogical relationship between the person and the spirit world. Persons are baptized at the time of the display of a *malanggan* figure and thus come to embody the name, and, with it, the ownership right over the image of *malanggan*. The peculiarity of the *malanggan* material is that names, as the carriers of a transcending body politic, are considered the property of the ancestral domain, are 'found' and recollected through dreaming, to be validated and transferred as images.

Names become 'skins' as a result of being shaped into figures, but they also become images through the figure's anticipated death and disappearance from sight. The imagistic character of names in New Ireland enables names to be recalled or 'found' in a controlled fashion using mnemonic techniques whose imprint is found in the process of giving form to figures. The control authorized over the recall and recognition of ancestral names stands in stark contrast to the New Ireland image for involuntary remembering encapsulated in bush spirits, 'rulrul,' who snatch human skin and appear in their disguise, haunt and trick the living with their sudden and momentous appearances and their seemingly affirmed identity.

The ownership over such imaged names distinguishes 'members of malanggan' (*raso*) from those who rely on the 'members' in finishing the work for their dead. One figure can finish thus the work for any number of deceased persons buried within a single cemetery since the last performance of *malanggan*. It is the death of an elder 'member' that initiates the planning of the final stage in the work of mourning. 'Members' are both male as well as female, their name associating them with an image that is considered, like names of *malanggan*, to be generative and reproductive. In old age, members carry a 'string' (*wuap*) of names, each name associated with a certain rendering of its imaged-form carved or woven during his or her life to finish the work of deceased relatives.

Names and their imaged form thus become increasingly inclusive as they are 'produced out' of a 'source' (*wune*). The ranking of names and images traces the structure of a tree with vertical 'stems', horizontal 'branches', and figurative 'leaves.' The first name given in infancy at the moment of the ritual death of a *malanggan* and the first image to be produced in the early years of adulthood is of the 'leaf' form, with further and ever more complex names and images to be rendered visible by a person throughout his or her life.

Names and the right to images are transmitted in a clear line within a matriclan that also lends or sells 'parts' of names and image 'sources' both internally within the clan and to other, affinally related, clans. The portability of a name and an image follows the figure's death, which is brought about by metaphorically 'stripping' the figure's 'skin;' the skin (*tak*), visible as the painted and carved olanes of the richly incised figure, is captured by relatives of the deceased person who offer money in exchange for the right to reproduce the named image for another celebration of death to take place in the future. If more than one clan has participated in the act of capturing, the hollow remains of the figure will be broken up into parts that act as symbolic reminders of shared rights to the image and its name.

The repeated dissecting of an image and its name has left its imprint in the numerous collected artworks. While not one *malanggan* figure is identical to any other figure, certain reoccurring patterns are easily discernible. Of these, the most important to be mentioned here is on the one hand the occurrence of framing and connecting motifs that enable the recognition of named image sources and, on the other hand, the greater or lesser number of motifs occurring in any single figure. As one may assume, over the 120 years of collecting, the figures have become progressively fragmented, with fewer motifs per figure typical for those collected in the 1970s. While this may be a discernible trend, there are enough exceptions to suggest the opposite – that ownership over images is periodically 'rewritten,' with complex figures reinventing patterns of inclusive ownership whenever possible. Such appropriation of ownership occurs whenever a social unit associated with a major *malanggan*-owning clan ceases to be represented in a particular locality due to the lack of female offspring in one generation.

The death of *malanggan* thus gives rise to a notion of 'corporation' that is pivotal to the fiction of the perpetuity of collectivities. When attending the reveal of a *malanggan,* everybody present is purposeful and prepared – their minds and pockets ready to attain at least a fragment of share in what is to be seen for only a matter of minutes. It is useful to compare the exotic complexity of the revealing of a malanggan house with similar occasions in the West. One might think of the dismantling of Christo's wrapped Reichstag in Berlin when a staggering number of souvenirs from fragments of the fabric to sketches and paintings were sold to the many thousands who came to witness the disappearance of a monument; or one may recall the immediate aftermath of fall of the Berlin wall, when thousands came not just to celebrate but also to acquire a fragment of a monument about to disappear. As with the Berlin wall, those who acquire shares in a *malanggan* in the moments after it is revealed, a right to own its memory and to use it as a source for future recollections of what was rendered absent through decomposition – with the notable difference that the fragment of the wall survives physically in the owner's possession, the *malanggan* only in the mental image.

Emerging as if from nowhere, monuments whose point of reference lies in absence allow us to be 'touched' by memory like an awakening from a dream.[47] When *malanggan* are revealed in their houses, many of those who have come to see this event burst into tears, being shocked to almost physically feel the presence of those who departed; others who remain silent reported afterwards that they saw in their minds *malanggan* that they had seen in the past and responded by comparing and integrating it into an ensemble of remembered images. Accusations of theft of ownership, hidden laughter at badly executed carving, or admiration are verbalized only during the days following *malanggan* when people have returned to their villages and the effigies have been removed from the graveyard. The memory of an image seen for a brief moment has once again become mobile with the figure's disappearance.

Conclusion

Malanggan thus documents a mode of forgetting, a mode brought about through rendering invisible the representations that act as temporary vehicles of social transmission. Once invisible and publicly forgotten, *malanggan* forms the generative and reproductive resource of an information-based economy in which proprietary rights pertain not to objects, but to their mental 'remains'.

Thus unmoored, memories produced by marking absences fashion, according to De Certeau, 'habitable spaces' within which past and present collapse; such spaces have shrunk in contemporary Western experience, yet their importance has immeasurably increased as they are driven into the cellars and garrets. Where are the spaces for memory, free of physical artefacts, to be found in modern Western experience?

Notes

1. See M. Bloch and J. Parry, *Death and the Regeneration of Life*, Cambridge, Cambridge University Press, 1982, on the concomitant

relation between political authority and the institutionalization of secondary burial.

2. A. Riegl, 'The Modern Cult of Monuments: Its Character and Its Origin', trans. K. Forster and D. Ghirardo, *Oppositions* 25 (1982), pp. 21–58.
3. D. Lowenthal, *The Heritage Crusade and the Spoils of History*, London, Viking, 1997.
4. F. Yates, *The Art of Memory*, Harmondsworth, Penguin, 1966, p. 99.
5. See E. S. Casey, *Remembering: a Phenomenological Study*, Bloomington and Indianapolis, Indiana University Press, 1987, on the nineteenth- and early twentieth-century definition of memory as forgetting, and U. Neisser, *Cognition and Reality*, San Francisco, Freeman, 1976, on the independence of remembering from cognition. Also H. Bredekamp, 'Der simalierte Benjamin: Mittelalterliche Bemerkungen zu seiner Aktualität', in A. Berndt, P. Kaiser, A. Rosenberg, and D. Trinkner (eds), *Frankfurter Schule und Kunstgeschichte*, Berlin, Dietrich Reiner Verlag, 1992, on computer simulation and its impact on our notion of 'reproduction'.
6. See selected texts by Aby Warburg and the material accompanying the exhibition 'Mnemosyne', Hamburg, 1992.
7. M. Proust, *Swann's Way*, trans. C. P. Scott-Moncrieff, London, Chatto & Windus, 1922.
8. C. Ginzburg, 'Repräsentation: das Wort, die Vorstellung, der Gegenstand', *Freibeuter* 22 (1991), pp. 3–23.
9. E. Kantorowitcz, *The King's Two Bodies: a Study in Medieval Political Theology*, Princeton, Princeton University Press, 1957, p. 7.
10. On the notion of the monument as 'dialogical space' see J. Young, *The Art of Memory: Holocaust Memorials in History*, New York, The Jewish Museum/Presto, 1994.
11. c.f. S. Küchler, 'Malangan: Art and Memory in a Melanesian Society', *Man* (n.s) 22 (1987), pp. 238–55.
12. D. Battaglia, *On the Bones of the Serpent*, Chicago, University of Chicago Press, 1990; R. Guidieri and F. Pellizzi, 'Nineteen Tableaux on the Cult of the Dead in Malekula, Eastern Melanesia', *Res*, 2 (1981), pp. 1–86; S. Kooijman, *Art, Art Objects and Ritual in the Mimika Culture*, Mededelingen van het Rijksmuseum voor Volkenkunde 24, Leiden, E. J. Brill, 1984.
13. R. MacDonald, *The Burial-Places of Memory: Epic Underworlds in Virgil, Dante and Milton*, Amherst, University of Massachusetts Press, 1987.
14. MacDonald, *Burial-Places of Memory*, p. 8.

15. Ginzburg, 'Räpresentation', p. 4.
16. M. de Certeau, *The Practice of Everyday Life*, trans. S. Rendall, Berkeley, University of California Press, 1984.
17. One may recall the story of Simonides related by Cicero. Simonides of Keos recollected the seating order of those who died during the devastation of the theatre and thus presented an example of the embeddedness of the 'art of memory' in the imaginary space of absence. The medieval visualization of the art of memory in architectural structures and painting reminds us of this intimate relation between forgetting and recollecting (see Yates, *Art of Memory*).
18. MacDonald, *Burial-Places of Memory*, p. 7.
19. A. Assmann and D. Harth (eds), *Mnemosyne: Formen und Funktionenen der kulturellen Errinnerung*, Frankfurt am Main, Fischer Taschenbuch Verlag, 1993.
20. M. Roth, 'Dying of the Past: Medical Studies of Nostalgia in Nineteenth Century France', *History and Memory* 3 (1991), pp. 5–29.
21. K. W. Forster, 'Monument/Memory and the Mortality of Architecture', *Oppositions* 25 (1982), p. 3.
22. R. E. Vinograd, 'Private Art and Public Knowledge in Later Chinese Painting', in S. Küchler and W. Melion (eds), *Images of Memory: On Remembering and Representation*, Washington D.C., Smithsonian Institution Press, 1991.
23. H. Morphy, *Ancestral Connections*, Chicago, University of Chicago Press, 1991.
24. G. Feeley-Harnik, 'Finding Memories in Madagascar', in Küchler and Melion, *Images of Memory*.
25. Benjamin, W., *Illuminations*, trans. H. Zohn, ed. H. Arendt, New York, Schocken Books, 1969.
26. cf. S. Harrison, 'Anthropological Perspectives on the Management of Knowledge', *Anthropology Today* 11 (1995), pp. 10–14; Harrison, 'The Commerce of Cultures in Melanesia', *Man* (n.s.) 28 (1993), pp. 139–58; Harrison, 'Intellectual Property and Ritual Culture', *Man* (n.s) 21 (1991), pp. 435–56; American Institute of Graphic Arts, 'Who Owns Cultural Images: The Property Issue', *Journal of Graphic Design* 14 (1995).
27. C. A. Kratz, 'Rethinking Recyclia', *African Arts*, 1 (1995), pp. 7–12; S. Sheriff, *Recycled Reseen: Folk Art from the Local Scrap Heap*, New York, Harry N. Abrams/Museum of New Mexico, 1996.
28. See M. Thompson, *Rubbish Theory: the Creation and Destruction of Value*, Oxford and New York, Oxford University Press, 1979, for the so-far single study of the category of rubbish in modern economy.

29. cf. V. Greenfield, 'Making Do or Making Art? A Cognitive- Behavioral Study of Recyclers, Material Transformations, and the Creative Process', PhD. thesis, University of California, Los Angeles, 1984.
30. Kratz, 'Rethinking Recyclia', p. 7.
31. The contemporary significance of recyclia in art goes back to the 1960s and has grown out of collage and assemblage in the modern art movement (cf. Kratz, 'Rethinking Recyclia').
32. See P. Springer, 'Paradoxie des Ephemeren: Ephemere komponenten in zeitgenössischen Monumenten', in M. Diers (ed.), *Mo(nu)mente: Formen und Funktion ephemerer Denkmale*, Berlin, Akademie Verlag, 1993; Young, *The Art of Memory*.
33. Young, *The Art of Memory*.
34. Springer, 'Paradoxie des Ephemeren', p. 259; Riegl, 'The Modern Cult of Monuments'. A large body of writing has sprang up in Germany around the ephemeral monument that epitomizes the monument's momentuous experience – cf. A. Assman and D. Mark (eds), *Kultur als Lebeswelt und Monument*, Frankfurt am Main, Fischer Taschenbuch Verlag, 1991; W. Lipp (ed.), *Denkmal-Werte-Gesellschaft: Zur Pluralität des Denkmalbegriffs*, Frankfurt am Main and New York, Campus Verlag, 1993; E. Mai and G. Schmirber (eds), *Denkmal-Zeichen-Monument: Skulptur und Öffentlicher Raum heute*, München, Prestel Verlag, 1989; Diers, *Mo(nu)mente: Formen und Funktion*.
35. Bredekamp, 'Der simalierte Benjamin'.
36. S. Harrison, 'Anthropological Perspectives on the Management of Knowledge', *Anthropology Today* 11 (1995), pp. 10–14.
37. Harrison, 'Anthropological Perspectives', p. 10.
38. Harrison, 'Intellectual Property'; Harrison, 'The Commerce of Cultures'.
39. De Certeau, *The Practice of Everyday Life*.
40. Ibid., pp. 88–9.
41. Ibid., p. 87.
42. J. R. Gillis (ed.), *Commemorations: the Politics of National Identity*, Princeton, Princeton University Press, 1994.
43. For the significance of place as 'burial place of memory' see D. Charmichel, J. Hubert, B. Reeves, and A. Schanche, *Sacred Sites, Sacred Places*, London, Routledge, 1994.
44. Marilyn Strathern ('Artefacts of History: Events and the Interpretation of Images', in J. Siikala (ed.), *Culture and History in the Pacific* Suomen Antropolisen Seuran toimituksia, 27, Helsinki, Finnish Anthropological Society, 1990) amplified recently the sense of surprise

linked to images that surface in ritual performance as if from nowhere, which totally negates our sense of a contingent relation between images and events. On the sense of 'finding' ancestral names see also S. Harrison, *Stealing People's Names: History and Politics in Sepik River Cosmology*, Cambridge Studies in Social and Cultural Anthropolgy, 71, Cambridge and New York, Cambridge University Press, 1990.

45. I have talked about this at length elsewhere, particular in Küchler and Melion, *Images of Memory*; S. Küchler, 'Landscape as Memory: the Mapping of Process and its Representation in Melanesian Society', in B. Bender (ed.), *Landscape: Politics and Perspectives*, Oxford, Berg, 1993.
46. Kantorowitcz, *The King's Two Bodies*; see also Ginzburg, 'Repräsentation'.
47. De Certeau, *The Practice of Everyday Life*, p. 88; Strathern, 'Artefacts of History'.

Part II
Remembering and Forgetting in Images Past

In eighteenth century Europe, the association between visual art and 'memory' reached its fullest development. The capacity of works of art to evoke memories became, at least in the view of some critics and philosophers, one of the highest goals of art. The three chapters here, all concerned with works of art produced in the eighteenth century, explore the ways in which memory's converse, forgetting, also formed part of the work.

Helen Weston's chapter considers the portrait of one of the few black representatives in the National Assembly during the French Revolution, showing how this work, ostensibly a memorial, was also a means of sealing off from the present a past episode.

David Bindman, in his chapter on English funerary monuments by the sculptor Roubiliac, considers the purposes of these monuments, and draws attention to the extent to which oblivion and forgetfulness was knowingly made part of the artistic theme in these works.

Tarnya Cooper's chapter explores ways in which the experience of real places and images of them assist each other, but also conspire against each other in the processes of memory. Reflecting on how memories of Rome were formed by the well-known engraved views of the city produced by Giovanni Battista Piranesi, she takes up the distinction between 'inscribing' and 'incorporating' practices put forward by Paul Connerton in his book *How Societies Remember*, and argues that the particular appeal of Piranesi's prints was to offer their viewers a sense of a metaphorical incorporation through which they interpreted their actual experience of Rome. She also draws attention to the way aesthetic perception occurs not only through the memory of, but also the willed forgetting of previously received images. A common response among eighteenth and nineteenth century visitors to Rome was that to experience the city itself, one had first to forget the images by which Piranesi had made it memorable.

– 3 –

Girodet's *Portrait of C. Belley, Ex-Representative of the Colonies*: In Remembrance of 'Things Sublime'

Helen Weston

> 'I shall often go and dream in front of this portrait. What sublime things! Raynal, freedom for negroes and the brush of Girodet.' Pierre Chaussard[1]

On 4 February 1794, (16 pluviôse, Year II of the first French Republic), one of the most important decrees in French legal history was passed.[2] Consistent with the revolutionary ideals of liberty and equality, this decree, following decades of wrangling in the National Assembly and the Convention, finally abolished slavery in France's colonies and gave full rights of French citizenship to all their inhabitants.[3] The imminence of the arrival at the National Convention of the 'men of colour' from the colonies had drawn attention to the anomalous survival of slavery in the colonies of a free nation:

> Since 1789 an important matter has remained unresolved: hereditary aristocracy and sacerdotal aristocracy have both been wiped out, but the aristocracy of the skin has remained a powerful force. The latter has now breathed its dying gasp; equality has been ratified; a black, a yellow, and a white man will take their seats among you in the name of the free citizens of Saint-Domingue.[4]

Jean-Baptiste Mars Belley was the sole black delegate present at the passing of this decree. The session of the National Convention on 4 February concluded with the proposal that the announcement of abolition should be relayed to all France's colonies without delay. However, some deputies dissented and arguments about its desirability continued throughout the year, until, in December, Belley made an impassioned plea to put an end to all objections, and reiterated the decree of 4 February, emphasizing the need to send the message to the colonies.[5]

The occasion of the passing of this decree was recorded in a number of graphic works, notably those of François Bonneville, Parisian engraver and print dealer, but only in one painting, exhibited at the Salon of 1796, and now lost, by a forgotten artist called Houzeau. From the catalogue description, it represented a conventional allegory of equality holding a level over a black and a white child, seen in fraternal embrace. Girodet's *Portrait of Citizen Belley, Ex-Representative of the Colonies*, shown in the 1798 Salon, is thus the only surviving painted commemoration of the abolition decree, to date from the revolutionary decade (Figure 9). It

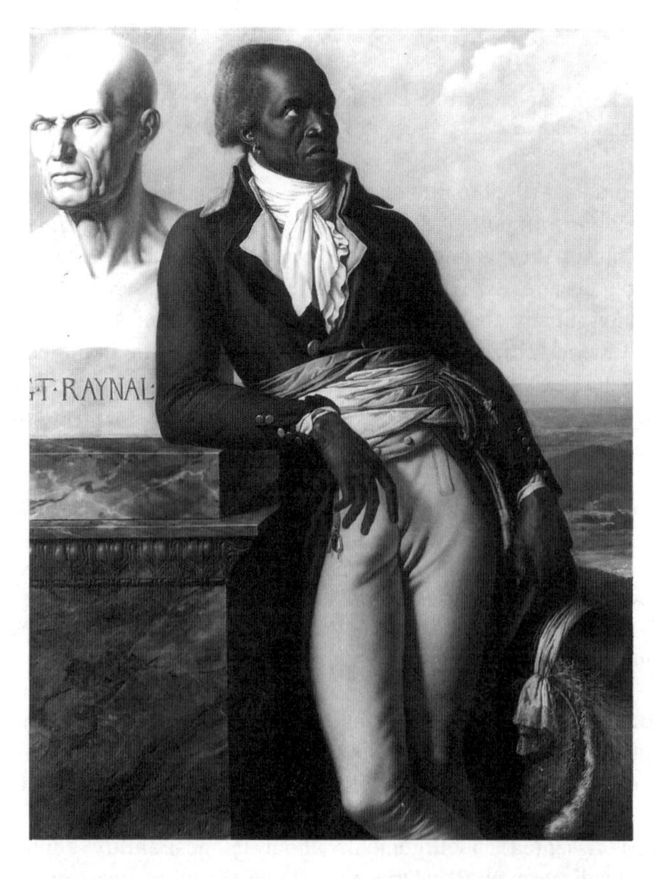

Figure 9 A.-L. Girodet-Trioson, *Portrait of Citizen Belley, ex-Representative of the Colonies*, dated year V (1797). Versailles, Musée National du Chateau de Versailles. (Photo: Réunion des Musées Nationaux.)

commemorates, on the one hand, the rise to rank of deputy in the Paris Convention of a man of humble African origin and, on the other hand, what abolition achieved in enabling a man who had once been a slave to hold national office.

Sites and Meanings

It is not known why Girodet painted this picture. There is no evidence that it was commissioned by the State or by any individual, nor even by Belley himself, although it is tempting to suppose that this might have been the case, as a reminder of his years of office in Paris. It is more probable that Girodet chose to paint it as a result of his already developed interest in people of non-European origin.[6] We also know of Girodet's republican enthusiasm while in Italy and this may have encouraged him to fix on canvas a direct image of the Revolution and the Republic without recourse to disembodied allegory. It is also likely that in exhibiting this likeness of Belley he was hoping to consolidate a reputation as a portraitist. He showed it first in the 1797 *Exposition de l'Elysée*, together with his 1793 *Endymion*, the work that had established his reputation as an artist working independently from David. Both works share an explicit and graceful sexuality, not part of David's repertoire in 1793. Nor, moreover, had David shown any interest in the representation of non-European figures, so Girodet's exhibition of the works in 1797 and 1798 may have been a further assertion of independence. In other respects Girodet's picture also breaks with earlier traditions of portraiture, especially of blacks. The usual format for portraits of black servants domiciled in France and of visiting men of rank was bust-length or head only. Girodet shows Belley in three-quarter length and in conjunction with an antique bust, which, by association, elevates him further.

The subversive nature of this picture and its rarity give it a peculiar value. Even more so does its present situation. For this painting is normally locked away, together with a number of works from the period of the French Revolution, on the attic floor of the palace of Versailles, where it is only visible by the public once a year on a specific day in August, and otherwise by special request. Thus, in this major national tourist site that focuses on the sumptuous splendour of France's royalist past, there is no space, or perhaps no will, to evoke or re-present the violent struggles of France's revolutionary history. The only references in these attic rooms to the ignominious fall of Louis XVI and Marie-Antoinette are the sentimental portraits of those who fell victim to the republicans.

The Belley portrait hangs in a room devoted to Napoleonic imagery and, curiously, it functions, through its format, size and location, almost as a pendant to a portrait of Bonaparte as First Consul on the same wall.[7] It is positioned on this wall so that Belley turns towards Bonaparte who, by contrast, confronts the spectator with all the authority invested in him as Consul. There may be practical considerations determining this choice of place but the result is problematic, since the *Belley* was produced in 1797, before Bonaparte came to power, and in fact refers the spectator, as I shall argue, to an even earlier period, to February 1794, that is to the period of high Terror when Robespierre and his committees governed France in the name of virtue and intimidation. It is arguable, therefore, that this picture should be placed in the room devoted to an earlier period. In 1802, shortly after Bonaparte had been made First Consul, he reinstated the *Code Noir*, revoked the 1794 decree and welcomed the reopening of the slave trade. Thus, in relation to Bonaparte's presence in this Versailles location, Girodet's portrait of Belley takes on an unfortunate new meaning; instead of standing as representative of the free people of the colonies, Belley here appears to turn his gaze towards the man who was soon to re-enslave the people Belley represents. What appear to have been its originally intended and perceived meanings are transformed by this location and juxtaposition.

I would like to argue first, that this work was conceived by its author and perceived by critics at the time of its exhibition in the 1798 Salon as more than a portrait of an individual, that it was in fact intended as and appropriated as a commemoration of the decree of abolition of 1794; secondly, that the strategies employed by the artist and the statements of critical response to the picture implied there was a need for this monument, lest the moment be forgotten and lest the great achievement of emancipation be short lived (as indeed it proved to be); and thirdly, that its positive reception in the 1798 Salon suggests that it was indeed understood as one of the many works representing the consensual ideology of the Directory government, supporting a unified centrist position.

Jean-Baptiste Mars Belley was the first black man ever to represent the people of France's colonies in the French parliament. He made his first appearance there on 3 and 4 February 1794,[8] and his whole identity was associated with the decree of that day. Born in Senegal in 1747 and taken to Saint-Domingue (present-day Haiti) as a slave, he gained his freedom when he was in his twenties and became an infantry captain fighting with French republicans in the summer of 1793 against French troops commanded by General Galbaud, who was trying to crush the slave insurrections. Belley's election in September 1793 as representative for the People of Saint-Domingue was largely a political triumph for the Robespierrist Jacobin supporters. They supported liberty and equality for all male citizens of France and its colonies. In the new context of discussions about rights of man they rejected – on grounds of irrationality – the notion that either skin colour or physiognomic factors could decide the question of political rights. The decree of 4 February 1794 marked for them an end to what they called *l'aristocratie cutanée*, aristocracy of the skin.

The decree would have been perceived less significantly by those earlier human rights campaigners among the *philosophes* of the 1770s and 1780s who were certainly concerned about the slave trade and the treatment of slaves but who, for the most part, had not called for immediate abolition of slavery. Among their number we can count the Abbé Guillaume-Thomas Raynal, author of a controversial book, *Philosophical and Political History of European Establishments and Commerce in the East and West Indies* (1770).[9] Raynal had died in 1796 and Girodet's inclusion of a large marble bust of him in the form of an ancient philosopher is an act both of homage and of commemoration by the artist. However, juxtaposed with Belley, it is anachronistic and it is very noticeable that Girodet has made Belley turn his back on Raynal; he does not, himself, gaze up in homage at him. Belley's election would likewise not have been perceived as a triumph by the members of the *Société des Amis des Noirs*. In 1781 the Marquis de Condorcet, one of the founding members of this society, had been among the first in France to denounce slavery and throughout the next decade this society would attack the *Club Massiac*, or *Société Correspondante des Colons Français de Saint-Domingue* for its hindering of all attempts at reform of the slavery issue.[10] The new president of the *Société des Amis des Noirs* in 1790 was Abbé Grégoire and he had included a clause in the draft constitution for the colonies that amounted to enfranchisement for free mulattos who met a property requirement and this could be seen as a first step in a move towards eventual abolition. The Society was short lived, however, as many of its members emigrated or defected or were guillotined by the Jacobins for their moderate views. Grégoire himself regarded the decree of 1794 as disastrous and probably counterproductive, because of its rushed and immediate implementation. Effectively, the aim of the *Société des Amis des Noirs* had been to achieve gradual abolition.

Raynal had been banished from France in 1781 and the 1780 edition of the *Histoire* was condemned by the Parlement of Paris to be burned for its anti-clericalism. In this edition an explicit parallel had been drawn between the oppression of the European people by church and state, and the oppression of the black slaves in the colonies. Thus in the pre-1790s phase of the Revolution's development Raynal had been championed by radical thinkers and reformers and his inclusion here is justified by the memory of those days. By the early 1790s Raynal had no sympathy with the egalitarian lines along which the Revolution was progressing and he was distinctly out of favour with the Jacobins. So at the time of the decree of 4 February 1794, Raynal and Belley held irreconcilably different views about liberty and equality. A set of contrasting notions is adumbrated in the picture between Raynal and Belley, amounting to a contrast between freedom of conscience claimed by the philosopher on the one hand, and freedom of the person and civil liberties fought for on the battlefield and in the political arena by the soldier and politician on the other.

Girodet shows Raynal in the conventional manner of honoured ancient philosophers and shows Belley in the official modern costume of Representative of the People. Belley, despite his solidarity with Robespierre's government under the Terror, continued in office after Robespierre's fall in July 1794. He was appointed *chef de bataillon* to the 16th infantry regiment in May 1795 and found himself in the new Assembly as a Deputy to the Council of Five Hundred and his appointment was renewed in March 1797. But by the time Girodet's portrait was painted Belley was fifty years old and had come to the end of his term of office. By the time the portrait was first exhibited at the Elysée exhibition, another delegate had taken Belley's seat in the Convention. There is some reference to him being promoted in June 1797 to *chef de brigade* and in July *Commandant en chef* or *chef de la gendarmerie de Saint-Domingue*.[11] It is believed that Belley died in 1804 at the age of fifty-seven, but the nature and circumstances of his death are the subject of conflicting accounts. One version relates that he returned to Saint-Domingue in 1797 still aligning himself with the convinced republicans as he had done in 1794.[12] There are claims that Belley was arrested by Bonaparte's forces during the insurrection at Haut Cap and brought back to Belle-Isle-en-Mer in Britanny, where he died at the end of 1804. Another source suggests that Belley was a member of an unsuccessful expedition to Saint-Domingue led by General Hédouville, sent by Bonaparte in 1798 to disband the black army and depose Toussaint-Louverture, leader of the black insurrections in Le Cap and self-proclaimed constitutional ruler of the colony.[13] The same source also suggests that Belley joined a second expedition led by General Leclerc against Toussaint in 1801. Again Toussaint defeated Bonaparte's army, although he was later tricked and captured, and died in captivity in the Jura mountains in 1803. It is believed by some that Belley was taken prisoner by the black revolutionaries and shot for collaborating with Bonaparte after the French had left Saint-Domingue. Although there is no evidence either way, it might be thought that the placing of Belley's portrait in relation to Bonaparte's in the rooms of Versailles corresponds to the latter version of events.

An Allegory to Commemorate Liberty and Equality

The 'sublime things' of my title are the words of Pierre-Jean-Baptiste Chaussard, a consistent Jacobin supporter and one of the more interesting critics of the period; for Chaussard these 'sublime things' were Raynal, whom he mentions by name (not surprisingly as the name is inscribed into the marble base of the bust within the painting), the brush of Girodet, whom he also mentions by name, and 'the liberty of negroes'. He does not refer to Belley by name, (nor does any other critic), despite Girodet's insistence on entitling the work 'Portrait of C. Belley, Ex-Representative of the Colonies', giving him title of respect, identity through naming and description of his office. Instead Chaussard uses the phrase 'la liberté des nègres' and understands the figure of Belley as an allegory. For Chaussard such liberty was a sublime thing.[14] A quite different view of this liberty was expressed by a second, anonymous critic, who likewise perceived in the painting more than a straightforward portrait. Like so many comment-ators on the painting over the last 200 years, this critic tried to shift the focus onto the importance of Raynal and away from Belley. He lamented the fact that Belley had not been shown embracing the sacred image of Raynal, so that one could then have entitled the painting 'Homage of Gratitude'.[15] Such an interpretation of course reveals the expectation that emancipation would be seen as a white achievement, and that the painting should represent gratitude and humility, with the conferral of rights by the superior paternal white figure onto the grateful black – a recurrent theme in abolitionist imagery, especially that of the period prior to the 4 February decree.[16] This critic of 1798 was uncomfortable with Belley appearing as Raynal's equal, clearly preferring praise of generalized white humanity and compassion to the recollection of Jacobin abolition and black assertion of right to equality in 1794. However, both for Chaussard and the anonymous critic of 1798, the figure of Belley went beyond portraiture and represented liberty and equality of blacks as achievements of an earlier period.

There had been some question of excluding from the Salon a number of works, including the Belley portrait, in order to make more room to display history paintings, especially those works that had been plundered from Italy. When the Minister of the Interior proposed that history paintings in the 1798 Salon, and those in the category of historic genre should be more favourably hung and thus be made more visible to viewers, Girodet wrote to the Minister supporting this decision, but insisted that his own portraits, that of *Belley* and *A Young Child looking at Images in a Book*, were in fact conceived not as portraits but as history paintings, that is in the appropriate style and format for conveying elevated and morally ennobling ideas. 'The two portraits are almost full-length and the manner in which they are treated necessarily calls for them to be placed in the historic genre. If these pictures are to be displaced at all it should be in order that they might be seen more advantageously'.[17] The artist's own perception of these works was matched by the critical reaction to them. Critics were impressed with Girodet's intelligence, with the ideas explored in the painting, with his sense of beauty, of composition, draughtsmanship and choice of gesture. Remarks about 'ce beau Nègre que l'on admire', (this beautiful Negro that is admired) even appear in a Vaudeville Comédie-Parade called *Le Déménagement du Sallon ou le Portrait de Gilles* (Moving from the Salon or Portrait of Gilles),[18] where the porters complain of having to move out so many works – a clear reference to the controversy over the status of Girodet's painting. In the same 'parade' Harlequin wins the affection of Columbine despite the black colour of his face – a tribute to the artist's ability to make blackness so beautiful and desirable that it has the power to change prejudice. Thus, both the artist's claims and the various types of critical discourse indicate that we are dealing with something grander than portraiture.

In the representation of equality, the careful levelling of heads of Raynal and Belley is a crucial device and is part of the currency of signs used against class or racial discrimination in prints dating back to the early phase of the Revolution's history. An example is *L'Egalité accordée aux Noirs*, an anonymous coloured acquatint, probably dating from 1791 (Figure 10); the same point is made by the title couplet, some lines of verse from Voltaire: *'Les Mortels Sont Egaux. Ce N'est pas la Naissance. C'est La Seule Vertu qui fait La Difference'* ('Mortals are equal. It is not birth. It is virtue alone that makes the difference'). A figure of Reason holds a rod above the heads of a black man with the Rights of Man and the Decree of 15 May, and a white man in the uniform of a French National Guard, signifying their equality as French citizens. As Anthony Halliday has recently pointed out, however, the levelling of the heads of Raynal and Belley is not presented as inevitable. Halliday suggests that Belley has lowered his head to the level of that of Raynal,

> because of the support which even posthumously the Man of Reason is supposed to afford him. Take that support away, and the Man of Nature would

Figure 10 Anonymous, *Equality accorded to Blacks*, coloured etching, *c.* 1791. Bibliothèque Nationale, Paris. (Photo: Service Photographique, Bibliothèque Nationale)

> once more rise to his full height, the ruins of Le Cap, still smouldering to the right of the painting, would burst into flame once more and Belley's compatriots in Saint-Domingue would once more commit atrocities . . . [19]

The notion of equality was also expressed through a single black male figure, as, for example, in new decks of cards.[20] *Égalité des Couleurs* (Figure 11) shows a man with African hair and physiognomy, seated on a coffee container and with sugar canes to his right. This replaced the knave of diamonds. His attributes are courage, written vertically down the side of the playing card, and weapons. Broken chains and yoke lie at his feet. Just as Belley had freed himself from slavery through sheer toil and service on the battle field, so this image constructs the black as one who has freed himself from his chains through courage and this has earned him equality with other men. Something of Belley's claim to equality through his military past and of the slave insurrections in 1793 is evoked in the bottom right hand corner of Girodet's painting, where it is possible to see intermittent bursts of smoke, the flat plains of Le Cap and the sea beyond, much as they had been depicted in prints.[21]

Girodet's juxtaposition of Raynal and Belley should not be seen as denigration of Belley.[22] Rather Girodet has explored the differences between the two men by invoking the new iconography of equality. Art

Figure 11 Anonymous, *Egalité des Couleurs*, playing card, *c.* 1794. Musée de la Révolution Française, Vizille. (Photo: Musée de la Révolution Française)

historians' concern to argue the issue of race in discussing this painting today supports Girodet's own claim, that he had invested the work with the intellectual and moral status of a history painting.[23]

Lest we forget . . .

Returning to Chaussard's 'sublime things', the second reference is to the fragility of the achievement of abolition. Chaussard's claim to often go and dream in front of this portrait, and the implication that he would continue to do so in the future, refers to freedom from slavery not as a reality achieved, but as a past, unfulfilled hope. There is a sentiment of the insecurity of the values represented by the decree of 4 February and the risk of losing sight of them.

Régis Michel writes of the melancholy of premonition in Belley's gaze and pose, suggesting that already, by 1797, the optimistic mood of 1794 no longer prevailed.[24] Certainly, by 1799 Bonaparte's policy on the colonies and the issue of slavery was becoming less libertarian and by 1802 he had rescinded the 1794 decree, forbidden mixed marriages and reinstated slavery in the colonies. In the same year Chateaubriand, praising the reasonable and humanitarian attitude of Catholic missionaries in the West Indies, was able to ask ' Who would dare to plead the cause of the blacks after the crime they have committed?'[25] This suggests that for Bonaparte's supporters the new image of blacks was of a brutal and bestial people, the very image that Belley had been trying to dispel in his speeches to the National Convention, and that Girodet had rejected in his portrait of Citizen Belley.

In terms of visual representation, it is not only the expression in the eyes turned to the heavens or the inclusion of the exotic landscape and reference to the dead Raynal that gives this picture a sense of the passing of a significant moment and makes one question whether abolition would endure. There is also the question of a *rite de passage*, for Belley and for an understanding of this we need to look at Girodet's Classical precedents for the figure of Belley, such as the mid-fourth-century BC figure of *Pothos* (Desire) by Scopas. Richard Brilliant has singled out the dissolute figure of the *Capitoline Satyr* as a source, in defence of the negative characterization he believes Girodet has produced of Belley.[26] It is possible that Girodet was also drawing on certain conventions in classical sculpture which, to the erudite amateur at least, could have signalled such notions as the transformation from slave to free man, dressed as he now is in his new clothes, and of the translation involved in the journey from one state of being to another. A possible ancient source for the representation of this change of status and for the sentiments of loss, hope and regret is that of the boundary herms. These might also offer a different explanation for the prominent genitals usually regarded as signifying excessive sexual appetites in eighteenth-century stereotypical theories of blacks. It is possible that the bust of Raynal on its pedestal and the curious decorative motif beneath is an adaptation of a herm such as that from Siphnos of the late sixth century BC. These were placed at boundary points, by the roadside or at street corners and other main public places, to invite worship from and give protection to passing travellers. These stone pillars were surmounted with the head of Hermes and usually had an erect phallus protruding from the stone. It is entirely in keeping with Girodet's practice of visual punning and witty but erudite referencing that, instead of an erect phallus on the pedestal beneath Raynal, which would have been wholly inappropriate for this Salon painting and would have detracted from the dignity of the philosopher, he should have painted an adaptation of the egg and dart motif to resemble penis and testicles. The herm reference would certainly have been apposite in view of Belley's imminent departure from France and return voyage to Saint-Domingue, his mission accomplished and the status of those he represented changed, at least temporarily. There is a sense in which Belley appears to be halting on his journey, taking time to reflect on his military and political past and perhaps on the writings of Raynal, and deriving support from these reflections. Thus, the image of a reflective (sad?) Belley invites similar reflections from the viewer, precisely of the type which Chaussard brought to his Salon comment. Two hundred years later, the reminder of colonial tensions and threats to freedom is no less salutary than it was in the 1790s.

An Ideology of Consensus

Remembering is a selective and recreative process. It can be argued that, within Girodet's painting of Belley there is also a deliberate will-to-forget. For, in recalling and glorifying the achievement of black emancipation through this reflective image, all violence and bloodshed, struggle and opposition are made invisible, are forgotten. Whereas in reality emancipation had been achieved at the cost of much loss of life, especially on the battlefield at Le Cap in the summer of 1793, the price the rebellious slaves paid for their freedom was to earn for blacks an image of barbarism and brutality. Yet, all traces of violence have been erased from the picture. In other words, in this work, as in many others of the post-Terror period, there appears to be an attempt at disavowing the Terror and at suppressing past racial and class hostilities in the interests of unity and of an imaginary consensus.

In the period following the Terror and the fierce reaction to it, the leaders of the Directory attempted to steer a middle course between the conflicting claims of Jacobins and royalists. Any consensus necessarily involved an act of will to forget the excesses of violence of the period from late 1793 to late 1794, with its warring political factions. Yet, Belley's whole identity was linked precisely with that tumultuous period. In his speeches he had insisted on his military record and devotion to republican principles, and had refuted accusations that were by then commonplace, that, given innate laziness, depravity and bestiality, the natural condition of the African was that of enslavement.[27] In Girodet's painting the only reference to the killing fields is in the bottom right-hand corner and Belley is not shown as a military man. He carries no sword but wears his official costume of representative of the people. His full name, Jean-Baptiste Mars Belley, was a play on words of war, but Girodet entitled his painting *Portrait of C. Belley*, where C. stands for citizen and 'Mars' is omitted. It would seem that, in the interests of burying the image of violence and savagery of the Terror régime, Girodet has constructed Belley firstly in his role of politician and secondly in poetic reflection or meditation. He states as much in his letter to the Minister of the Interior.[28] Had Belley been presented as aggressively militaristic or brutish instead of graceful and passive, there would have been a likelihood of seeing his image as an allegory of the Terror.

Girodet had produced a portrait of a black man that was neither violent nor ugly and was in no way threatening. It was acknowledged from all quarters as being a thing of beauty. To a large extent this quality must be associated with the handling of colour, light and finish, for the overall effect is graceful, harmonious, clear and smooth. Girodet has chosen his colours carefully. For example, there is no vermillion. What would once have been a bright red, white and blue cumberband around the People's Representative's waist is here rendered as soft pink, cream and grey. No hue or texture even suggests the colour and viscosity of blood. This is in sharp contrast with David's use of red in *The Death of Marat* (Musées Royaux des Beaux Arts, Brussels), for instance, of late 1793. In that painting the thick glutinous texture of the vermillion red on the blade of the knife on the floor and the warm, liquid quality of the red blood in the bath had been manipulated by David to very different effect. It is as though Girodet has drawn a veil over the memory of violence and bloodshed that might be associated with black and white antagonisms.

We can accept the close juxtaposition of Raynal and Belley as non-anachronistic only by forgetting their opposing views on the issue of emancipation in 1794. Both men found acceptance under the Directory and making this acceptance visible was Girodet's contribution to the metadiscourse of the history of the French Revolution. The costume worn by Belley did not identify him solely with the days of 1794. When he was elected to the Council of Five Hundred – and until 1798 – he would have worn the same costume in his continuing role of representative of the people of Saint-Domingue. So, despite being identified with 4 February 1794 and with Robespierre's government, Belley could be seen as a member of this subsequent Council and of the legislative body with which he had served for three years since the Terror. After Robespierre's death Raynal had been received back into the Academy as a member of the history section of what was by then the Institut. Before his death in 1796 he had started on a revised edition of his *Histoire des Deux Indes*, which served as a reminder that he had once been the philosopher who had campaigned for freedom of speech and had fought against oppression of blacks in the colonies, even if he had not gone so far as to recommend their enfranchisement. So, within Girodet's painting the period when Raynal's views diverged from the Jacobins can be forgotten and the excesses of the Terror with which Belley was so closely connected can be disavowed.

As mnemonic history, this image asks the spectator to remember abolition as a non-violent moment in France's revolution, achieved jointly by blacks and whites, for whom Belley and Raynal are metaphors. At the time of its display it was conceived and perceived as allegory on the same scale and with the same solemnity as grand history painting. By bringing these two figures together in seeming harmonious accord Girodet enabled the Directory to be seen as embracing shades of opinion that had once represented extremes of the political spectrum, an image reinforced by the critical acclaim the picture received. That these achievements and relationships cannot be acknowledged by the visitor to Versailles today is, presumably, the result of an official decision to forget the Revolution and the notions of equality that, 200 years ago, had destroyed the French royal family.

Notes

1. J'irai souvent rêver devant ce portrait. Que d'objets sublimes! Raynal, la liberté des nègres et le pinceau de Girodet. *Exposition des ouvrages de peinture, sculpture, architecture, gravure, dans les Salles du Muséum, premier Thermidor, an VI par Chaussard,* Collection Deloynes, XX, 539, pp. 117–18.

2. I am grateful to the organizers and audience of the 1994 conference, *Remembering and Forgetting*, where this paper was first delivered and which was, in itself, an act of remembrance of the February 1794

decree. Girodet's painting was the subject of a different discussion in an article of 1994 by the author. See H. Weston, 'Representing the right to represent: the *Portrait of Citizen Belley, ex-representative of the colonies*, by A.-L. Girodet,' *Res* 26 (1994), pp. 83–99.

3. For a discussion of the coverage of the debate on abolition in approximately thirty newspapers, see Y. Bénot, 'Comment la Convention a t-elle voté l'abolition de l'esclavage en l'an II?', *Annales historiques de la Révolution française* 34 (1993), pp. 349–62. See also Florence Gauthier, *Triomphe et mort du droit naturel en Révolution*, Paris, Presses Universitaires de France 1992, pp. 155 ff., for a discussion of the issue of natural rights in the French colonies.

4. > Depuis 1789 un grand procès restait en suspens; l'aristocratie nobiliaire et l'aristocratie sacerdotale étaient anéanties, mais l'aristocratie cutanée dominait encore; celle-ci vient de pousser un dernier soupir; l'égalité est consacrée; un noir, un jaune, un blanc vont siéger parmi vous au nom des citoyens libres de Saint-Domingue.

   National Convention, sessions of 3 and 4 February 1794, *Le Moniteur*, no 137 (17 pluviôse l'an II) in *Réimpression de l'ancien Moniteur, seule histoire authentique et inaltérée de la Révolution française*, vol. XIX, Paris 1847, pp. 385–8. See also H. Honour, *The Image of the Black in Western Art, 4: From the American Revolution to World War 1*, Part 1, Cambridge MA, Harvard University Press, 1989, p. 104 and n. 267, 271.

5. 'Je termine, citoyens collègues, en vous proposant le décret suivant. Art. 1. La loi du 16 pluviôse qui abolit l'esclavage dans les colonies françaises, sera incéssament envoyée dans tous les endroits où elle n'a pu être encore promulguée.'
   ('I conclude, citizen colleagues, by proposing the following decree. Art. 1. The law of 16 pluviôse, which abolished slavery in the French colonies, shall be constantly relayed in all the places where it has not yet been promulgated'.) See *Le Bout d'Oreille des Colons, ou le Système de l'Hotel de Massiac, mis au jour par Gouli*, Belley, Député Noir de Saint-Domingue, to his Colleagues, n.d., p.8.

6. Girodet's biographer confirms that the artist was often in the company of non-Europeans and was much impressed by their beauty. See P.-A. Coupin, *Oeuvres posthumes de Girodet-Trioson, peintre d'Histoire, suivies de sa correspondance, précédées d'un notice historique et mises en ordre par P-A. Coupin*, vol. 1, Paris, Jules Renouard Librairie, 1829, p. xviij.

7. I would like to take this opportunity to correct the long-standing attribution of the *Portrait of Bonaparte as First Consul* to Girodet, which I erroneously repeated in 1994, (Weston, 'Representing the right to represent' p. 99). It is in fact thought to be by Robert Lefèvre. See Nicole Hubert, 'Musées de Malmaison et de Bois-Préau. Nouvelles Acquisitions. Peinture, miniatures, gravures', *La Revue du Louvre et des Musées de France* 3 (1986), pp. 210–15.
8. The other two men who appeared with Belley on these occasions were Louis-Pierre Dufay, a white man, and Jean-Baptiste Mills, a mulatto. On 30 May 1794 Belley officially took his seat in the Convention.
9. G.-T. Raynal, *Histoire philosophique et politique des établissements des Européens dans les deux Indes*, vol. IV, The Hague, Gosse fils, 1774. A collaborative work to which Denis Diderot contributed, and first published in 1770 as reflecting official enlightenment policy in French colonial matters, the book was expanded in 1774 and again in 1780 and went through more than thirty editions in France before 1822. In the 1774 edition an added passage (probably by Diderot) referred to the possible consequences of retaliation if emancipation were to be achieved through the effort of some modern Spartacus. At that point, it predicted, the *Code noir*, understandably hated by black slaves, would be replaced by a *Code blanc* that would be equally hateable to whites. See p. 227, 'Alors disparaîtra le *Code noir*; et que le *Code blanc* sera terrible, si le vainqueur ne consulte que le droit de représailles!'
10. On the machinations of the Massiac Club, see Gabriel Debien, *Les colons de Saint-Domingue et la Révolution: Essai sur le Club Massiac (août 1789–août 1792)*, Paris, 1953.
11. For details of Belley's life, see Paris, Archives Nationales, C352, no 40, *Isle Saint-Domingue*; Paris, Archives Nationales, AD XVIII_b 125, AD XVIII_b 135; and Service historique de l'Armée de Terre, Yb 379. See also Auguste Kuscinski, *Les Députés au Corps législatif, Conseil des Cinq-Cents, Conseil des Anciens de l'an V à l'an VI*, Paris, Au Siège de la Société, 1905, pp. 106, 137, 192; Victor Schoelcher, *Vie de Toussaint Louverture*, Paris, Ollendorf, 1889, pp. 430–42; A Mathieu-Meusnier, 'Lettre de Girodet', *Archives de l'Art Français*, 2e série, I. (1861), pp. 317–19; Adolphe Robert, Edgar Bourloton and Gaston Cougny, *Dictionnaire des parlementaires français*, vol. I, Paris, Bourloton, 1891, p. 245, 'Belley (Jean-Baptiste)'; Michel Prévost and Charles Roman d'Amat, *Dictionnaire de biographie française*, vol. V, Paris, Letouzey et Ané, 1951, col. 1355, 'Belley (Jean-Baptiste)'.

12. For further speculation about Belley's moves after his departure from France, see Stephanie Brown, 'Girodet: a Contradictory Career', PhD thesis, University of London, 1980 pp. 147–9.
13. A. Mathieu-Meusnier, 'Lettre de Girodet', pp. 317–19.

14. C'est un des tableaux le plus scavamment peint que je connoisse; je conseille à plusieurs artistes d'interroger ce tableau, il fera leur desespoir ou leur guide; j'irai souvent rêver devant ce portrait. Que d'objets sublimes! Raynal, la liberté des nègres et le pinceau de Girodet.
    (It is one of the most cleverly painted pictures that I know of; I recommend several artists to go and learn from this picture; it will cause them to despair or to be guided. I shall often go and dream in front of this portrait. What sublime things! Raynal, liberty for negroes, and the brush of Girodet). Chaussard, *Exposition*, pp. 117–18.

15. *Le Mercure de France*, 19 July 1798, Collection Deloynes, XX, 538, p. 34.
16. The frontispiece engraving entitled *Soyez Libres et Citoyens* by Pierre Rouvier to Benjamin Sigismond Frossard's sentimental novel, *La Cause des esclaves nègres et des habitants de la Guinée, portée au Tribunal de la Justice, de la Religion, de la Politique*, Geneva, Slatkine Reprints, re-impression of edition de Lyons, 1789, is probably the kind of image this anonymous critic had in mind. It shows genuflecting black men and women released from their chains by an allegorical representation of France, she all benevolence and divine power, they all gratitude and servile humility.

17. Les deux portraits sont presque en pied, et la manière dont ils sont traités les fait nécéssairement rentrer dans le genre historique, en conséquence. Si ces tableaux pourraient être déplacés, ils ne devaient l'être que pour être vus plus avantageusement' (30 fructidor an VI).

    For the exchange of correspondence between Girodet and the Minister of the Interior, see Mathieu-Meusnier, 'Lettre de Girodet', pp. 317–19.
18. Collection Deloynes, *Exposition*, XX, 542, pp. 268–70.
19. A. B. Halliday, 'French Portraiture under the Directory and the Consulat', PhD thesis, University of London, 1996, p. 195. Halliday refers to Benjamin Constant's cautionary words published independently in a pamphlet, *De la force du gouvernment actuel de la France et de la nécéssité de s'y rallier*, later printed in *Le Moniteur* of 12 floréal an IV (1 May 1796) warning of the danger of further revolts,

not only among the slaves of Saint Domingue, if the voices challenging inequality were ignored.

20. This deck of cards was published by Jaume and Dugourc in 1793. See Henri-René d'Allemagne, *Les cartes à jouer du XIV*[e] *au XX*[e] *siècle,* vol. 1, Paris, Librairie Hachette, 1906, pp. 139–42, and Jean-Pierre Séguin, *Le Jeu de cartes,* Paris, Bibliothèque Nationale, 1968, p. 114.
21. See, for example, engraving by Pierre-Gabriel Berthault after Jean-François Swebach-Desfontaines, *The Fire of Le Cap Français, June 20, 21, 22 and 23, 1793*, Bibliothèque Nationale, Paris, De Vinck 6040.
22. Weston, 'Representing', pp. 97–8.
23. Thomas Crow confirms this reading:

    > In the midst of the political drift of the Directory years, Girodet has managed to turn a demonstration of his mastery of portraiture into an ambitious tribute to the cause of abolition, to the improving force of Enlightenment ideas, and to the general expansion of life possibilities for the low-born – indeed to the lowest-born – under the Republic.

    Emulation: Making Artists for Revolutionary France, New Haven and London, Yale University Press, 1995, p. 228. For a discussion of the theory of denigration of Belley, see Richard Brilliant, *Portraiture*, London, Reaktion Books, 1991, pp. 32–7.
24. Régis Michel, *Aux Armes et Aux Arts! Les Arts de la Révolution 1789–1799*, Paris, Editions Adam Biro, 1988, p. 79. Halliday also points out that by the time of its exhibition, Girodet's portrait of Belley was out of date 'Portraiture', p. 201. It was no longer possible to have a universalist notion like liberation of blacks serve as a 'lesson in how society could be governed by the power of ideas . . . It was now clear that whoever could call on the support of the army would rule the Republic.'
25. François-René de Chateaubriand, *Génie du Christianisme,* ed. Maurice Regard, Paris, Bibliothèque de la Pléiade, 1978, p. 1000.
26. Brilliant, *Portraiture,* pp. 32–7.
27. For a discussion of these speeches see Weston, 'Representing the right to represent.'
28. Mathieu-Meusnier, 'Lettre de Girodet', p. 317.

–4–

Bribing the Vote of Fame: Eighteenth-Century Monuments and the Futility of Commemoration

David Bindman

The futility of erecting monuments in the hope of achieving remembrance by posterity was one of the great themes of eighteenth-century English essays, satire and religious poetry. For writers like Joseph Addison and James Hervey and many others, monuments were affecting and morally instructive not because they might prolong the life of an individual into posterity, but, on the contrary, because of their very inability to resist oblivion. What could be more forlorn than a grand and costly tomb, put up to prolong a reputation beyond the grave, but now long neglected and falling into ruin, with the name of the deceased completely forgotten? Monuments with extravagant inscriptions had their own form of poignancy; as Addison noted in his classic account of a walk around Westminster Abbey, in the *Spectator* for 30 March 1711: 'Some of them were covered with such extravagant Epitaphs, that if it were possible for the dead Person to be acquainted with them, he would blush at the Praises which his friends have bestowed upon him'.[1] On the other hand monuments that simply recorded the name and dates of birth and death were equally forlorn in their expectation that the name would mean something to a passers-by of a later generations: 'I could not but look upon these Registers of Existence, whether of Brass or Marble, as a kind of Satire upon the departed Persons; who had left no other Memorial of them, but that they were born, and that they died'.[2]

For Addison monuments were vain attempts to resist the inevitable fading of the dead from memory, poor substitutes for more enduring forms of remembrance. In effect, a family that erected such a monument, by making public a name that would be unrecognized, only ensured the deceased's oblivion more completely. Nor were great deeds enhanced by a monument; on the contrary they were diminished by what James Hervey called 'these ostentatious Methods, of BRIBING the VOTE of Fame, and purchasing a little posthumous Renown!'[3] A monument, then, was a form of conspicuous consumption that not only failed to guarantee immortality, but on the contrary tainted the name of the deceased forever with the suspicion of vanity and luxury.

How then should a life be remembered if not through a monument? Hervey's answer was that the deceased should have carried out 'a Set of memorable Actions' which would ensure renown; another was to live the life of an exemplary Christian eschewing all desire for fame, seeking in one's desire for personal oblivion to provide a model of human conduct. Yet such ideal prescriptions did not alter the fact that monuments continued to be erected regardless of the disdain of moralists because by giving 'a second life, among the living'[4] to the deceased, they frequently fulfilled other purposes than the assuagement of grief.

What did monuments do for those who commissioned them? This depended first of all on who was responsible for the commission, and private grief may not have played a large part in the decision to erect a monument, though monuments based on sentiment, such as those set up in memory of young wives who died in childbirth, did become more frequent towards the end of the century.[5] In many cases the purposes were dynastic or self-serving, to aggrandise a family or a profession, but the most common reason was an obligation towards a benefactor felt by those who had unexpectedly inherited great wealth or an estate.[6] In some instances a large monument might be set up to vindicate the reputation of a politician falsely accused of treachery or a crime, or of a military man who had lost a battle, but in practice the size and elaboration of the monument might be quite out of proportion to the loss the deceased's relatives might have been expected to feel. It would, despite the touching images of grief so often used in the monuments, be misleading to see them as necessarily concerned primarily with the preservation of the memory of an individual.

I want to argue that an acceptance of the inability of monuments to resist the certainty of oblivion, as well as a need to suppress the essentially worldly purposes they served, profoundly conditioned the imagery of the monumental work of the most thoughtful sculptors of the age. I propose to look at a small number of works by the sculptor Louis Francois Roubiliac (1702–1762), who worked in London on a group of highly dramatic monuments for Westminster Abbey and other churches throughout the country.[7] In general Roubiliac's response to the barrage of disdain for the overblown monument was to avoid conventional triumphalism, even in military monuments, in favour of meditative themes of loss and redemption that might capture the respectful attention of Addison-like visitors to church, in their search for 'pleasing Melancholy'. In Roubiliac's monument in Westminster Abbey to Field Marshal George Wade,[8] which commemorates a high-ranking soldier who had died in 1748 under a cloud of failure for having, as commander-in-chief for England, allowed the Jacobites to get as far as Derby in the 1745 Rebellion, the monument's inevitable neglect and decay in the future are at the very heart of the

Figure 12 L. F. Roubiliac, Monument to Field Marshall George Wade, Westminster Abbey, London, 1750. (Paul Mellon Centre for Studies in British Art)

image's central conceit. The monument shows a Roman-style trophy, adorned as if for a field funeral, while two allegorical figures are engaged in combat. The theme was expressed by a contemporary periodical as 'exhibiting a contest between *Fame* and *Time*, whether the Trophy behind them should endure or not'.[9] We see in the monument itself the enactment of a scene in the distant future; the Field Marshal has begun to fade from human memory and the monument has fallen into terminal neglect. Wade has reached the point of oblivion and Time himself 'is eagerly approaching to pull down the Pillar with the Ensigns of Honour that adorn it'. At this moment Fame bounds into the picture and stays Time's hand, granting the Field Marshal eternal renown.

Time is thus the bringer of oblivion, destroying inexorably human memory and its symbols. Nothing material can stay the hand of time or preserve memory, least of all the physical substance of marble, though of course the monument is, paradoxically, itself made of marble. In Roubiliac's Hargrave monument,[10] also in Westminster Abbey on the same range on the south side of the nave as the Wade monument, the provisional nature of the monument is taken a stage further in a representation of its actual destruction. The scene is a kind of flash-forward to the end of time prophesied in the Bible, when the dead shall arise and go to judgement before entering the Kingdom of Heaven. The figure of Time creeps up on the monument at the right to consign it to final oblivion, as he would have done with Wade if not thwarted by Fame, and had done with the unmemorable subjects of so many other monuments. In the central conceit of the monument's imagery, however, it is Time itself who is sent to oblivion, along with all signs of the material world: the skeleton representing Death which itself dies, and the symbol of perpetuity in the pyramid behind, which explodes and collapses. At the moment of the end of time the deceased breaks out of the tomb at the sound of the Last Trump, and, glimpsing eternity, destroys the monument itself which exists only in time. We are perhaps intended to read the monument as lying among the ruins of the Abbey, for the sarcophagus appears to rest upon the collapsed masonry of the Abbey itself. Also, by implication, fame is destroyed, for though rhetorically eternal, it too is bounded by existence in the material world.

The Wade and Hargrave monuments in Westminster Abbey were erected to soldiers whose careers were notably unheroic,[11] at a time when there was much sensitivity about the poor calibre of the British army. The richness, even profundity of the imagery, can be seen as a distraction from the dispiriting reality of their careers, but the monuments were also designed to appeal to urban visitors, looking, as Addison had, for objects of contemplation and meditation. The complexity of the allegories had the effect of displacing the individual commemorated in favour of a kind of universal sermon on the vanity of the world and the certainty of resurrection. The triumphal imagery of the Wade monument can be related to his career by the suggestion that he will ultimately be vindicated, but no connection is made, understandably, between Hargrave's sleazy career as a military profiteer and the imagery of his monument. Hargrave is transformed into a kind of Everyman, experiencing the joyful fate of all good Christians at the moment of resurrection. Far from being commemorated as an individual Hargrave has become a cipher; as Oliver Goldsmith noted in an ironic reference to these and other monuments: 'I found several new monuments erected to the memory of several great men [in Westminster Abbey]; the names of the great men I absolutely forget, but I well remember that Roubiliac was the statuary who carved them. Alas! Alas!, cried I, such monuments as these confer honour, not upon the great men, but upon little Roubiliac'.[12]

The Wade and Hargrave monuments are in no sense about grief or the loss of an individual; Fame preserves and vindicates Wade, and eternity welcomes Hargrave. They live on fictively, in Wade's case in the memory of future generations perhaps yet unborn, and in Hargrave's case in the world beyond this one. There are, however, many other monuments which express grief, and whose iconography is directly concerned with the loss experienced by surviving relatives. In the face of time, the eraser of memory, how could a monument prolong the life of the deceased in the memory of the grieving family, of dependants and friends, or preserve the name for posterity?

It is precisely this issue that seems to be the ultimate subject of the rich and complex pair of monuments by Roubiliac to the Duke and Duchess of Montagu[13] in the chancel of Warkton Church, Northants. The monument to the Duke, erected on the order of the Duchess, represents a moment in the erection of the monument itself. As visitors to the church we are intended to imagine the period after the Duke has been laid to rest in his own church following his funeral, with all his honours and emblems of rank and office waiting to be attached to the monument. A figure of Charity accompanied by weeping children (presumably recipients of the Duke's charity) is hanging up a medallion of the Duke on the monument, while the marble figure of the mourning Duchess, leaning against the actual tomb, holds the Duke's honours ready to attach them to it. She pauses to reflect on his face, an action in itself implicitly critical of the elaborate dynastic tomb encrusted with coats-of-arms and emblems of power, for her grief at her husband's loss far transcends the merely earthly matter of

Figure 13 L. F. Roubiliac, Monument to the Duke of Montagu, Warkton church, Northamptonshire, 1754. (Paul Mellon Centre for Studies in British Art)

rank. We are clearly intended to feel empathy for her plight and marvel at her loyalty as she stands, like an antique heroine, by her husband's tomb, rekindling perpetually her inconsolable grief.

The primary conceit of the monument, then, is of a grief that achieves permanence through the medium of marble, yet is also actively renewed in the person of the Duchess who remains both inside and outside the tomb itself. If we imagine the half-finished monument as it might have become if it were finished, then it would be a fairly conventional affair, with the Duke's medallion hung on a kind of temple by a lamenting group of Charity with children, celebrating the Duke's reputation for charitable conduct, whereas his elevated rank would have been signified by hanging emblems, the ones still clutched as traces of his existence by the widow. Her presence and the unfinished nature of the monument, with the funeral hatchments and weaponry in the background, remove it from a kind of temporal void, and place it precisely in the aftermath of an exceptionally grand funeral befitting a great Duke. We enter the chancel as if entering a private space, intruding on the Duchess's grief, further dissociating the imagery of the monument from conventional rhetoric. The imagery and setting by alluding to and yet marginalizing the material consequences of rank, make of the monument a human drama of remembrance, hopefully proof against the ridicule normally applied to a grand tomb for a great duke, and interesting enough to encourage visitors, perhaps in the far distant future, to seek to unravel its meanings.

The monument on the opposite side of the chancel in Warkton church is to the Duchess, and was also made by Roubiliac, a few years later. The moment represented is even more specific than in the Duke's monument. If we can associate the latter with the days after the return of the Duke's body from his funeral, the Duchess's monument records the precise moment of her own death, when the Fates cut the thread of her mortal life. She has no commemorative medallion; her presence is eternally at the side of her husband on the other side of the chancel. The unexpected and thought-provoking disjunctions between the two monuments have the effect of further distancing the experience of being in the chancel from viewing a conventional family memorial. Meditation here becomes an active process. We are obliged to move from one monument to the other and from one moment of fictive time to another; the Duke's funeral, the erection of the monument, the Duchess's mourning period, which we must assume to last for the rest of her life, her own death, her meeting with the Duke in the world beyond as her gaze suggests she longs to do, and finally to the real time when the viewers themselves relive the emotions called up by the monuments.[14]

The reading I have given of the Montagu tombs has involved entering fully into their fictions, central among which is the assumption of a transcendent love between husband and wife. Whatever the nature of their real relationship we need to be clear that the elaborate structure of emotionally charged fictions that make up the monument was the work of Roubiliac and also of the Duchess's adviser on the project, Martin Folkes.[15] Such tombs would have originated not in a spontaneous effusion of grief,

Figure 14 L. F. Roubiliac, Monument to the Duchess of Montagu, Warkton church, Northamptonshire, 1754. (Paul Mellon Centre for Studies in British Art)

but in a desire to fulfil traditional obligations; in the case of the Duke's tomb, on the part of the widow to show gratitude for her inheritance, despite 'failing' to produce a male heir to prevent her husband's dukedom from becoming extinct with the consequent loss of the name embodied in his title. The couple did, however, have two daughters and after their mother's death they in turn inherited the family estate with a similar obligation to demonstrate their gratitude,[16] though they were in dispute with each other over the inheritance.

For monuments erected by an inheriting widow, there appears to have been an established typology that might involve the fictive presence in the monument of the widow herself. The touching and more modest monument by Roubiliac to the minor landowner George Lynn[17] in Southwick, Northamptonshire, not far from Warkton and made a short time later, shows a widow lamenting by her husband's medallion, seemingly longing to join him in heaven. Mrs Lynn had inherited the estate from her husband in the absence of a male heir, and she was personally responsible for the negotiations with the sculptor. The monument was, then, the fulfilment of her obligation as a widow to commemorate her husband's name and his endowment of his property upon her, but the emotional power of the monument results from the sculptor's interpretation of what an ideal widow might feel. She is represented, like the Duchess of Montagu, as if one has come upon her unawares in the chancel, gazing on a medallion of her husband. Her desperate longing to leave behind the material world and her eagerness to join him in heaven is wonderfully suggested by the detail of her slipper hanging off her foot. The vividness and immediacy of the imagery, as in the Montagu tombs, acts, then, also as a kind of veil over the complex and often unpleasant realities surrounding death and inheritance, which were so important to eighteenth-century property owners.

It would be useful at this point to say some brief words about inheritance in the eighteenth century. The ideal method was for an estate to pass from father to eldest son through the generations, but in practice this did not happen in all or even the majority of cases. If the eldest son died it would go to the brothers and then the male cousins on the father's side to preserve the family name. Failing this, and there frequently were no possible male heirs, it would go through the female line, to a daughter and her husband at best, or to sisters, aunts or cousins. As Lawrence Stone has demonstrated, most families were likely to endure some break in the line over the period of a century, and a number would lose the family name altogether.[18]

It was not the custom in eighteenth-century England for a family where there was a son and heir to erect a memorial to the father; in dynastic terms a male inheritance did not represent a rupture, or loss of the family name, but a natural continuity from generation to generation. Accordingly major monuments were rarely erected by close family members, but almost invariably when inheritance went to first, second or even third cousins. Indirect inheritance was the consequence of a failure of a family's male line, resulting in the extinction of the family title or even the name, and the symbolic closure of the family vault.[19] It is clear that an obligation to preserve the memory of the family lay as heavily upon a distant heir as upon a widow, while he (for the distant heir was bound to be male) might feel a genuine sense of gratitude at coming into a large estate with its attendant wealth and standing, and be prepared to express that gratitude in a splendid monument to the defunct line, which he would now be able to afford.

Of course such monuments also bestowed some honour on the donor who had so magnificently carried out his obligation to his knowing or unknowing benefactor, and the name of the donor was usually prominent in the epitaph. Even so the original circumstances behind the monument were usually well concealed behind the rhetoric of the imagery and epitaph, which would almost always claim that the monument's existence followed inevitably from the need to proclaim the deceased's exceptional virtues. Roubiliac's spectacular monument to Bishop John Hough in Worcester Cathedral[20] is a good example of the discrepancy between appearances and the circumstances that lay behind the erection of the monument. Hough had been something of a Protestant hero in his youth; in 1687 he defied James II's efforts to take over Magdalen College, Oxford, of which he was President, but for over sixty years after that incident until his death in 1743 he did little else of note. His piety, generosity and staunch Protestantism are dwelt on at great length in the epitaph, and the bishop himself is shown on his deathbed rising in exultation at his first glimpse of heaven. What could be more fitting than that a grateful congregation should wish to commemorate such a great and benevolent cleric, particularly as his monument was erected shortly after the '45 Rebellion when Protestant feeling was at its height? Though such considerations undoubtedly affected the imagery and the epitaph of the monument, in reality the decision to erect the monument had nothing at all to do with the bishop's virtues. Bishop Hough happened to be a man of great wealth who owned much property in Worcester and elsewhere. He was childless and his wife (represented in the monument by a tablet and mourning putto) had long predeceased him. On his death his fortune passed to a distant cousin, John Byrche,[21] who did the decent thing in terms of his obligation by commissioning a promising London sculptor to design an appropriate monument to the Bishop.

The Bishop had no close family to grieve over his death, nor would it have been appropriate for a distant heir to express grief, especially as he may not even have met his munificent benefactor. As a bishop piety could in a formal sense be assumed, and Hough had in his youth defied a Catholic king as President of Magdalen; both these aspects of his life are represented in the monument. The bishop is shown in the traditional manner of episcopal tombs with the lid of his sarcophagus acting as his deathbed, and Roubiliac has dramatized his sense of joy at the first sight of heaven as he looks upward in exultation. The bishop died at the age of 92 and his moment of heroism, which took place nearly 60 years before, is represented in a long bas relief below the sarcophagus, the cloth covering it held up by a mournfully gazing figure of Religion. His wife, represented by a tablet, had died 20 years before. These moments are all represented as being at different fictive times, reflecting the way in which epitaph moves insistently between Hough's 'dangerous and important station' in the bad times of James II, and the 'happier Times' in which as bishop he could display his characteristic benevolence.

Hough, in the absence of emblems of personal grief, becomes a type of 'good Christian' who can expect to reach heaven as the reward of a well-spent life; there is nothing here of the empathy and personal feeling that pervades the Montagu and Lynn monuments. Yet it is still distant from the 'luxurious' architectural structures that proclaimed the glory of a specific dynasty by a display of marble heroics. Despite its size, its existence could be justified to Evangelical doubters like James Hervey on the grounds that it provided an image of ideal behaviour and Christian conduct that enhanced the religious aura of the cathedral in which it was placed. It was an example of what were later to be called 'sermons in stone', designed to uplift the congregation and provide virtuous examples rather than to seek fame for the deceased.

Many of the most extravagant and imaginative monuments of the period were commissioned by distant heirs. The distance between deceased and patron could allow the sculptor to achieve an unusual autonomy, releasing him from the need for conventional expressions of grief, and from any obligation that close family members might have imposed to represent the deceased as an individual or as part of a group. Indeed, the sculptor might be able, by playing on the heir's lack of personal involvement with the deceased, to make the commission suit his own purposes and create something that would attract attention to his own abilities.

By any measure the monument to Miss Mary Myddelton[22] in the parish church of Wrexham is an arresting work. Miss Myddelton, though she had died at the age of 59, is represented as a young girl breaking through the heavy granite of her coffin, rising exultantly to judgement and to eternity. The monument reveals the theatrical imagination and ingenuity the sculptor was able to command; it is probably not fortuitous that he was commissioned soon afterwards to carve in the Hargrave monument an even bigger and more elaborate version of the motif, and also a commentary on the transience of the monument itself and the memories it carries.

The patron of this commission, a Mr William Lloyd, a clerk in the Exchequer Office of Pleas in London, was distant in two senses; he inherited a large part of Miss Mydelton's estate and considerable fortune though he was not a relation, and he did not live in the same part of the country.[23] Mary Myddelton had been the last survivor of an old line of a distinguished family. She had inherited money but had also supplemented it by money-lending, and her principal attachment was to her clerical advisor the Revd Thomas Lloyd, to whom she left a large part of her estate, allowing it on his death in 1734 to be transferred to his son. The son inherited the money on her death in 1747 and in 1751 he signed a contract with Roubiliac for the monument, for the impressive sum of £300.[24]

We can assume that William Lloyd had a predilection for the fashionable, and in going to Roubiliac was commissioning a sculptor known above all for the imaginative and dramatic disposition of figures, an artist who had built his clientele on creating novelty. In such circumstances the monument to Miss Myddelton has moved as far away as possible from the act of individual commemoration, except possibly in the epitaph, which apart from referring to 'the Eminence deriv'd from Birth', could, in its conventional pieties, apply to almost anyone. The monument, then, has achieved something of the independence of a work of art which 'belonged' to the artist rather than the patron or the family of the deceased. It is surely not coincidental that Roubiliac was closely allied in this period with artists who were beginning to challenge the authority of the gentleman in matters of taste, arguing for the superior authority of their own professionalism.[25] As Goldsmith remarked, Roubiliac's monuments in reality commemorate not the deceased, whose name is rapidly forgotten, but the artist himself. It is a thought worthy of eighteenth-century meditations among the tombs that the names of most of Roubiliac's subjects have only been saved from oblivion because of the artistic interest his monuments have attracted among later generations.

Notes

1. *The Spectator*, no. 26, 30 Mar. 1711 (new style), p. 2.
2. *The Spectator*, no. 26, 30 Mar. 1711 (new style), p. 1.
3. J. Hervey, *Meditations among the Tombs*, London, 1796, I, p. 58.

4. The words are those of Aaron Hill, quoted in M. Brownell, *Alexander Pope and the Arts of Georgian England*, Oxford, Clarendon Press, 1978, pp. 350–1.
5. See N. Penny, *Church Monuments in Romantic England*, New Haven and London, Yale University Press, 1977.
6. For a pioneering account of the conventions of obligation see Matthew Craske's as-yet unpublished thesis, 'The London Sculpture Trade and the development of the imagery of the family in funerary monuments of the period 1720–60', PhD. thesis, University of London, 1992.
7. For Roubiliac see D. Bindman and M. Baker, *Roubiliac and the Eighteenth-Century Monument: Sculpture as Theatre*, New Haven and London, Yale University Press, 1995.
8. Bindman and Baker, *Roubiliac*, pp. 102–4 and 294–8.
9. *The Remembrancer*, 1750, pp. 514–15.
10. Bindman and Baker, *Roubiliac*, p. 85 passim.
11. Bindman an Baker, *Roubiliac*, p. 116.
12. O. Goldsmith, *A Citizen of the World*, London, 1761, p. 45.
13. Bindman and Baker, *Roubiliac*, p. 24 passim.
14. This discussion is indebted to Alex Potts's review of Bindman and Baker, *Roubiliac*, in *Burlington Magazine* 139 (1997), pp. 879–81.
15. Bindman and Baker, *Roubiliac*, p. 125.
16. Bindman and Baker, *Roubiliac*, p. 308.
17. Bindman and Baker, *Roubiliac*, pp. 133ff.
18. I am indebted to L. Stone and J. C. Fawtier Stone, *An Open Elite? England 1540–1880*, Oxford, Oxford University Press, 1986, pp. 66ff for this information.
19. Craske, 'The London Sculpture Trade', pp. 84ff.
20. Bindman and Baker, *Roubiliac*, pp. 109–12.
21. Bindman and Baker, *Roubiliac*, pp. 279–80.
22. Bindman and Baker, *Roubiliac*, pp. 112–16.
23. Bindman and Baker, *Roubiliac*, pp. 112–13.
24. For further details see Bindman and Baker, *Roubiliac*, pp. 304.
25. Bindman and Baker, *Roubiliac*, pp. 75–6.

–5–

Forgetting Rome and the voice of Piranesi's 'Speaking Ruins'

Tarnya Cooper

Arriving in Rome for the first time in 1857, the English writer Augustus Hare's initial impression of the city was that it seemed 'new yet most familiar, strange, yet well known'. He attributed this to his recollection of the engraved views of the city he had poured over in his childhood – 'their images were even at that early age, as distinctly impressed on my mind as if I had actually seen them'.[1] An even more curious encounter with Rome, this time before even visiting the city, was recounted by Sigmund Freud in *The Interpretation of Dreams:*

> I dreamt once that I was looking out of a railway-carriage window at the Tiber and the Ponte Sant' Angelo. The train began to move off, and it occurred to me that I had not so much as set foot in the city. The view that I had seen in my dream was taken from a well-known engraving which I had caught sight of for a moment the day before in the sitting-room of one of my patients.[2]

The image that caused Freud to remember a place he had not yet visited was, in all probability, the print of the Ponte Sant'Angelo by the most famous of all eighteenth century topographical engravers, Giovanni Battista Piranesi (Figure 15). In this particular print, the viewpoint is suspended in mid-air above the river, and might well have suggested being on a bridge to Freud; the pictorial depth of the image gives the impression of a scene glimpsed through a window, while the large area of shaded wasteland in the foreground could be seen as a railway embankment. The effect of these devices, if this was indeed the print Freud had seen, were sufficiently strong for him to have unconsciously translated the scene into his own experience.

Over and over again from the late eighteenth century onwards, visitors to Rome remarked upon finding it a city that they already knew, and in which the greatest pleasure lay not in discovery of the new, but recognition

Figure 15 G.-B. Piranesi, 'View of the Bridge and Castello Sant'Angelo', from *Vedute di Roma*, *c.* 1748–1778. British Museum.

of the familiar.[3] The cause of this sensation was, in very many cases, put down to a knowledge of the city previously gained from prints of Rome. For instance, Goethe, on his arrival in Rome for the first time in November 1786 at the age of 37, wrote:

> Now I see all my childhood dreams come to life; I see now in reality the first engravings that I remember (my father had hung the prospects of Rome in a corridor); and everything long familiar to me in paintings and drawings, copperplates and woodcuts, in plaster and cork, now stands together before me. Wherever I go I find something in this new world I am acquainted with; it is all as I imagined, and yet new.[4]

Of all the artists responsible for creating this Europe-wide collective visual memory of Rome, Piranesi must be considered the most important. What concerns us here are the particular pictorial devices through which Piranesi succeeded in creating a sense of intimate familiarity with a city as yet unvisited, and which caused the actual experience of Rome to become, for many visitors, a matter of relating what they saw to the remembered images. By means of the tension in Piranesi's prints between record and invention, and through pictorial relationships between the viewer (surveyor) and the etched figures (*cicerone*), Piranesi created a shared currency of memory, which in many cases displaced recollection of the direct experience of the city itself.

Topography as Pictorial Fiction

Before the invention of photography, printed images provided the main means for collective recollection of a city. The conventions of topographical art included the use of multifarious viewpoints and a schematized language for the representation of natural and architectural landscape, essentially attempting to conceptualize cites within a harmonious set of memorable motifs. Thus the mechanisms of the visual genre of Western topography were rarely based on the corporeality of cities. Truth to nature, if it could ever exist, had to be subverted to allow comprehensive representation of as complex an object as a city. An engraver or draughtsman often needed to compress the features of a city into a single view, even if that view did not exist in actuality. The effect of these 'adjustments' to reality was frequently commented upon in nineteenth-century guidebooks and visitors' accounts of Rome, and their effect upon the perception of city, and its collective misremembrance, often noted.

Artists over several generations such as Jacob van Ruisdael, Claude Gellée, Wencelaus Hollar, Antonio Canaletto and Richard Wilson all felt the need to invent imaginary or ideal viewpoints, to transport existing monuments or features to new locations, or to supply imaginary vistas as the backdrop to recorded landscape, for the purpose of compositional harmony or heightened dramatic effect. By the mid-eighteenth century the artists' view had conditioned an expectation of Rome that allowed greater harmony, more spacious surroundings, heightened dramatic scale, enhanced preservation and more readily assimilated vistas, than were in reality present. The practice of the *capriccio*, the imaginary constructed topographical viewpoint, had been part of the eighteenth-century understanding of the picturesque, practised to great effect in Italy by Canaletto and Venetian school engravers. Piranesi drew on this genre to evolve an approach whose principal theme was that the invention and ingenuity of the architects of ancient Rome ought to be equated with that of their topographer.

The association within a single image of factual topographic details and free invention could often cause memories of a physical site to become condensed with memories of its representation in the viewer's mind. Not surprisingly, this refashioning of the cityscape had the greatest impact on developing collective memories of a city when presented in the medium of printmaking. Across northern Europe printed visual 'records' of the physicality of cities were commonly produced and on occasion sponsored or promoted by civic authorities or prominent local dignitaries to foster the identity of that city, for the purposes of trade, and civic dignity. In Holland for example printmaker publishers such as Claes Janz Visscher working in Haarlem gained privileges from the Stathouder for various maps of cities in the province. Visscher and Esaias van de Velde also produced panoramas and topographical views of Haarlem, that attempted to site the city in the mind of the viewer as a place of abundance and social order that could ultimately celebrate long awaited peace following its siege and the removal of the Spanish forces. Such images rarely have the didactic function of maps: they offer a vision to be held in the memory and associated with specific activities occurring in particular places.[5] The movement of the eye across such views of a city could, given the inconveniences of travel, replace the experience of visiting the city itself. The anthropologist Paul Connerton in *How Societies Remember*,[6] defines this type of recall as a feature of '*inscribing* practice' where information is imparted through a secondary source and incorporated into a social or collective memory. In assessing how Piranesi's prints operated as '*inscribed*' memory, it is necessary to consider Piranesi's market and to examine how the monuments of Rome were understood through earlier visual and literary accounts.

Piranesi's Audience and the Marketing of Ancient Rome

The audience for topographical views of cities expanded throughout the eighteenth century, as grand tourists commissioned painted views or reproductions of topographical paintings of both modern and ancient sites in Rome, and in other Italian cities such as Venice and Naples. This practice helped to establish a collective pictorial memory within which there was a selective forgetting of a city's totality; Venice, or Rome, could for example become succinctly represented by Canaletto's or Piranesi's *manneria*.

A trade in topographical prints extended throughout Europe, but people were most likely to buy prints of a particular city within that city as travel mementoes. In Rome, print shops were concentrated along the Corso, and most guidebooks drew attention to their location.[7] The material on display at these shops would undoubtedly have included topographical views of monuments, key sites within and outside Rome, as well as reproductions of paintings and other tourist memorabilia.

Before Piranesi settled permanently in Rome in 1744, several professional engravers and a number of artist-printmakers had produced documentary records of the city. The printmaker Giuseppe Vasi, Piranesi's early master in Rome, produced highly accomplished and technically accurate panoramas and views of the ancient and modern city. His style combined formal clarity with technical virtuosity and his compositions were carefully delineated; his vision of Rome was recorded with the precision of a detached observer and populated with orderly citizens and travellers. Compared to Vasi's work, and that of other contemporary engravers, Piranesi's prints of the city were startlingly original, both in terms of their scale and their inventive content. The sizeable etchings published as part of the *Vedute di Roma* would have been within the means of the majority of tourists – unlike painted views, which were becoming increasingly expensive. In 1787 one James Robson recorded purchasing 'some old drawings and some Piranesi prints in Rome'.[8] For those who had visited Rome, such prints became part of their recollection of the city, establishing a collective, if deceptive, memory of it; for those yet to visit the city, these prints created a mental image of the city through which they were to see its reality, as they had for Goethe.

Piranesi may have learnt from Vasi's approach, but he soon left Vasi's practice to establish his own studio in an attempt to find visually more challenging topographical 'truths'. Piranesi's perception of his own endeavour is well documented. In the dedication to Piranesi's first publication *Prima Parte di Architetture e Prospettive* . . . of 1743 he describes the monuments of Rome as 'speaking ruins' that fill his 'spirit with images that accurate drawings, even such as those of the immortal Palladio, could never have succeeded in conveying'.[9] Thus for Piranesi the architecture of Rome resounded with the essence of ancient glory, and it was the modern architect's task to fill the spirit of the present with this inheritance. His aim was to show the monuments of Rome within a more dynamic context that could match the grandeur of the ancient Roman architecture and, ultimately, assert the achievements of the Etruscans – the original Italian race – as designers and architects of genius. In the preface to the four volumes of the *Antichità Romane*, published in 1756, Piranesi states his purpose not as an architect or artist, but as an archaeologist and an architectural historian with a key role in re-presenting Roman space: 'When I first saw the remains of the ancient buildings of Rome lying as they do in cultivated fields or gardens and wasting away under the ravages of time, or being destroyed by greedy owners who sell them as materials for modern building, I determined to preserve them forever by means of engraving.' His motives as expressed here are fired by a desire for a type of pictorial 'conservation' where monuments are rescued thorough the process of visual depiction, accurate archaeological description and presented with enhanced dramatic grandeur in large-scale printed format.

To Piranesi's subscribers and antiquarian audience, the essays and subtext of the imagery had topical relevance. During the 1760s, Joachim Winckelmann's approach to antiquity, championing the Greek historical supremacy and influence over Roman architecture, had gained general acceptance. Piranesi's viewpoint within this debate altered dramatically during his lifetime, principally because of the increasing importance he attached to invention within his own work.[10] From the 1760s Piranesi's artistic persona appears at odds with the thesis expressed in the text of *Della Magnificenza ed Architettura de Romani*, where he maintained that necessity, truth and simplicity were the cornerstones of supremely great architecture – qualities Piranesi found manifested in the buildings of the Etruscans, whom he considered the true fathers of Roman architecture.

The overall audience for Piranesi's work was large, and it increased throughout the nineteenth century as further editions of the plates were printed.[11] Many literary accounts of the monuments of Rome specifically mention Piranesi's depiction's of specific sites; Piranesi is recalled in Lady Anne Miller's *Letters from Italy* published in 1776, as an eccentric figure whose 'prints are sufficiently known to rank him amongst the first engravers on copper. He sometimes is carried by his taste, into romance.'[12] Having seen the monuments of Rome at first hand Lady Miller could afford to categorize some of his works as more capricious than topographical.

There is some evidence about who it was that bought the complete volumes of prints from contemporary accounts of the libraries of antiquarians, connoisseurs and the nobility, some of whose collections have since found their way into museums and libraries.[13] The sale of the library of William Beckford of Fonthill in 1823 included almost all of Piranesi's major works bound in over sixteen volumes as well as an additional set of 'the most brilliant impressions' of the *Vedute di Roma*.[14] An indication of the use to which Piranesi's prints were put in an English domestic context is provided by the set of his work owned by Fredrick William Hope, whose loose-leaf collection of prints from the *Vedute di Roma* series shows signs of candle wax spilt upon their pages. Evening viewing of gentlemen's print collections was no doubt common, but few prints bear such obvious marks of this, and it is tempting to think it was the result of an attempt to replicate at home the so-called 'moonlit' viewing of Roman monuments recommended by all the travel guides.[15]

Expectation and Literary Accounts of Rome

Late eighteenth-and nineteenth-century descriptions and guides to the eternal city provide some evidence of how Roman monuments were perceived, and may help us assess the extent to which Piranesi's concept of Roman antiquity contributed to the commonly experienced gulf of disappointment between expectation and reality. Typically guidebooks and accounts of the city and its monuments reject some of the illusions created by Piranesi's prints; J. C. Hobhouse, author of one of the most popular guidebooks, asserted that a man in confidence of the common fame of Rome 'must have the conviction of imposture and mistake forced upon him at every turn'.[16] The conflict between imagination fed by a visual and literary inheritance and the bald reality of the city was frequently exacerbated by the 'deplorable' state of both the fabric of the modern city and of the morality of the modern citizen. Joseph Forsyth, author of another popular guide to the antiquities, commented that one's attention would continually be 'divided between filth and magnificence'.[17] Prior to the French excavations, many ancient monuments were still, as Forsyth complained, in 'their half buried state', their proportions being 'difficult to grasp'. Other authors spoke of ruins being 'grand rather from association than in reality'[18] and it was this that had led Piranesi and other subsequent engravers who followed, to emphasize the grandeur belonging to literary memory rather than their present ruinous state.

The experience of looking often came into conflict with the recollected images: the English neo-classical sculptor John Flaxman recalled to his friend Joseph Farington in 1795 how on arrival in Rome he found the streets 'narrow and dark; and when he came among the ruins of ancient building he found them on a smaller scale, and less striking than he had been accustomed to suppose them after having seen the prints of Piranesi'[19] Flaxman's passing remarks to his friend reveal the power Piranesi's prints had to evoke a vision of Rome yet more majestic and imposing than the tumble of ruins that were its monuments. Several authors went further and were keen to deconstruct the exclusively visual concept of Rome propagated by the engravers, of whom they regarded Piranesi as the prime exponent. Forsyth opens his introduction to Rome with a tirade against the falsehood of the visual impressions of Rome: 'That rage for embellishing, which is implanted in every artist, has thrown so much composition into the engraved views of Rome, has so exaggerated its ruins and architecture, or so expanded the space in which they stand, that a stranger arriving here with the expectations raised by those prints, will be infallibly disappointed.'[20] That Forsyth's attack is directed at Piranesi is made plain by his comments on a temple sited near the Via Appia that he calls the 'Temple of Honour and Virtue'. Here, he complains, is an 'enormous frieze or belt of defaced stuccos, which appear very beautiful and perfect in Piranesi . . . – those lying engravers!'[21]

Like Flaxman, William Beckford who visited Rome in 1781–2 experienced a gulf between reality and pictorial fiction. At the Pantheon 'I was very near being disappointed, and began to think Piranesi and Paolo Panini had been a great deal too colossal in their view of this venerable structure. But though it is not so immense as I expected, yet a certain venerable air, an awful gloom, breathed inspiration, though of a sorrowful kind.'[22]

Despite his disappointment here Beckford embraced the spirit of Piranesi's work in his descriptions, and he continued to look at Roman ruins through Piranesi's visions, finding Piranesi's evocations of the contrast between ancient greatness and present degradation particularly moving.

On his arrival in Rome in the 1820s William Hazlitt expressed even greater displeasure than Beckford: this was not the Rome that Hazlitt had expected to see and the monuments did not correspond to his previous images of them. His appreciation of the spaces of ancient Rome was constantly invaded by modern degeneracy, 'the vulgar looking streets where the smell of garlick prevails over antiquity'. Hazlitt continues, 'I had thought that here were works immovable, immortal, inimitable on earth, and lifting the soul half to heaven . . . I find them not, or only what I had seen before in different ways'.[23] Informed by Piranesi's compelling vision of the architecture of Rome, Hazlitt concludes that 'Rome is only great in ruins.'

For very many visitors to Rome, a major aspect of the visit turned out to be the reconciliation of the reality of Rome with their previous mental image of it, formed from images, literary descriptions and classical texts. As Beckford, Goethe, and Hazlitt all found, being in Rome became a sort of dialogue between the remembered and the real. In this dialogue, Piranesi's prints played a particularly important part.

Piranesi's Pictorial Devices and the Imaging of 'Magnificent Rome'

How exactly did Piranesi succeed in creating in people the sense of a memory of what they had not yet seen? This may be explained by two elements of Piranesi's work. The first concerns his ability to combine, simultaneously and in heightened form, the two properties of 'age value' and 'historical value' described by Alois Riegl in his 1903 essay *On The Modern Cult of Monuments*. 'Age value' Riegl defined as the general sense of the passage of time produced by the contemplation of monuments, whereas 'historical value' referred an object's value as the document of a moment of past time.[24] The second element of Piranesi's success relates to his use of figures in the images as aids to the eye, so as to set up a sense of a metaphorical journey around monuments. A desire on the part of both artist and viewer to exalt the status of ancient Roman monumental structures, to see and experience the anticipated magnificence of Rome infused with the intensity of the sublime, established a sense of empathy between the viewing subject and the artistic intention. Piranesi's stated purpose was to record Roman architecture graphically for perpetuity, acting as its orator and reviving its eloquence. Yet the 'speaking ruins' that Piranesi describes command their intensely poignant impact precisely through his interpretation of this melancholic contrast between their past glory and their present dilapidation.[25] For the eighteenth-century viewer, a sense of what Reigl was to describe as the contrast between 'ancient greatness and present degradation' was a key part of the equation. As with William Beckford, the stimulus Piranesi provided to recognition of the differences between past and present could have a compelling effect upon a romantic imagination.

In Riegl's terms 'age value' was a mode of appreciation triggering an emotional understanding of an object's past and was the logical conclusion of historical value. Uniquely, Piranesi was able to combine an appreciation of both 'age value' and 'historical value' seamlessly within his work; monuments are presented as objects of hallowed magnificence more pleasurably evocative exactly because of their deterioration through time. For Riegl, age value was not dependent on a knowledge of history but on signals that both feed and evoke the memory of a universal past, though held subject to individual preference. The cult of ruins that Riegl described is part of a wider esteem and desire for association with symbols of power structures, which is in part why Piranesi's ennobling treatment of Roman ruins has such immediate satisfying appeal. However, Riegl's 'historical value' is also addressed by Piranesi, although more subtly through the use of keys to the principal sites, details of inscriptions, visual descriptions of archaeological finds and in particular within the whimsical analysis of ancient civilization provided in essays prefacing the *Antichità Romane* and in the *Parere su Archittetura*.

The presentation of 'historic value' is found in Piranesi's enlighteningly detailed technical descriptions of the construction of ancient sites, or the mechanics of Roman engineering, such as the body of work on the waterworks at the Lago Albano. While rarely in either the pictorial plates of the *Antichità Romane* or the *Vedute di Roma* does Piranesi provide the spectator with clear or even accurate accounts of the city, in the technical diagrams that follow the engraved views, his presentation is meticulously factual. This paradoxical combination of supreme pictorial eloquence and factual precision, part of his attempt to prove the superiority of Roman architecture over Greek, demands that at one level his work be judged as free invention and on another level be accepted as an archaeological record of the achievements of both Roman and Etruscan civilizations on Italian soil.

His exposition of the waterworks at the source of the two aqueducts at the Lago Albano and Castel Gandolfo, published between 1762 and 1764, provided a thorough archaeological analysis within an exceptionally inventive format. In the view of the plan of a drainage outlet from the *Descrizione e Disegno dell' Emissario del Lago Albano* (Figure 16), the viewer could play 'surveyor'; a *trompe l'oeil* page laid out like an overlaid drawing board offered ground plans, elevations, cross sectional diagrams, and contemporary pictorial views, tacked over each other and divided across the page by a cunningly depicted length of string complete with its

Figure 16 G.-B. Piranesi, 'Plan of the drainage outlet at Lake Albano', from *Descrizione e Disegno dell'Emissario del Lago Albano*, 1762. University College, London.

own shadow. Lady Anne Miller, whose visit to the Lago Albano between 1770–1 was probably inspired by Piranesi's visual description of the ruins there, noted, after a description of the waterworks: 'Piranese, in his Antichita d' Albano, & c. has given a most curious account of this work, with very ingenious conjectures of the manner in which it was carried on, & c.'[26]

The figures with which Piranesi populated his views of Rome were a further important means by which people's vision of the city was conditioned. In particular they account for the ease with which spectators were mentally able to position themselves within his constructed space, and imagine themselves physically in Rome, even without travelling there. The figures, as in the views of the tomb of Cestius, were often so loosely etched as to indicate no more than theatrical gestures, such as hat-raising or bowing, and could not be identified as individual citizens or travellers. Figures of all types appear to use the same gestural language, be they the connoisseurs with three cornered hats or the vagabonds resembling *comedia del arte* characters that hover and clamber in rags over rough ground and at impossible heights. It is this common gestural language between figures that allows the spectator to identify with any of Piranesi's figures, who as a collective group appear engaged in a bodily assault upon the spirit of ancient monuments.

As an artist Piranesi used figures in endlessly resourceful schemes that recall Venetian carnival scenes or the frenetic theatrical characters of Salvator Rosa or Stefano della Bella. Piranesi positions figures in uniquely artistic adventures, placing them high in the distance in an act of compression at the apex of a ruinous structure, as in the *Foundations of Castel S. Angelo* from the *Antichità Romane* or amid the decaying contents of partly excavated tombs as in the view of the *Tomb of L. Arrunzio* (Figure 17). As well as providing a cast, the figures allow the spectator a clear opportunity to visualize themselves in the depicted environment and recognize their own relationship to the vastness of the space.

Piranesi's figures draw us into a narrative that expresses the tension in the contrast defined by Riegl between 'ancient greatness and present degradation'. Their bewilderment and fiery passion amount to a desire and an attempt to repossess the ancient, a commodity that through an act of fantasy, becomes the spectators' own world. The figures Piranesi used throughout his work display a repertoire of movements that could be described using Paul Connerton's analysis of how memory is assimilated in the body as '*incorporating* practice'. Connerton uses this definition to group the 'bodily practices' of signs that are imparted by bodily movements or words spoken. The 'incorporated' actions of Piranesi's cast

Figure 17 G.-B. Piranesi, 'View of the tomb of L. Arrunzio' (detail), *Antichità Romane*, vol. III, plate XXII, 1756. University College London.

of characters essentially stresses desire for mental and physical possession of their ethereal vision through gesture and posture. The posturing of figures with arms outstretched or swaggering with hands on hips and the placing of figures in apparently inaccessible positions suggests human power over monumental structures. This metaphorical form of 'incorporated' bodily practice – received by the eighteenth-century spectator of images as an '*inscribed*' practice – was fundamental in situating the viewer's memories of the city of Rome. To know the city, one must walk it, and climb the monuments. It is this act of incorporation that Goethe described soon after his arrival in Rome:

> We walk diligently here and there, I acquaint myself with the street plans of ancient and modern Rome, view the ruins, the buildings, visit this and that villa, and deal quite unhurriedly with the main objects of interest. I just keep my eyes open, look, and go, and come again, for only *in* Rome can one prepare oneself for Rome.[27]

Likewise, William Beckford in his first few days in Rome spoke of his intention to 'wander soon in the catacombs, which I am half inclined to imagine communicate with the lower world,'[28] – but Beckford's phantasy owes much to his recollection of Piranesi's views of gloomy catacombs, or his views of the *Camere Sepolcrali* where eerie figures loom from dark corners. For Beckford, the act of incorporating the city into his own memory was a reliving of the metaphorical incorporation that he had already experienced in viewing Piranesi's prints. Looking at Piranesi's views, the viewer saw the city *as if* they were themselves already gauging the space of the catacombs, or scaling the monuments. But when they came to do this for themselves in reality, Piranesi's images became part of that reality, which some, like Goethe, felt they had actively to forget, and to unlearn, before they could acquaint themselves with the city. In this sense, incorporating the space became an active dialogue between remembered images and present experience, a dialogue in which elements of one or of the other usually ended up displaced from memory.

Only in comparison with other contemporary engravers of ancient sites does Piranesi's fascination with human energy, expressed through movement appear as a supremely well orchestrated melodrama. *The Tomb of Arrunzio* (Figure 17) is an example of the extreme theatricality Piranesi brings to ruinous structures, turning the space to the status of stage scenery. Curiously Piranesi incorporated the work of another artist along with his own studies of this site in Vol III of the *Antichità Romane*. Engravings originally published in 1727 by Bianchini, illustrate various rooms from the tomb interior. In prints by Girolami Rossi the solid inert figures and the spatial flatness of the compositional structure reveal a difference of intent. Plate XXVI from Bianchini's *Tomb of the Household of Augustus* (Figure 18) depicts gentlemen archaeologists who methodically record, transcribe plans and note inscriptions with orderly presence. If Piranesi's figures are those of acrobats playing at being connoisseurs or vagabonds then Rossi's figures maintain the regimented solidity of wooden puppets untouched by the spirit of the speaking ruins. This approach also has a very different effect on the spectator's sense of space, as the figures do not attempt a physical or spiritual possession of the ancient environment. Rossi's figures do not make aesthetic judgements, nor like Piranesi's imp-like connoisseurs and spirited vagabonds loot the contents of burial chambers. The difference is that Rossi's figures promote an 'inscribed', but not an 'incorporated' memory of the space. Piranesi's inclusion of these plates within his own publication starkly draws attention to the quality of his own figures.

In Piranesi's repeated depictions of the pyramid tomb of Caius Cestius we see a subtle refashioning of his own techniques. This monument had fascinated artists since the sixteenth century, and particularly northern European visitors, as the Protestant Cemetery was sited directly adjacent

Figure 18 Girolami Rossi, after Antonio Buonamici, 'Tomb of the Household of Augustus', published in Francesco Bianchini, *Tombe di Agosto*, 1727, and in *Antichità Romane*, vol. II, plate XXVI. University College, London.

to it, causing travel guides to evoke comparisons between the glorious dead of great nations. Above all the site was described during the eighteenth and nineteenth centuries as picturesque; Eustace comments 'its form, in the whole, is graceful, and its appearance very picturesque . . . it rises in a lonely pomp, and seems to preside of these fields of silence and mortality'.[29] Many travellers familiar with views of Rome attempted to read actual monuments with the same 'syntax and grammar' used for representational images, and often looked for similar viewpoints. Emphasis was put upon viewing monuments from the proper distance, and allowing the monument, as Eustace says of Cestius to form the 'principal feature of the picture'.[30] Hester Lynch Piozzi actually mentions Piranesi's 'admirable' depiction of Cestius in her description of the monument for the traveller, encouraging individual memories to become fused with the shared, collectively available image.[31]

In the view of the Pyramid of Cestius published in *Antichità Romane*, (vol. III pl. xl) two vast facades of the pyramid dominate the approach to the Porta S. Paolo. The image is framed on both sides, on the right by the tower of the city gate and on the left by a building in use as a modern dwelling. The absolute distinction between the stark, terminally unchanging monument and the contemporary degeneration is made evident by the motif of hanging clothes that jut out towards the pyramid from a makeshift balcony, tacked in a temporary fashion on to the side of a building. Unlike the other later views of Cestius' pyramid from the *Vedute di Roma*, the steep facades of the angular structure are also represented as clear of foliage, thus outlining a remade monument cleanly tooled as a symbol of ancient permanence defining for the eighteenth century the laws of Roman architecture as understood by the Renaissance. The four consecutive prints in this bound volume offer aerial views and intersections of the monument that provide technical information concerning the scale, physical structure and position of the interior burial chamber. The inserted texts also include historical and archaeological information, specifically the details of the restoration of the pyramid in 1663 by Pope Alexander VII when a new entrance was cut into the stone. It is exactly this type of information recorded in the pages of the *Antichità Romane* that is repeated in many of the travel guides.

In the two versions of the tomb of Cestius from the *Vedute di Roma, Vedute del Sepolcro di Cajo Cestio* and *Piramide de C. Cestio* (Figure 19) the concern is more with atmospheric effects than didactic explanation.

Figure 19 G.-B. Piranesi, 'The Pyramid of Cestius', from *Vedute di Roma*, c. 1761. University College London.

Fragments of ancient ruins lie embedded in the ground and in both views the monument is curiously lit, light emanating from background, while the front or side facades remain dark and heavily worked by the burin. In the later view of the *Piramide de C. Cestio* published in 1761 with substantial reworking, the ruinous nature of the site is developed to supreme dramatic effect. Piranesi's cast of disreputable male characters attempt to clamber up the monument's facade, over rubble and distorted trees; following their progress, the spectator realizes the size of the monument, and in the figures' relationship to it, their own insignificance to its monumentality. The figures in this composition typify Piranesi's approach, they act as visual tour guides to the eye or *cicerone*, offering up the pyramid as a cultural circus to be explored, consumed and digested, by following their sinuous human forms across the darkened facades. A single figure is silhouetted against a scroll-like inscription and gestures theatrically in the far right of the image, acting as a type of ingression to the composition and thus the site itself. This sense of entry for the eye is reinforced by the figures positioning right up against the picture plane and in the corner of the plate, so that bodily access to the two-dimensional image by the viewer image appears almost conceivable.

Conclusion

The existence of a collective memory held over time is the conceptual basis of all intentional memorial objects. As Riegl showed, this memory held by a transient collective has a tendency to become substituted by the materiality of the monument itself: thus what began as a commemorative monuments turns into a historical object. This is the case with ancient Roman ruins. Piranesi used the transmutability in the meaning of monuments – from memorials for an ancient Roman élite, to monuments of the history of antiquity – to provide powerful images that conveyed a highly effective, dramatically heightened representation of Rome that the eighteenth-century spectator both expected and demanded to see. His focus on the complexities of architectural construction of monuments combined with his abilities as a *vedutista* put greater emphasis on monuments as cultural artefacts, and eloquently helped to restyle the ruins of Rome as monuments to the memory of a great civilization.

By using and presenting monuments as commemorative of the grandeur of history, Piranesi posited 'age value' above 'historical value', without denying the efficacy of the latter. While pictorially asserting the general dramatic view before the particular historic detail, Piranesi stimulated a selective forgetting that helped to increase the accessibility of the visionary landscape of ancient monumental space for a wider European audience. His recognition of decay, but not destruction, as part of the enchantment of monumental ruins, allows an understanding of monuments as pieces of history never forgotten – yet remembered only within a fluid historical framework, to meet specific ends.

The literary sources cited here that both documented and conditioned the expectation and reality of Rome show that many spectators of the city felt disappointment on their ultimate encounter with it. However, an inestimable number of visitors to the city, such as William Beckford, were determined not to relinquish the vision of sublime majesty and grandeur that Piranesi's work evoked, and which justified his position as orator of their memory. This was Piranesi's unique accomplishment, achieved in part by his inventive use of figures within the city constructed on paper. These human figures in the images could act as the *cicerone*, or tour guides for the eye to follow across the page, a metaphorical act of incorporation which spectators assimilated into their own, corporeal, experience of Rome.

Notes

1. Augustus Hare, *Walks in Rome*, London, Strahan, 1871, p. x.
2. S. Freud, *The Interpretation of Dreams*, Harmondsworth, Penguin Books, 1976, p. 282.
3. See S. Rogers, *The Italian Journey of Samuel Rogers*, ed. J.R. Hale, London, Faber & Faber, 1956, p. 94.
4. J.W. von Goethe, *The Italian Journey*, trans. R. Heiter, Princeton, Princeton University Press, 1994, p. 104.
5. See C. Levesque, *Journey through Landscape in Seventeenth- Century Holland, The Haarlem Print Series and Dutch Identity*, University Park Pa., Pennsylvania State University Press, 1994, for a critique of work by Claes; and E. de Bievre 'The Urban Subconscious: The Art of Delft and Leiden', *Art History* 18 (1995), pp. 222–52.
6. P. Connerton, *How Societies Remember*, Cambridge, Cambridge University Press, 1989, pp. 72–3.
7. *The Handbook for Travellers in Central Italy*, London, Murray, 1843, mentions the papal government's own enterprise where 'beautiful engravings from the masters' (p. 252) could be purchased and Mariana

Starke in her *Travels in Europe for the use of travellers on the Continent*, London, John Murray, 1833, list view of Rome available on the Corso where a 'large assortments of prints and coloured drawings are to be found' p. 585.

8. J. Black, *The British Abroad, The Grand Tour in the Eighteenth Century*, Stroud, Sutton Publishing, 1992, pp. 264–5.
9. Text from the *Prima Parte di Architetture e Prospettive* . . . of 1743, quoted in *Giovani Battista Piranesi: Drawings and Etchings at Columbia University*, New York, 1972, p. 117.
10. There is a translation of the *Parere su Achittetura* by M. Nonis and M. Epstein: 'Piranesi's "Thoughts on Architecture"', *Oppositions* 26, (1984), pp. 6–25. For a discussion on the Polemical Texts, see R. Wittkower, 'Piranesi 's "Parere Su Archittetura"', *Journal of the Warburg Institute* II (1938–9), pp. 147–58.
11. Piranesi's work was still being published into the nineteeth century. Following Piranesi's death in 1778 his sons Franceso and Pietro Piranesi republished some of his work and in the late 1790s established a workshop in Paris, reissuing his graphic works in twenty-seven volume editions between 1800 and 1807.
12. Lady Anne Miller, *Letters from Italy describing the Manners, Customs and Antiquities &c of the Country in the Years MDCCLXX and MDCCLXXI*, vol. III, London, Edward and Charles Dilly, 1776, pp. 166–7.
13. The eighteenth- and nineteenth-century audience for Piranesi's work deserves further research and initial enquiries in libraries has revealed the following ownership and the number of works by Piranesi that record their ownership : Thomas Parry (artist and antiquarian 1816–1888) four publications at the Brotherton Library, University of Leeds; George John, Second Earl Spencer (1758–1834) fifteen publications at the John Rylands University Library, University of Manchester (Spencer was travelling on the continent between 1778–80 at which time the volumes may have been purchased); Mr. David Roberts RA (artist, 1796–1864) one publication ; Samuel Angell Esq. (biography unknown) two publications in the Department of Manuscripts and Rare Books, University College London. Certain Oxbridge colleges also ordered the key works by Piranesi soon after publication for their own libraries, All Souls College, Oxford purchased eleven separate publications including the *Vedute di Roma*, *Antichità Romane*, and the *Della Magnifcenza de Architettura de' Romani* in March 1768. Volumes held by the Royal Academy Library show no trace of early ownership and were in the library by 1802.

14. *The Valuable Library of Books in Fonthill Abbey, sold by Auction, 1823*, London, Phillips, 1823, lot 1711.
15. This collection is now held by the Ashmolean Museum, Oxford.
16. Broughton, Rt. Hon Lord [J. C. Hobhouse], *Italy: Remarks Made in Several Visits from the Year 1816–1852*, London, John Murray, 2 vols., 1859, p. 288.
17. *On Antiquities, Arts and Letters in Italy*, London, John Murray, 1835, (first published 1813), p. 123.
18. Rogers, *Italian Journey*, p. 209.
19. J. Farington, *The Diary of Joseph Farington*, eds K. Garlick and A. Macintyre, Vol. II, January 1975 – August 1796, New Haven and London, Yale University Press, 1978, p. 444.
20. J. Forsyth, *On Antiquities, Arts and Letters in Italy*, London, John Murray, 1835, p. 123.
21. Forsyth, *On Antiquities*, p. 139.
22. W. Beckford, *Travel Diaries of William Beckford of Fonthill*, ed. G. Chapman, Cambridge, Constable/Houghton, 2 vols, 1928.
23. W. Hazlitt, 'Notes on a Journey Through France and Italy', in *The Complete Works of William Hazlitt*, ed. P. P. Howe, London, Dent and Sons, 1932, p. 232.
24. A. Riegl, 'The Modern Cult of Monuments: Its Character and Its Origin', trans. K. Forster and D. Ghirardo, *Oppositions* 25 (1982), pp. 21–51.
25. *Prima Parte di Architettura e prospettive . . .*, 1743; quoted in *Giovanni Battista Piranesi: Drawings and Etchings at Columbia University*, New York, 1972, p. 117.
26. Miller, *Letters from Italy*, vol. 3, p. 114.
27. Goethe, *Italian Journey*, p. 107.
28. Beckford, *Travel Diaries*, p. 190.
29. J. C. Eustace and R. Colt, *A Classical Tour through Italy and Sicily*, London, Mawman, 1819, p. 225.
30. Eustace, *Classical Tour*, p. 225.
31. 'Caius Cestius' Sepulchre . . . one of the most perfect remains of antiquity we have here . . . and it is a very beautiful pyramid, a hundred and ten feet high, admirably represented in Piranesi's prints, with an inscription in white marble of which it is composed, imploring the name and office and condition of its wealthy proprietor: C. Cestius, Septem vir epulomum.'

Part III
War Memorials

War memorials – an almost exclusively twentieth-century phenomenon – constitute one of the principal artefact-related memory practices of Western societies. From long before the end of the First World War, their value, their purposes, and their appropriate form, have been matters of exhaustive debate.

The three chapters here are related to these debates, but concentrate on what has hitherto been relatively little discussed, out of a fear that it might overshadow the memory of the dead – that is the purposes that these memorials have served amongst the living in allowing them to forget not just the fallen, but also certain aspects of their own societies.

Michael Rowlands's chapter draws attention to the way in which war memorials fit within anthropological theories of sacrifice, and serve both to allow the living to forget the realities of the deaths, but also to remember the purpose of the sacrifice.

Alex King's discussion of British memorials to the First World War stresses the extent to which these arose out of debates among the survivors as to the appropriate forms of commemoration, and shows how any one choice of a memorial involved the necessary closure of certain memories, even if it allowed the preservation of certain others. This dynamic, he suggests, formed the true subject of the memorials.

Neil Jarman's account of the relative differences between Northern Irish Protestant and Catholic commemoration of the First World War in Northern Ireland makes clear how the same event can be differently appropriated within a single culture. His analysis of banners and murals shows how the strikingly different icons of memory are exploited by each religion, each calculated not merely to remember one particular version of events, but to maintain oblivion of the other.

– 6 –

Remembering to Forget: Sublimation as Sacrifice in War Memorials

Michael Rowlands

The last two decades have witnessed a tremendous growth in both the building of war memorials and in writings about them. The memorial sites of the First World War now receive more visitors than ever before; since 1988 there have been several new competitions for memorials for Holocaust victims and the Vietnam Veterans Memorial on the Washington Mall has become perhaps the most famous and one of the most visited monuments of the late twentieth century. The need to build memorials is also beginning to spread outside the West as can be seen in the monument built to commemorate the war of independence in Zimbabwe and the debate on how to remember the victims of genocide in Cambodia. This, of course, does not inevitably mean a late twentieth-century or late capitalist obsession with mass death, nor that the experience of traumatic violence inevitably becomes a public act of relief from private misery in public bereavement and mourning, but it does suggest that the need to 'find out' what happened, that the process of 'coming to terms' is now and probably always has been more complicated than a passive acceptance that 'they died for a good cause'.

The question I wish to ask is why some monuments 'work' at the personal level of healing and reconciliation whereas others evoke distaste and condemnation. The latter is particularly true of the minimalist architecture of some recent memorials that have aroused considerable controversy. Rachel Whiteread's winning composition (Figure 3) for the new memorial to the Holocaust victims to be built on the site of a medieval Jewish synagogue in Vienna remains, because of local opposition, a design waiting to be unveiled. James Young explains popular resistance to modernist memorials as due to the inadequacy of these sites to gather together personal memories into a collective space.[1] The implication that the visual structure of a monument fails to encourage certain kinds of remembering and forgetting as part of a healing process raises an interesting point that we may better be able to understand how it works negatively, through what people dislike. However it is also true that some memorials are successful not by encouraging remembrance but rather by the demands they make for recognition of what was done, to whom and by whom. The expectation for confessions, expiations and reparations are therefore not too distant from these controversies over the aptness of visual form.

Mourning and Memorials

The art historian Arthur Danto, writing on the Vietnam memorial, distinguished memorials from monuments on the principle that the former are about the healing embrace of remembrance and reconciliation whereas the latter are usually celebratory and triumphalist.[2] The ambiguity of the statement suggests the distinction may not be so simple, since one of the features of nationalist war memorials has been their capacity to turn traumatic individual deaths into acts of national celebration and heroic assertions of collective value. Freud, writing on the death instinct, saw this transition from negativity to positivity as a fundamental feature of mourning (as active practice since death like time for Freud is negativity and could not be part of the unconscious, which only knows repression and forgetting). The death of significant others is experienced as externalized violence and, like rape, as a breach in the unity of identification. Trauma is a demonstration of personal and collective impotence that has to be reconciled through mourning as a process that culminates in the restitution of mastery over one's world. It is then, Freud writes, that the reverse movement, the preservation and continuation of death into life may culminate in the introjection of the absent loved one into the foundation of the ego.

In his essay 'Mourning and Melancholia', Freud[3] describes mourning as an outpouring of grief aimed at keeping the love object alive. Bereavement is a period in which the subject identifies with the absent person, idealizes the person and attempts to become him or her, yet comes to realize the impossibility of this fusion. Mark Cousins described this recently in a discussion of the work of Rachel Whiteread, as a process of being moulded by the absence of the other; an identity which cannot be sustained. Succinctly put – he describes this as:

> In a way the object must die twice, first at the moment of its own death and secondly through the subject's unhitching from its own identification. It is

> only then that the object can pass into history and that the stones can be set – for mourning and memorial are a phase apart.[4]

Memorials become monuments as a result of the successful completion of the mourning process. The dead are dead as an active process of remembering to forget, through the creation of an appropriate memory. Such a successful resolution implies self-sacrifice (the aim of identification in mourning is to become the dead person and make him/her live again and the outcome of reconciliation is the acceptance of its impossibility via the unpicking of this identification through ambivalence, refusal, jokes and so forth). War memorials should ideally allow the fusion of the living with the dead as an act of remembrance whilst eventually providing a way out of melancholia through an act of transcendence. Triumphalism, the reason why most memorials are monuments, achieves this through the assertion of collective omnipotence and by banishing from memory those acts of humiliation when the nation failed to protect its own young. The temporal gap between mourning and memorial is the outcome of a successful closure; a stage reached when a reassertion of mastery makes it possible to remember to forget the pain.

Violent death, however, particularly of the young, may be seen as unnatural and not open to this process of closure through the restitution of omnipotence. A 'bad death' implies injustice and a desire for revenge. The pain of death unresolved and unjustified compromises those selective acts of remembering achieved through the reparation of loved objects. War memorials, in their capacity to represent traumatic deaths as an outcome of self-sacrifice, become objects of contestation. Moreover it is their visual form that generates most disquiet.

What are the cultural resources available at any particular time for experimentation? The role of national hero was a contentious proposition even during the First World War and was only put together in a rather shaky manner in the inter-war years. Dying for a good cause has never been a wholly convincing description and one can only guess at the means by which people individually and personally came to terms with what had happened and recovered, if at all, from their loss. The fact that we have access to the public space rather than personal trauma describes the difficulty of talking about such things; yet recent controversies over sites such as the Vietnam war memorial do not appear to affect the memorial's ability to create a sense of place (which this one clearly does) but refers more to the unease aroused by the capacity of the memorial to recall rather than resolve painful memories. The contrast this makes with the heroic mould of earlier memorials where human sacrifice is justified for the greater good suggests that we have two radically different visual modes of forgetting at work: one that promotes ambivalence and moves people to remember as much as possible of what suffering meant to the victims, and another that effectively transforms suffering into something else – a form of collective validation that transcends personal trauma.

I would argue that a second element, temporality, has to be added to Freud's writing on mourning. The synthesis that opens between mourning and memorial takes place through repetition; the return of experience, grounded in a solid archetypal model, is established by its truth in correspondence with the past. (In *The Logic of Sense*, Deleuze describes this as Platonic repetition.) In the visual imagery of war memorials we experience Platonic repetition as synthesis in architectural form (classical temple style of architecture, white marble, monumentality, the triumphalism of bronze and so forth) but we may be unconsciously disturbed by another, accompanying form of repetition in the frightening anonymity of names inscribed on memorials without origin, dates or personality. Repetition, where the real is saturated with a destructive ideal, implicates the Eros /Thanatos theme which unbinds and returns energy to pure formless time (Deleuze's 'time out of joint' – literally off its hinges/ hors de gonds). And, of course, the memorials that achieve this best are those that appear as models of Platonic repetition that hide the second, more disturbing, Deleuzian form of repetition. Yet ambivalence, disturbance and unease may be experienced visually more directly as, for example, in Rachel Whiteread's still-to-be-unveiled Vienna memorial, about which she has said:

> When I was thinking about the Vienna memorial, I was thinking about having lived in Berlin and the things that most affected me there. There was a rubble mountain over by the Teufelsberg that was made from all the rubble of the bombing of Berlin and it's on the outskirts of the city. People use it, they fly kites on it and paraglide off it. It's just a very strange kind of monument.[5]

Sacrificial Acts

If the visual imagery of war memorials demands remembrance, then how can this encourage 'a living through', as repetition of an emotional experience? Clearly it does not function as a vehicle for dredging emotions to the surface but rather as a means of giving them narrative form. If memorials that simply repeat the visual forms of the past can appear empty and lifeless then counter-memorials appear equally lifeless in their minimalist desire to disturb. Freud's answer would be that the successful visual form is one that liberates an unconscious compulsion to return to the time in which a pathogenic trauma occurred (the psychoanalytic concept of re-enactment contrasted with the 'open endedness of mere succession'). The war memorial as site would therefore encourage individuals as survivors or sharers of collective memory to be led back into the nature of the traumatic situation both to evoke a sense of fear (anxiety usefully encourages future avoidance) and to reassert effective mastery over their environment.

How this might be achieved is best explored through cases where there has been considerable debate over what constitutes an appropriate visual form for a war memorial. The form of a memorial usually mediates between memories of brutal, tragic events involving, in the twentieth century, death on a massive scale with ideals that these were not in vain. The idea that the deaths were not wasted but were constitutive of collective memory is implied by the often strongly egalitarian and democratic ideologies presented in the material form of the memorial. The names of the dead are inscribed often without reference to rank or class. The emphasis is either on their collective heroic (masculine) contribution signified in various signs of death and military honour or the figure of the nation saved, usually in female form, dressed in classical garb.

Bruce Kapferer's analysis of Australian war memorials that commemorate the dead of Anzac day share both these features.[6] No town in Australia is without a memorial to the Anzacs. The Sydney war memorial has more visitors annually than Ayers Rock, that other great symbol of Australianness. The Australian war memorial in Canberra is set opposite the Parliament building, which it physically dominated until 1978 when a new and much larger state building was erected. The memorial is built as a tomb to the sacrificed dead of the Australian nation. The names of the dead are inscribed on marble slabs around the pool of reflection, arranged alphabetically without reference to rank or seniority. The symbolism of the death and suffering of the Anzac troops in Europe evokes egalitarian ideals of 'the digger', of Australian mateship.[7] Moreover it resolves what Kapferer has termed the 'dilemma of the cultural cringe', a form of Australian self-presentation that fears devaluation and aggressively asserts a range of ideas and practices identified as a uniquely home-grown national identity. The celebration of the Anzacs reverses the ignominious creation of Australian identity in colonial serfdom as a penal colony. Instead, to be Australian acquires an historically forged identity that has saved the 'other', and in particular saved the 'cradle of Western civilisation' through the blood and sacrifice of Australian egalitarian ideals. The 'Old World' was both saved and repossessed by the shedding of Australian blood and the burial of Australian dead in its earth.[8] These ideals are objectified in the monumental form of the Canberra memorial that combines elements of a Middle Eastern mosque such as a dome and twin towers with gothic features such as stained glass windows. As Kapferer notes, the 'cultural cringe' still functions to validate and naturalize these signs of dependency that constitute the audience as a moral community through a shared sense of shame.

Representing these ideals requires their temporal synthesis in the form of a memorial. In the case of the Sydney war memorial to the Anzacs, there was fierce controversy over how this could be achieved. The design was open to public competition and a jury was established to make an award. The original design that was at first selected and subsequently rejected after much controversy was of a single naked, female figure with the jumbled figures of the slain, clothed, male soldiers at her feet (Figure 20). Objections were made against the naked female form and the ugliness of the broken bodies of the dead soldiers.[9] The birth of the nation as a literal description of male death was incompatible with its idealization in martyrdom and the regenerative aspects of sacrifice. The ideal of Australian sacrifice was captured in the successful design by a figure of a naked male lying on a shield and a naked sword in a semi-crucified pose, supported by a column of three clothed female forms, representing the living sacrifice of those who mourn; the mother, the sister and the wife. Sacrifice of the nation embodies a classical theme of the warrior as a heroic, young and sexually potent male whose death is justified by the preservation of the regenerative powers of women.

There is a tradition of anthropological writing on sacrifice stemming from Robertson Smith and Durkheim and found particularly in the classic work of Hubert and Mauss,[10] which sees the core of the rite as a gift of a human life or a substitute (animal sacrifice) by humans to gods. The bearer of the gift (sacrifator) embodies pollution, sin or guilt and the act provides the means by which the social body is cleansed of these moral stains. Society, by surrendering its most valued quality, expiates its sin and cleanses itself as an act of renewal. It has rightly been said by some that this is merely characteristic of a particular Christian vengeful notion of the relation of community to its god, whereas others have said that it has a more universal significance. Moreover, like trance and spirit possession, sacrifice is a ritual form that, as Bloch and others have argued, overlaps in form and content with initiation, funerary rites and spirit mediumship.[11] This has led to what has been termed a 'family resemblance' approach to the study of sacrifice in which no clear boundaries can be established between these different ritual forms.[12] This is undoubtedly true as long as

Figure 20 Rejected design for war memorial, Sydney.

it is the act of giving or surrendering that is used to establish formal similarities in different ritual forms. However the point stressed by others as distinctive of sacrifice is that it requires the act of ritual killing and that this should ideally be a human life.[13] This quite correctly emphasizes that it is the violence of killing that is central to sacrifice and not giving per se. Sacrifice justifies the taking of significant forms of life for an ulterior symbolic purpose. Yet the sacrificed life as retribution, compensation or expiation shares in common with the sacrifice as gift the idea that something of the highest value has been surrendered or destroyed in order that something may be given in return.

This allows us to give a rather different slant to the understanding of war memorials as sites of sacrifice. What is claimed by the nation in the act of remembrance is that it has sacrificed its youth for its own cause and the enemy who actually killed their young was merely its instrument. In the Freudian sense of 'fort/da', the crime committed by enemies as an act of humiliating violence to the nation is symbolically inverted and claimed to be instead an expiatory sacrifice made on behalf of the nation for its own survival and renewal. The living bodies of the young are represented as impure and morally stained, carrying with them all the undesirable features of the lived tradition. They are prepared for sacrifice through invocation and dedication to the spirit of the nation and by inculcating their willingness to die for it. Those who have died appear to have made the sacrifice, but it is in fact the nation that has sacrificed them and it is the body of the nation that has been regenerated and is now capable of cleansing the social body of injustices, crimes and humiliations. The dead as the sacrificed play their role not as physical bodies that are left behind in a 'foreign field' but as an idealized icon, cleansed of transitory weaknesses and moral stains. The inevitable but painful act of mass death is internalized as a justifiable act of ritual killing carried out by the high priests or priestesses as a dedication to the nation.

The rite of national sacrifice differs from archaic forms of sacrifice in the lack of emphasis on 'giving' to a god. The idea of the nation attempts to subsume the religious into its own purpose and make itself the focus of popular devotion. Hence the furore over the inappropriate form of the failed Sydney memorial was due to its non-adherence to the scheme of sacrifice outlined above. The figure of the sacrificed female indicates that it is the nation that has been sacrificed rather than male youth for the nation. The jumbled realistic figures of the dead soldiers denies the expiatory role of sacrifice to reclaim the dead as purified and cleansed. Overall the failed design signified disaster and destruction whereas the one eventually built expressed both anxiety over irretrievable loss and a restoration of mastery by the nation.

However the question remains why should the objectification of sacrifice take the form of war memorials and in particular why has this become an essential feature of modernity and become part of a more global response to twentieth-century events? The relation between memory and sacrifice emphasizes that intertwining two modes of forgetting is a key aspect of a symbolism that simultaneously provokes and soothes anxiety. Perhaps this is why a suitable period of time has to take place between the brutal realities of the event and the public act of re-collection. Moreover the public internalization of memory is emphasized by opening a public subscription and choosing the memorial by open competition. This emphasizes that the sacrifice was made by 'the people' for the nation and that the state, in the role as sacrificer, should be excluded from the shaping of memory through the building of monuments to the dead. Consciousness towards forgetting reshapes experience, which is at the same time 'in the world' and embodied.

Memory and sacrifice

A successful design for a certain kind of war memorial has to achieve resolution of mourning, loss and grief through the overcoming of negativity. A wasted, destroyed life that has proved to be of no importance is humiliating to the living. In Castoriadis's sense of society as the imaginary, this cannot be allowed; people have to be given the means to reassert their mastery and to reconcile the trauma through the assertion of higher, positive ideals. An active process of forgetting (the realities of actual deaths) in order to remember (the purpose of the sacrifice) creates a realm of ideas and associations that may attach themselves to any object. What puts this reconciliation beyond doubt is the fixing of these ideals in the enduring form of a memorial and the social context in which this is done. It is this metamorphosis that harnesses intensities and ideas to a process of individuation and explication; providing narrative form to the relationship between repetition, temporal synthesis and ideas. But what form successfully manages to convey this closure?

Built by the veterans of the Vietnam War and paid for out of the veterans memorial fund, the Vietnam Veterans Memorial was inaugurated on Veterans Day 1982. The final design for the memorial was the result of a competition open to any American citizen over eighteen years of age. Over 1,400 entries were judged anonymously and the winner, Maya Lin, was a Chinese–American, a senior at Yale studying architecture. The criteria on which the competition was judged claimed that the winning design should be:

1. Reflexive and contemplative in character.
2. Harmonious with its site and surroundings.
3. Provide for the inscription of 58,132 names.
4. Make no political statement about the war.
5. Occupy up to 2 acres of land.

The winning design in the form of an extended V made of two walls of black granite set in the earth at an angle of 125 degrees extends over 500 ft with the angle of the vertices pointing towards the Washington Monument and the Lincoln Memorial. Each arm tapers from a central hinge ten feet in height. The names of the dead are inscribed chronologically, listed according to their 'casualty day', beginning and ending with the dates 1959 and 1975 at the memorial's vertex. From the announcement of the winning design, the Vietnam Memorial has been controversial for its seemingly minimalist, unheroic design. At the inauguration of the memorial in 1982, Tom Wolfe called it 'a piece of Modernist orthodoxy that was a tribute to Jane Fonda' associating the alienation of modern architecture with a sense of betrayal.

Several commentators have noticed that the Vietnam memorial is in many ways an inversion of other monuments on the Washington Mall. For example, in contrast to the Lincoln and the Jefferson Memorials, the Vietnam memorial is sunk in the earth and you step down into it. The black granite of the memorial violates the heroic monumentality of the white marble of all the other monuments on the Mall. The names of the dead are inscribed starting from the west to east on each of the arms and the monument faces south. The memorial is literally read from darkness to light and symbolically from death to regeneration of life. The vertex of the monument points towards the Lincoln memorial where the seated figure of Lincoln inside faces east, like Zeus in his temple on Mount Olympus, and he looks out to the monument of Grant, the Civil War general, seated on a horse and facing west. Lincoln who was assassinated and died for the sake of the nation, had a memorial built to him in 1922 more than sixty years after the events that are commemorated. The memorial, built to copy an ancient Greek temple, embodies repetition in a Platonic essentialist form that identifies a modern hero with an original ideal. Lincoln is identified with the classical pattern of the Greek hero whose deeds have won him immortality combined with a Christian ethos of dying to cleanse the sins of others. Excerpts from the Gettysberg address and his second inaugural speech are carved on the wall behind his figure. Beneath these is the inscription 'In this temple as in the heart of the people for whom he saved the Union, the memory of Abraham Lincoln is enshrined forever'. No mention is made of slavery, the cause of national division, and the Civil War. Erected so long after the event, the scars of conflict forgotten, the memorial perhaps no longer has the function of healing but emphasizes rather the duty to remember (selectively) the origins of the nation.

By contrast, the Vietnam memorial built only eight years after the end of the war, by and for the veterans without national support sought or offered, has produced a considerable academic discourse about the healing qualities of ambivalence. Maya Lin claimed the aim of her design was 'to bring out in the American people the realization of loss and a cathartic healing process'. The listing of the names emphasizing the reality and individuality of each of the deaths contrasts with the harmonious repetition of the classical Greek temple form of the Lincoln Memorial. Lin characterized her design as 'a rift in the earth bringing the Vietnam memorial into historical context'. A number of commentators have seen it physically as a gash in the earth, a scar only partially healed by the growth of trees and grass over the mound in which the marble slabs are set. Clearly this was intended by Maya Lin who explained her feelings about the design:

> I thought about what death is, what loss is . . . a sharp pain that lessens with time but can never quite heal over. A scar. The idea occurred to me there on that site. Take a knife and cut open the earth and with time the grass would heal it.

There are many indications that the Vietnam memorial is an extremely successful site for the expression of grief. People go there to remember and feel too much. They touch and caress the names carved on the wall (Figure 21). They trace the names on to pieces of paper to take away. These are more than souvenirs or mementoes as expressions of having been there. They are perhaps less than trophies, although a certain triumphalism of repossession of lost ones is undoubtedly part of these acts. In Rosalind Krauss's sense we are presented with a site that speaks with a symbolical tongue about the meaning or use of that place.[14] Thousands of things have been left at the memorial – photographs, letters, identity bracelets, teddy bears, clothes and medals of honour. They are regularly collected up by the national park service and stored in the Museum and Archaeological Regional Storage Facility (MARS for short!). Thousands of daily acts of personal appropriation of the monument by

Figure 21 Vietnam Memorial, Washington. (Photo: M. Rowlands)

the victims kin and others, encouraged by the original design, are countered by attempts to domesticate the monument for the nation. The sequence of names of the dead inscribed on the granite slabs of the memorial lack the singularity appropriate to the extinction of lives as specific events. These deaths are not recorded as made in a glorious cause. As one commentator said at the time 'they (the names) might as well have been traffic accidents'. Moreover, the inscriptions deny the passive gaze of the viewer as curious spectator. The black granite on which the names are inscribed acts as a polished mirror, so that you see your reflection reading the names. An anti-monumental, individualizing motive is suggested that denies the inscriptions an existence as a timeless, numinous image of the nation to which the viewers might submit themselves.

Decontextualizing the dead from glorious causes also accuses the nation of unwillingness to claim the dead as sacrificial victims. It is part of the ambivalence felt about the monument that an emotional closure around possession of the dead by the nation has not taken place. The construction of the monument emphasized the debt by the nation to the Vietnam soldiers and veterans. It is the nation (not the state) that has refused to honour the sacrificial debt by not adopting the role of sacrificer. The inscription on the memorial is to the Vietnam veterans (living and dead) and not to the sacrifice made by them to the nation:

> Our nation honours the courage, sacrifice and devotion to duty and country of the Vietnam veterans. This memorial was built with private contributions from the American people, November 11, 1982.

As Griswold has argued, the Vietnam memorial is essentially interrogative whilst the Lincoln memorial is an act of closure around the figure of the nation.[15] The Vietnam memorial implies terrible questions about futility, dying in vain, and about when and for what Americans should die in war? The structural inversions of black versus white marble, the gash in the earth versus the temple on a mound, abstraction versus figurative realism articulate this questioning and a repudiation of a desire to forget the past. The fact that the memorial has not been desecrated suggests that a therapeutic solution has been sought and found to these questions in the memorial. Tom Wolfe's objections to the abstract modernism of the memorial was widely shared at the time and people complained that it denied a triumphal celebration of the heroism of those who died. Soon after the original inauguration, triumphalism was allowed back in the form of a realistic figure of three soldiers in warlike pose (two white and one black), cast in bronze and set about fifty yards back from the memorial (Figure 22). Soon after a flagpole was erected and a figure of a group of nurses was added to the complex. The inscription reads 'this flag represents the service rendered to our country by the veterans of the Vietnam War. The flag affirms the principle of freedom for which they fought and their pride in having served under difficult circumstances'.

The certitude of the Lincoln memorial has still not been achieved in the Vietnam memorial complex. The form of the latter is a memorial made by and erected for the sacrifices at a time when the nation, as defined by

Figure 22 Vietnam Veterans' Memorial, Washington. (Photo: M. Rowlands)

the power holders, wished for a long period of forgetting. Physically encompassed by these additional elements in a more heroic mould, classical repetition in form allows the closure of sacrifice not allowed by the formalism of the original Maya Lin design.

Conclusion

It is the essential justification of war memorials that they should allow the resolution of suffering yet it is by no means obvious how they do this. For the sense of personal sacrifice to be validated, war memorials have to be to some extent a special category where resolution is achieved by the extent to which visual forms unproblematically affirm 'that they did not die in vain'. Such cannot be said of Holocaust memorials, for example, where nobody can claim that the deaths served any purpose whatsoever.

What all memorials share is the drive to resolve the conditions of negativity and impotence. The apparent unsatisfactoriness of modernist memorials only seems evident when contrasted with heroic, triumphalist forms. Maya Lin went on to several other commissions that have been no less popular than the Vietnam memorial. In part this may be because her work is not really modernist at all, a point made recently in an interesting article by Daniel Abramson.[16] In the statement accompanying her competition entry, she wrote

> the descent to the origin is slow, but it is at the origin that the meaning of this memorial is fully understood. At the intersection of these walls, on the right side, at this wall's top is carved the date of the first death. It is followed by the names of those who have died in the war, in chronological order. These names continue on this wall, appearing to recede into the earth at the wall's end. The names resume on the left wall, as the wall emerges from the earth continuing back to the origin, where the date of the last death is carved, at the bottom of this wall. Thus the war's beginning and end meet; the war is 'complete', coming full circle.[17]

I started by making a link between Freud's discussion of the resolution of mourning as the moment when non-consent is filled in, when the victims of bereavement implicate themselves retrospectively and thus reassert their omnipotence, with anthropological ideas on sacrifice as exchange. Who is giving, what are they giving up and to whom, what is the nature of the internal economy of sacrifice, the need for the gift to be destroyed for it to mark as a sacrifice, and the extent to which this allows a certain resolution of suffering? These are all questions that underlie our fascination with memorials. I began with a simple idea that this fusion of mourning and of sacrifice is experienced visually. This may be either through the harmony of repetitious form, the denial of negativity in the reproduction of enduring image of sacrifice, as in the Anzacs memorials or the Lincoln memorial, or interrogatively by statements about the reality of the deaths, and the pain and suffering caused made explicit in the modernist memorials (and here I would include some of the Holocaust memorials). Working through the subject again, I find myself focusing on the manner in which memorials differ in their moralistic concerns with narrativity and in the desire to rid themselves of moral burdens in order to tell it as it really was. The Vietnam memorial is, as Abramson argues, history without narrativity and moralizing. It lists an open-ended chronological sequence that finally circles around to an arbitrary closure. The deceit the author wishes to avoid is the use of chronicle-like narrativity to claim a morality of what really happened, to make it appear orderly, causal and objective. The minimalism is in the raw, bureaucratic information given, listing names as 'one thing after another' in seeming objectivity and neutrality rather than in the material form of the monument.[18] Yet a memorial where Deleuzian repetition runs wild may be no more objective than a Lincoln memorial in the sense that there is no mention of the thousands of

Vietnamese who died or the social inequalities hidden in the representation of the American dead.

Our comparison suggests that monuments become memorials when they satisfy three functions for the living. First they should acknowledge the importance of the death and destruction that constituted the sacrificial act. Acknowledgement in detail of the loss incurred by relatives, communities and nations is also an acceptance that the violence and the suffering took place and a sacrifice will not be forgotten. Secondly, this acceptance of violence takes place in a context where it is claimed that something has been gained instead, which is effectively the transformation of a sense of collective loss into an object of devotion and passion. Thirdly, the dead are deified as part of that devotional logic in the sense that they become embodied in the idea of the collective. It is the role of the living to recognize the debt and express a willingness to reciprocate.

What is it that the living give to the dead? In a sense it is the remembering of names and actions as real events that constitutes the sacrificial act by compressing both past and future in the present. For victims and relatives it is the fear that the past no longer constitutes 'facts and events' in the present, that an absolute forgetting has taken place, voiding the sacrifice that energizes the debt. Visually empty repetition of the same image or the rupturing of identity through modernist imagery signifies an absence of debt by the living to the dead. 'Feeding the dead' is a matter of providing sustenance for memory, achieving significance for past sacrifice in order that future devotion will require further commitment to confirming the social order and establishing the key social relationships that make life worth having or at least worth bearing. The relief from trauma lies in the detail. Recognizing the nature of sacrifice as an act of surrendering the self is in this sense part of a wider understanding of what constitutes humanity, which is the ideal object of devotion imaged in the war memorial.

Notes

1. J. Young, *The Texture of Memory*, New Haven, Yale University Press, 1993.
2. A. Danto, 'The Vietnam Veterans Memorial', *The Nation*, 31 Aug. 1986, p. 152.

3. S. Freud, 'Mourning and Melancholia', *Standard Edition*, vol. 14, London, Hogarth Press, 1957.
4. M. Cousins, 'Inside, Outside', *Tate Magazine*, Winter 1996, p. 6.
5. Cousins 'Inside, Outside', p. 6.
6. B. Kapferer, *Legends of People, Myths of State*, Washington D.C., Smithsonian Institution Press, 1988.
7. Kapferer, *Legends of People*, p. 124.
8. Kapferer, *Legends of People*, p. 125.
9. Kapferer, *Legends of People*, p. 182.
10. H. Hubert and M. Mauss, *Sacrifice: Its Nature and Function*, London, Cohen & West, 1964.
11. M. Bloch, *Prey into Hunter: the Politics of Religious Experience.* Cambridge, Cambridge University Press, 1992, p. 25.
12. L. de Heusch, *Sacrifice in Africa*, Cambridge, Cambridge University Press, 1986.
13. R. Girard, *Violence and the Sacred,* Baltimore, Johns Hopkins, 1977; W. Burkert, *Homo Necans: the Anthropology of Ancient Greek Sacrificial Ritual and Myth*, Berkeley, University of California Press, 1983.
14. R. Krauss, *The Originality of the Avant Garde*, Cambridge MA, MIT Press, 1986, p. 279.
15. C. L. Griswold, 1986 'The Vietnam Veterans Memorial and the Washington Mall: Political Thoughts on Political Iconongraphy', *Critical Inquiry*, 12 (1986), p. 713.
16. D. Abramson, 1996 'Maya Lin and the 1960s: Monuments, Time Lines, and Minimalism', *Critical Inquiry* 22 (1996), p. 688.
17. Quoted in Abramson, 'Maya Lin and the 1960s'.
18. Abramson, 'Maya Lin and the 1960s', p. 705.

–7–

Remembering and Forgetting in the Public Memorials of the Great War

Alex King

The commemoration of the dead of the First World War was probably the largest and most popular movement for the erection of public monuments ever known in Western society. As the culmination of the 'statuomanie' of the nineteenth century described by Agulhon,[1] it had precedents in earlier civic art, but it was on a far greater scale. Patterns of commemoration, and the resulting memorials, differed from country to country according to the character of the official and voluntary institutions that promoted them. Britain, discussed here, was not representative of commemoration in all the belligerent nations, either in its range of memorial types, nor in the interpretations given to them.[2]

Expressions of public mourning were not new in the practice of monument building, but the commemoration of the war dead with its purely private recollections by millions of individuals was altogether different from the official mourning of even the most popular public figures. War memorials had to allow those who had lived through the war to mark their lives and the places in which they lived with symbols expressing the degree of importance they attached to their experience, and to share this sense of importance with others.[3] At the same time, erecting memorials was a public, collective process, conducted through institutions. No matter how personal the motives of participants may have been, they had to be realized through the procedures that civic monument building offered, if the result was to be an acceptable public memorial.[4]

A number of writers have seen modern public commemorations as a socially integrating process that obtains assent to a particular code of values or view of society, and thereby prompts people to orientate their everyday actions towards the more harmonious pursuit of common goals. The work of Clifford Geertz is often cited as the model for this approach. I argue that this view is neither convincing in principle, nor does it fit the evidence of war commemoration. On the contrary, commemoration of the Great

War accommodated differences of outlook, often fundamentally irreconcilable, within a framework of common action that avoided attachment to a specific code of values, and permitted participants to express their divergent beliefs. To act together did not presume a common interpretation of this action.

In the late nineteenth and early twentieth century, the social function of civic commemoration was, in general, to allow participating groups to form working relationships with each other in pursuit of mainly local, civic political goals.[5] In this respect it was the extension and culmination of much charitable and voluntary activity. War commemoration, in its turn, undoubtedly served civic political purposes, which influenced the form it took. However, many participated for the more personal purpose of making sense of the impact of war on themselves, in which they appealed to a wide variety of often conflicting values. The result, I shall argue, was that no common basis for giving meaning was found in remembrance of the dead. Lack of agreement, nonetheless, allowed participants to continue to conduct their search for meaning, and to resist the unspeakable prospect that the pain and loss of war might ultimately have been worthless. The work of setting up suitable physical memorials contributed to the cohesion of remembrance of the dead, as a social and symbolic activity, in the absence of a general scheme of values to which all involved could subscribe. Memorials were symbolic objects that transcended differences amongst participants through the practical activities, not the abstract ideas that were associated with them.

Public Commemoration

As a means of representing the dead, public commemoration was confined to no particular material or genre.[6] It included sculpture, architecture, ceremonies and other forms of performance, and the written or spoken word. Although we are used to treating these as separate media of expression, there is a good reason for seeing public commemoration as a medium in its own right, which exploited a variety of means of representation. As with any other medium, particular techniques and capabilities were required to manage it – principally those of local politics, and the negotiation of relationships between groups within town and village communities. In the erection of permanent monuments, the skills of creative professions such as architects and sculptors were also required, but these were secondary to the formation of a consensus amongst participating groups about the nature of the memorial project, and the raising of resources for it. It is in these administrative and political tasks that we should see the primary medium of commemoration.

John Bodnar has attempted a systematic account of the process of 'public memory', drawing on the examples of state and national commemorative occasions in the United States.[7] In his American cases, Bodnar finds a dichotomy of intentions and interests between the official groups who institute commemorations and the various public groups who make up the mass of participants and audience. While the former interpret the acts of commemoration that they initiate as expressing abstract ideals to which they believe the whole of society should aspire, the latter interpret them in terms of their divergent concrete experiences and achievements within that society. Between one group and another, the same commemorative act may be seen as signifying quite different things, even though a common historical focus, such as the admission of a state to the Union, will be acknowledged by all as something they value.

As Bodnar puts it, 'the major focus' of commemoration 'is not the past . . . but serious matters in the present'. Through it 'various parts of the social structure exchange views' about questions of importance to them. In the events Bodnar surveys, these questions principally concern the relationship between the individual (often as part of a specific interest group) and the state. The function of commemoration, he maintains, is to give authority to one interpretation of social reality against competitors. This is achieved by encouraging holders of competing views to participate in commemoration, and then negotiating a form of commemorative event that all parties see as compatible with their interests. Officials, as holders of municipal or state power, remain the dominant power in the negotiations. Since they dominate the organization of the proceedings, they have the dominant share in determining the form of commemorative expression and the matter expressed. Bodnar argues, following Geertz, that their interpretation of what they are doing thus becomes the predominant interpretation of the celebrations amongst the population at large, and imposes a general framework of understanding within which people locate their own particular viewpoints.[8]

The extent to which a common framework of understanding actually exists in American commemorations has changed over the course of time. The difference between official and vernacular interpretations of commemorative events was at its greatest in the periods of frontier expansion and massive European immigration in the nineteenth century, but has gradually diminished. The public understanding of the past, as it is represented in commemorations, has become more homogeneous. To explain this, Bodnar suggests that it is the result of increasing penetration by the socially homogenizing power of official administration and policing into American society as a whole.[9]

However, this explanation presents a problem in understanding the social role of commemoration. Such a comprehensive extension of official power will affect not only the organization of commemorative events, and the image of society they present, but also the order of society as a whole. It will, therefore, alter the very nature of the everyday experience on which participants' interpretations of commemorative symbols are based. There is no reason to see an increasingly homogeneous social understanding as being particularly the result of the public memory fostered in relatively infrequent acts of commemoration. A more plausible source would be the institutions through which state power, or that other great homogenizer, the market, affect the lives of individuals through constant exposure to them, such as schools, national political parties and legislative programmes, or the press. Susan G. Davis,[10] writing about civic parades in Philadelphia, alludes to the importance of increasingly efficient police services in shaping public behaviour, and consequently influencing the conduct of and response to parades.[11] She also points out the weakness of parades in temperance recruitment drives, suggesting that, where their effectiveness in influencing people can be assessed, it may not be very great.[12]

There must, therefore, be considerable doubt about the power of commemoration to achieve, through representation, a degree of unanimity amongst members of the public beyond that which already exists or is imposed as part of the conduct of everyday affairs. Here, I want to explore the question of the creation of unanimity, and the social purpose of commemoration, from a different point of view. I shall concentrate on the actions and organizations involved, rather than the ideas – the cognitive schema relating to the understanding of society – which might or might not be communicated through it.

Remembrance ceremonies and physical memorials may appear to be quite different kinds of things. Ceremonies are composed of occasional human actions with a special place in the social calendar; memorials of static, permanent material, always present. In two important respects, however, memorials, no matter how solid, are no less part of a pattern of human action than ceremonies. In the first place, they require constant attention to ensure their permanence. Physically, they are sustained by organizations dedicated to maintaining them, such as local authority works departments. It is organizations of this sort that give memorials their permanence, maintaining their integrity and sanctity, protecting them from desecration and enabling them to defy the attrition of time.[13] An outstanding example is the Commonwealth (originally Imperial) War Graves Commission, which maintains the memorials and cemeteries of the British Empire forces of both world wars throughout the world. In the Commission's care there are also a number of memorials erected on the battlefields of the Great War by military units; lacking originally any arrangements for maintenance, their decay would have caused them to be lost within a few years of the War had they not eventually been entrusted to the Commission.[14]

No monument can resist the effects of time and nature, and the effectiveness of a memorial demands not only investment in its structure, but also a commitment to its upkeep. In Suzanne Küchler's and Nicholas Argenti's contributions to this volume, they describe cultures in which what might be called the institutional structure around monumental objects works to the opposite end, towards rendering the objects ephemeral: their fate, and their relation to memory, is equally determined by the way in which the connection of human beings with them is deliberately organized. No less than the memorials of the Great War, they acquire and retain their significance through the organization of human actions.

It was not only the survival of the physical structure of a memorial that depended on human attention directed towards it through institutions. Its continued place in the social and ideological life of a community also depended on organized action which took the memorial as its focal point. This started with the erection of the memorial, which was seen by contemporaries as a symbolic act in its own right. It was performed according to a familiar etiquette of voluntary subscription and publicly accountable decision-making, intended to represent communal unity, generosity, appreciation of the self-sacrifice of the dead, an acknowledgement of obligation to them, and a claim also that the community respected and, in its lesser way, shared their moral vision and qualities.[15] Equally, once the memorial was complete, it was the organization of public action around it that ensured it remained both respected and meaningful. If we look at the ways people in the 1920s and 1930s portrayed the war dead in memorials and ceremonies, we shall see that the images of them propagated by commemoration were far from secure, and that attempts to attach specific moral and political values to commemoration was a source of conflict rather than unity. That commemoration was a widely respected public observance was more a result of the influence of institutions over it than of the spontaneous welding together of individual sentiments or the expression of shared ideas.

Symbolism

Through its combination of monuments, ceremonies and words, commemoration attributed to the dead a variety of qualities: self-sacrifice, personal excellence – especially moral excellence – comradeship, devotion to the good of others, anti-militarism, emotional buoyancy in adversity. One other important aspect of their character was given by omission rather than assertion, and this was avoidance, as far as possible, of any suggestion that the dead had, in life, been violent or aggressive. Where soldiers were directly represented in memorials, denial of violence and aggression was frequently a consideration in the design of the image. It was fairly easily accomplished through posture and gesture. The figures on the London memorial at Mansion House (Figure 23) are typical in their attitudes. The tableau on Port Sunlight memorial (Figure 24) is nearer to a combat scene, but still, the figures are waiting and watching. The standing figure has his weight on the back foot to resist an impact, rather than to attack.

The commemorative characterization of the dead, therefore, suppressed both the violence of war and such profane compensations of war service as sex and drink. It promoted a peculiarly 'good' (in moral terms) memory of the dead. This good memory was not secure, however. At various junctures a 'bad' memory – an unidealized memory – could return. The 'bad' memory became especially prominent in the years after 1929, when a number of books appeared representing soldiers in the Great War as commonly human, fearful, undisciplined, and far from morally excellent. The most famous of these was Erich Maria Remarque's *All Quiet on the Western Front*. There was considerable controversy about these books at this time, but in fact the image of the dead that they provided had been available ever since the war in various forms, especially in the writings of the journalist Philip Gibbs, where it was mixed awkwardly with Gibbs's own idiosyncratic idealization of the common soldier.[16]

Memorials in particular might be criticized if they appeared in some way to convey an image of the dead as people who approved of violence. Bradford war memorial, unveiled in 1921, was bitterly criticized by some for containing figures whom they thought (perhaps mistakenly)[17] were engaged in close combat with bayonets (Figure 25; the bayonet blades are now missing, but their handles can still be seen). A number of influential people took exception to these figures, seeing in them the implication that the dead had themselves been aggressive killers. A Baptist minister who was one of the main complainants said: 'the idea of the fixed bayonet was not the motive which led some of our best to lay down their lives' and he wished the city 'had handed down to posterity not an

Figure 23 Sir Aston Webb and Alfred Drury, Memorial to London Troops (detail), Mansion House, London, 1920. (Photo: A. King)

Figure 24 Sir William Goscombe John, Lever Brothers' War Memorial (detail), Port Sunlight, Cheshire, 1921. (Photo: A. King)

affirmation of might but of ideals, not of physical but spiritual power'.[18] New books, pictures, films and plays about the war were tested against the moral idealization represented in commemoration, rather than against aesthetic or documentary criteria, lest they should introduce doubts about the virtues of the dead. Even R. C. Sherriff's enormously successful play, *Journey's End*, was initially criticized for representing the dead as morally flawed.[19]

Of course, the things that ought not to be said about the dead did not thereby become unavailable to individual recollection. There was, in fact, a lively sense of threat from them. The bad, worrying, memory had constantly to be fought off by reiterating the idealization, and this is one reason why, for twenty years after the Armistice, speakers and writers annually repeated the same platitudes. The characterization of the dead given in commemoration as morally excellent was far from secure in the

Figure 25 Walter Williamson and H. S. Wright, Bradford City War Memorial (detail), Bradford, Yorkshire, 1922. (Photo: A. King)

public recollection of them, and had to be reasserted constantly, in the most explicit terms, against the discord of other representations.

Exhortations to moral virtue were a constant accompaniment to the commemoration of the dead. They were presented in sermons, unveiling speeches, and newspaper editorials on Armistice Day and other anniversaries. They concerned not only the moral character of the dead, but the behaviour expected of the living if they were to remember and honour the dead in a fitting way. To judge from what was said in the talk and writing that surrounded any commemorative act, consolation for loss, and a sense that the enormous number of deaths could be given some meaning, depended on the survivors continuing the tasks in which the dead had been engaged while alive, and preserving the ideas that had actuated them. In this way the hopes and achievements of the dead might be preserved through the actions of the living.

The Christian hope of resurrection, to which most public speakers and writers were at least nominally committed, seems to have been ineffective in providing consolation and a source of meaning. Clergymen, as much as anyone else, insisted that the living must impose meaning on their bereavement by the moral rectitude of their subsequent actions. Those who were not themselves bereaved were equally required to participate in this process, partly out of respect for the sufferings of the bereaved, but also in order to repay the debt they owed to those who had defended them in war and had made the supreme sacrifice in doing so. A typical example was given by the Bishop of London when he dedicated the parish war memorial at Stoke Newington in 1920. He quoted a letter from an officer's widow who had written: 'I would not mind if I saw a better world, but I feel that my husband died in vain. That is the cause of my bitterness.' The Bishop's answer to this complaint was that whether or not the sacrifice of life had been in vain would 'largely depend on what the people in that church did to make the sacrifice worth while'.[20]

Although hardly consistent with the traditional Christian conception of resurrection, there was a widespread sense that the dead were still in some way present. A number of contemporary accounts, not only by spiritualists, refer to a sense of their presence at ceremonies or near memorials, but frequently as judges, issuing warnings and requirements, rather than as souls at peace. This was a common feature of newspaper rhetoric. The dead could only be at peace, and the living at peace with their losses, if the living dedicated themselves to continuing in some way the struggles the dead had been engaged in. They were expected either to continue the tasks the dead had started, or to preserve what they had achieved. This meant that the living must emulate the dead and act as they would have done. The sense of loss was not allowed to pass into the past. The mere memory of the dead as good and courageous was not sufficient to give meaning to their absence.

This feeling was, to a considerable extent, the result of the over-developed sense of moral purpose expressed in much wartime propaganda, which had asserted that the war was not just about winning battles and preserving national security, but about the elimination of a satanic force, the cleansing of the world. At the same time, the fact that the dead men were largely young, that they were not professional soldiers, and that few mourners knew what had really been happening to them when they died made the losses all the more unnatural. Honouring the dead for their heroism in a conventional military sense was not adequate. Instead, the meaning of these deaths was predicated on the transformative power of self-sacrifice, and this transformation had to be realized in some concrete way if the deaths were to become meaningful.

To many people's minds, the most pressing practical task was to prevent such a war occurring again, as that would mean that all the suffering had achieved nothing permanent. When the Prince of Wales unveiled the memorial to the missing of the Somme at Thiepval, he illustrated how uncertain the value of such a memorial was. His speech implied that it was not the monument itself, but only the actions of the living in preventing another war, which could preserve and give value to the memory of the dead. He said

> these myriads of names carved in stone . . . must form no mere book of the dead if they are to 'live for evermore'. They must be . . . the foundation and guide to a new civilization from which war, with all the horrors which our generation have added to it, shall be banished before the spirits of the dead.[21]

Concern with practical activity as a response to death has been seen as a symptom, verging on the neurotic, of repressed grief,[22] but there were entirely realistic reasons for anxiety about the social and political questions with which such activity was concerned. In particular, the war remained, in certain respects, unfinished business. There was a growing sense throughout the 1920s and 1930s that the end of the war itself had settled nothing. The Treaty of Versailles was criticized as both too harsh and too lenient, but widely regarded as unsatisfactory, with a lively fear that it contained the seeds of another war. There were also the distress and grievances caused by economic problems in the aftermath of war to contend with, especially those of ex-servicemen.

However, the idea that the living must give meaning to death in war through their practical action was not easy to implement, for what kind of action best affirmed the ideals and aims of the dead? Editorials and speeches accompanying commemorative events tried to answer the question, and their answers were, on the whole, unashamedly political and partisan. Newspapers in particular dressed up their opinions on domestic and foreign policy as the authentic views of the war dead. Speakers at memorial unveilings were a little more circumspect in attributing their own political views to the dead, but, basically, they were doing the same thing.

On the one hand, the memory of the dead was invoked, as at the unveiling of Brancepeth war memorial, to remind the congregation about 'the horrors and the wickedness of this war' and that 'they should each do their best to produce a peaceful atmosphere'.[23] More controversially, the *Daily Herald* urged readers to see that never again will 'the heroic common people of any nation . . . kill their fellows at the bidding of their masters'.[24] On the other hand, the London Brighton and South Coast Railway's memorial was supposed to inspire in onlookers a sense of duty to their country, and to reject 'an impartial tie with all countries, a sentimental sympathy with humanity at large with no preferential regard for . . . their native land'.[25] The *Daily Mail* even invoked the memory of the dead in support of the Italian invasion of Abyssinia.[26]

It is hard to see how commemorative symbols could represent commonly shared values if the interpretation of them was so open to differences of view. The symbols did not, it seems, embody or express a code of behaviour, but rather contained a clash between codes founded on the familiar divisions of political life. Beneath a general collectivist and altruistic ethic, there was no clear sense of who the collectivity was towards whom altruism was due, or even what kind of action was genuinely altruistic. When these vague ideals were elaborated, fundamental differences of outlook and values amongst participants were likely to emerge.

The symbolism of remembrance did not close the question of the meaning of death in the war: it simply reiterated the problem without settling it. Consequently, I think it is not right to argue that commemoration as a symbolic act – in other words, as an act deliberately intended to have meanings attached to it – was a socially unifying, or even a personally healing process. For the individual bereaved person, commemoration constantly rubbed in how much had been lost through death in the war, how much poorer life was without the dead, how seriously the dead would be betrayed if their virtue and example should be diminished in the memories of survivors. Indeed it exaggerated all this to a considerable degree. This is not to say that grief and mourning were not important reasons why people should have wanted to join in public commemorations, only to ask to what extent it really did contribute to their attempts to come to terms with life after their losses. Answers to the questions posed by war and death were only to be had through discussion and argument, perhaps with oneself but frequently with others.

Building Memorials

The disputatious aspect of commemoration, which I have been emphasizing, also appears in the production of memorials. Conflicts of purpose frequently arose when a town or village memorial committee discussed how it should give physical form to the ideals involved in honouring the dead, and disagreements were often reported in the press. It was no secret that deciding what to erect as a war memorial could be contentious, even acrimonious.[27]

There was a wide choice of possible types of memorial. Following precedents established mainly in the late Victorian period, the basic distinction was between the utilitarian and the artistic. Among the first were such things as hospitals, village halls and recreation grounds; the second consisted principally of monuments and plaques. Advocates of a particular solution frequently appealed to purposes beyond simply remembering the dead to support their preferences. Just as right action by mourners was thought necessary to adequately honour those they had lost, so a constructive purpose was demanded of a memorial. The purpose of a utility was obvious. In the case of artistic memorials, the expectation was that they should educate and inspire. The most arduous task for war memorial committees was to choose something from amongst this range of possibilities that would satisfy the views of a sufficiently large proportion of the public.

Arguments could not, by themselves, lead to a decision on the choice of a memorial, for, at the level of mere logic, they were thoroughly ambiguous, and could often be applied equally well to opposing proposals. In the borough of Islington, in London, alternative proposals for an extension to the local hospital and for a sculptural monument, amongst other things, were put forward. A supporter of the monumental solution wrote, '"Who gains the eyes gains all" is a true saying, and in nothing more so than in when we must comfort the emotions . . . a noble piece of sculpture would be the best anodyne and inspiration'.[28] The advocates of a memorial extension to the hospital claimed that practical philanthropy would have the same effect, however, arguing that 'alleviating the suffering of humanity' would serve 'to commemorate the fight of Humanity against threatened oppression and added sufferings', and would be 'a direct and tangible expression of sympathy'.[29]

Such arguments did no more than assert the preferences of participants, and reflect the particular interests they had in participating in the memorial project. In the absence of clear and universal principles for judging the propriety of a proposal, the choice was largely determined by institutional and financial power. Memorials were usually chosen by a committee that consisted of leaders of the local authority and delegates from other local institutions representing the variety of economic, social and religious groups in the community. The form of organization adopted was intended to encourage public participation and maximize the financial support for the memorial project, while, at the same time, giving it the symbolic value of a gift from the community as a whole, not merely its leaders, or certain sections of it. The organizers raised funds, made decisions by majority votes in committee, and then put the results to public meetings for ratification.

This structure was open to manipulation in ways entirely familiar to local politicians and voluntary organization activists, who knew very well how to get their preferred policies implemented. The surviving records of war memorial committees show agendas being controlled, superior resources marshalled to back one project against another, awkward groups of people marginalized, and so on. Memorial funds often depended on a few large donors to realize projects that were too ambitious for the small amounts usually donated by ordinary members of the public, and this gave the individuals in question considerable, sometimes decisive influence. Islington hospital's casualty department was selected as a memorial partly as a result of influence of this sort. Lord Northampton, a leading patron of the hospital, offered a large sum of money to the Islington memorial fund on condition that the hospital was the beneficiary, and a councillor promised to raise the same amount on the same conditions.

The memorial for the Borough of Stoke Newington, in London, was a particularly vivid example of how the profane methods of civic politics could contribute to the sacred task. Here, the Borough Council's original project for a monumental entrance to the borough library fell foul of political divisions within the local Conservative Party. Opponents of the project advanced various schemes that involved confining the bulk of the memorial fund to a charitable, not monumental purpose. Their manoeuvres included raising money that the donors specifically requested should not be used for the library. The project's supporters fought back by restricting attendance at a decisive meeting to subscribers of 10/- or more, so excluding many people, especially ex-servicemen, more interested in charity than in the civic dignity of the borough.[30] A rather similar situation is recorded in Enfield, where the deployment of funds became a matter of contention between left and right in local politics.[31] Many choices that were portrayed as those of the entire community were made through this kind of manipulative process.

Yet, in spite of the manifest differences of opinion, memorials were not only built, but were generally revered by everyone, whatever side of the controversy they may originally have taken. On Armistice Day too there was practically complete unity of action, for although certain groups such as the Peace Pledge Union and Women's Co-operative Guild held their own, increasingly visible, ceremonies, especially in the later 1930s,[32] the two minutes' silence and local memorials remained the essential focal points for ceremonial actions by everyone.

This unanimity in action was aided by the reticence of the imagery and ceremonial of commemoration. The significance of the Great Silence in this respect, as the central form of expression of homage to the dead, can hardly be missed. In memorial design, simplicity and reticence were urged by artists and critics, and it was also much appreciated by lay people – at least those whose views are recorded in memorial committee records. The Cenotaph in Whitehall, designed by Sir Edwin Lutyens, was a particularly successful embodiment of reserve and iconographical emptiness, allowing it to become a container for the emotions of those with widely different attitudes and beliefs. In 1921, the then President of the RIBA praised it as 'austere yet gracious, technically perfect, it is the very expression of repressed emotion, of massive simplicity of purpose'.[33]

Probably the most common free-standing memorial type is the cross. Many of these are in ecclesiastical gothic, especially, of course, where they are parish memorials in churchyards, but many are in a characteristically simplified style. The prototype for this spare kind of cross was Sir Reginald Blomfield's design for the Imperial War Graves Commission which was also used for many civic memorials. The design was published in 1918, and became widely known and respected. Many local memorials are copies of it. Obelisks, too, were a conveniently simple form, associated by tradition with death. As war memorials they frequently carry a cross in some form, or the cross-like inverted sword that appears in Blomfield's design. Another widely approved form of memorial was the simply lettered plaque, or an inscription cut directly onto a building, in which the simplicity and clarity of the design and lettering was understood to have a moral meaning.

Silent action and simple or reticent images made possible a still, calm centre or focal point amongst the controversies that any retrospect on the war was likely to arouse. It opened up a fragment of space or time that could be universally respected as containing the essential significance of commemoration where no explicit significance could be agreed. It was something to cherish and defend as a transcendent moment, transcending the problems of meaning and the divisions of opinion, especially political opinion, within each community. Not all memorials were of a conspicuously simple design. Allegorical or naturalistic figures appear on some, but these more elaborate images were often adjuncts to large architectural elements, such as obelisks, versions of the cenotaph or other funerary symbols. Bradford war memorial is an example. The controversial bayonet-carrying figures stand either side of a cenotaph-like structure with a cross and stone feature suggesting an urn or sarcophagus at its top. Such memorials, despite their figurative additions, therefore retain a transcendent symbolic abstraction at their centre.

In their simplicity and reticence, ceremonies and memorials made only the most minimal or general propositions about the dead, but the variety of hortatory activities with which they were surrounded offered interpretations of them in far more explicit terms. The ritual silence on Armistice Day was accompanied by religious services, speeches and the publication of newspaper editorials or other writing, which reiterated standard moral judgements about the dead and drew political conclusions from them. Memorial unveiling ceremonies also combined a ritual core – the dedication of the completed memorial – with more explicitly interpretative activities, especially moral and political exhortations in dignitaries' speeches, and, once again, commentaries presented in the local press.

The interpretations commonly uttered in these circumstances elaborated on the virtues of the dead – which constituted what I have called the 'good' memory of them – and on the lessons the living should learn from them. Here, the sacred and transcendent aspect of remembrance was linked to specific and worldly conclusions that interpreters wished to see drawn from the experience of war. However, it was important that the sacred and the worldly in this relationship should remain separate. If a memorial, or indeed a ceremony, seemed to allude too clearly to a contentious view of the dead, the consensus on which its sacred status rested would be threatened. The military ceremony at the Cenotaph on Armistice Day raised difficulties of this sort, being seen by some as militaristic.[34] Figures of combat troops on Bradford memorial created, as I have said, a similar difficulty, evoking a negative image of the dead for several commentators.

The controversy at Bradford shows us how the difficulty of combining consensual sanctity and controversial interpretation was negotiated, because it brought into the open a process that normally went unnoticed. Criticism of the memorial could not just be brushed aside as mistaken, as the views that lay behind it were respectable and valid. War, as a reviewer of Wilfred Owen's poems wrote, 'involves savagery; it demands of men such cruel outrage against their human instincts that as a moral experience it is essentially unbearable'.[35] But it was precisely in the idealization of the moral experience that a meaning for the suffering which war inflicted was to be sought.

Even critics of the memorial did not want to reject it as an object of veneration, nor as a representation of the ideals of the dead. Someone writing to the press as 'Peace wisher', described the figures as 'crude and mistaken' but insisted that the memorial 'is and must remain a shrine of reverent remembrance' whatever might be wrong with it.[36] Alderman Gadie, a member of the City Council, who had been closely involved in erecting the memorial, showed the way out of the dilemma. The physical reality of the memorial should be submerged in what onlookers knew to be its moral significance, he said.

> [W]hat mattered in a memorial was not so much its form as the sacredness of the thing it stood for . . . Even though a memorial called attention to certain things that happened in the war – and the war was no kid-glove affair – we forgot that in a moment, and remembered that whatever the lads passed through, they did so to crush a tremendous evil.[37]

It was this capacity to forget that conferred 'sacredness' on the monument and constituted the transcendent moment in which consensus was possible. The abstract tomb-like element at the centre of the memorial assisted the process, providing an alternative focus in the imagery. It enabled the Lord Mayor to make the necessary distinction between what was sacred and what was controversial. 'The monument itself is plain and dignified,' he said, although 'the figures . . . are quite out of place.'[38]

Sanctity, which focused on the fact of death while eschewing the details of war and judgements upon them, was essential in achieving the communal unity that commemoration prescribed. Nevertheless, without the conscious imposition by individuals of their own preferred meanings on commemorative symbols, the sacred space contained no answers to questions raised by death in war. The *Manchester Guardian*'s comment on the burial of the Unknown Warrior in Westminster Abbey in 1920 acknowledged this: 'What remains to do today is the greatest effort of all – to put into the chosen symbol all the meaning it should have . . . All the virtue and energy of its significance come from the heart and mind of him who uses or accepts it.' For the *Birmingham Post*, the effort required to give meaning to commemorative symbols was not merely one of creation but of discipline; 'our true task is to make sure the memory is a right memory'.[39] Alderman Gadie's forgetting of the things which divided those who commemorated the dead, his imposition of reticence on otherwise loud details, could only be temporary. The sacred moment of unity was indispensable, but so was the divisive business of interpretation and argument.

Just as the work of memorial committees in creating objects sacred to the dead depended on the use of power, so it is important to recognize the part played by official and unofficial power in creating and protecting the sacred moment of transcendence in the two minutes silence. A royal proclamation ordained that for two minutes all activity should cease throughout the country at 11.00 a.m. on 11 November. Local authorities arranged for the police to co-ordinate the stopping of traffic. The managers of factories and shops organized the cessation of work and movement by their employees and customers. A great many people went out into the open air as the time for the silence approached, and an active element amongst them intimidated anyone who appeared to be ignoring the silence. There were, in fact, a number of public disturbances arising out of action directed at people who had not wished to join in.[40] Civic leaders and police also controlled political leafleting or speech-making in the public areas of town centres where people assembled for the silence, forming a large potential audience. In this way they could keep the controversial side of Armistice Day activities out of its immediately sacred element.[41] Both in ceremonies, and in the production of memorials, power made a unifying transcendent act possible, and reticence made it universally acceptable.

Conclusion

I have argued that there was an underlying lack of confidence in the efficacy of the attempt to impose meaning on war death through the symbols of commemoration. In both the social and the personal spheres, their significance for contemporaries seems to have been shot through with doubts, disagreements and clashes of values. Much of the public interest in commemorative acts of the sort I have been discussing was that they focused attention on the question of what was the right memory, and assembled an audience to whom answers could be proposed. Such occasions were appreciated by those who participated in them as opportunities to enact their commitment to their own understanding of the war, rather than to share in a commonly accepted understanding of it. However, commemoration did achieve a very considerable degree of social unity in action. It could do so because all the controversial activity centred on a carefully preserved area of the unsaid, the inexplicit. It was an area that could be approached from many points of view, an area for common action, rather than for the expression of common values. As such, it was created and maintained by local administrative and political power, and by the co-operative effort of all who were interested in the opportunity to express elsewhere their senses of how the dead should be remembered.

Building monuments was an opportunity to establish more substantial working relationships between participants than were required in ceremonies, involving, as it did, negotiation, co-operation, the suspension of differences, and a prolonged commitment to seeing the project through. The unanimity that had, ultimately, to be achieved in order to realize the project, announced in advance the transcendent, unifying character of the memorial. It showed that such unanimity was not merely an ideal, but could be achieved in practice when the living adequately remembered their dead. The unity thus established formed those who commemorated the dead into a movement that could, up to a point, police the memory of them. They might not have had an agreed view to offer about the significance of that memory, but they could campaign together against the sheer forgetfulness that withdrew attention from the war completely, and abandoned the search for constructive meaning, or against an alternative memory that seemed demeaning. Against these they set a more limited form of forgetting, in which the meaning of suffering and war was not closed, but rather kept entirely open, so accommodating the contradictions between nobility and horror, heroism and victimization, sacrifice and homicide, in a momentary suspension of choice.

Notes

1. M. Agulhon, 'La "Statuomanie" et l'histoire', *Ethnologie Française* 8 (1978), pp. 145–72.
2. George Mosse, working from German examples, presents a very different view of war commemoration from that given here, seeing it as the expression of thoroughly nationalist politics, but generalizes unjustifiably to other countries. See G. L. Mosse, *Fallen Soldiers: Reshaping the Memory of the First World War*, Oxford, Oxford University Press, 1990. R. Koselleck, 'Kriegerdenkmäle als Identit-

ätsstiftung der Überlebenden', in O. Marquard and K. Stierle (eds), *Identität*, Munich, Fink, 1979, pp. 255–76, offers a less tendentious general approach but lacks the specific details concerning institutions and contemporary interpretations that are required, in my view, to elucidate the relation of memorial-building to society. Studies from outside Britain that do supply useful local detail are J. Giroud, *Les monuments aux morts dans le Vaucluse*, L'Isle sur Sorgue, Editions Scriba, 1991; M. Bach, *Studien zur Geschichte des deutschen Kriegerdenkmals in Westfalen und Lippe*, Frankfurt-am-Main, Lang, 1985; and G. Armanski, *'und wenn wir sterben müssen': Die politische Ästhetik von Kriegerdenkmälern*, Hamburg, VSA-Verlag, 1988.

3. Jay Winter makes mourning the centre of his wide-ranging account of many forms of cultural reflection on the Great War. See J. M. Winter, *Sites of Memory, Sites of Mourning: The Great War in European Cultural History*, Cambridge, Cambridge University Press, 1995. T. Laqueur, 'The Past's Past', *London Review of Books*, vol. 18, no. 18, 1996, pp. 3–7, also sees grief as central, but disagrees with aspects of Winter's argument. D. Sherman, 'Art, Commerce and the production of Memory in France after World War I', in J. R. Gillis (ed.), *Commemorations: The Politics of National Identity*, Princeton, Princeton University Press, 1994, pp. 186–211, concludes war memorials are primarily places of mourning because of the prominence they give to the names of the dead (p. 206), but has little to say about how people originally interpreted them.
4. Other forms of mourning for the war dead, not enacted in communal space, could and did exist. 'A woman correspondent' wrote of the dead, 'to-day they live in many a household shrine as canonized saints' (*Bradford Daily Telegraph*, 1 July 1922). Lord Leverhulme considered the idea of installing memorial windows to individual casualties in houses at Port Sunlight; see W. P. Jolly, *Lord Leverhulme*, London, Constable, 1976, pp. 166–7. Home memorials were offered, intended to incorporate the medals of dead men (*Architectural Review*, vol. 40, July–Dec. 1916, p. 39) or the memorial medallion, called a 'plaque', which was issued by the government to next-of-kin (advertisment for 'Wright war memorial plaque holder' *Bradford Daily Telegraph*, 10 Sep. 1921). There are still, it seems, many objects of this sort in private collections; I am particularly grateful to Nick Mansfield of the National Museum of Labour History for an illustration of one in his family's possession, probably a colour lithograph, with pictures of war leaders and a central space for mounting another document, most likely a photograph.

5. A. King, 'Acts and Monuments: National Celebrations in Britain from the Napoleonic to the Great War', in A. O'Day (ed.), *Government and Institutions in the Post-1832 United Kingdom*, Lewiston and Lampeter, Mellen, 1995, pp. 237–68.
6. Laqueur argues that the commemoration of the war dead could no longer employ traditional symbols with conviction, and writes 'a solution [was] to eschew representation and the production of meaning as far as possible', and merely to name those who had been lost. See T. Laqueur, 'Memory and Naming in the Great War', in Gillis, *Commemorations*, p. 160. He seems here to confuse representation and figuration. Allegories attributing qualities to the dead, or idealized images of them may have been less common than in earlier periods, but an enormous effort was made, none the less, to represent the dead and give meaning to their deaths. Much of this effort went into words, either on monuments, or uttered around them. The considerable amount of work that still went into the production of meaning through figuration is described in C. Moriarty, 'The Absent Dead and Figurative First World War Memorials', *Transactions of the Ancient Monument Society* 39 (1995), pp. 7–40.
7. J. Bodnar, *Remaking America: Public Memory, Commemoration, and Patriotism in the Twentieth Century*, Princeton, Princeton University Press, 1992.
8. Bodnar, *Remaking America*, pp. 15–16.
9. Bodnar, *Remaking America*, pp. 32–7.
10. S. G. Davis, *Parades and Power: Street Theatre in Nineteenth-Century Philadelphia*, Berkeley and London, University of California Press, 1988.
11. Davis, *Parades and Power*, pp. 164 and 167.
12. Davis, *Parades and Power*, p. 165.
13. Alois Riegl made this point in a paper on conservation policy written for the Austro-Hungarian imperial authorities in 1903. It is reproduced as A. Riegl (1982), 'The Modern Cult of Monuments, its Character and its Origin', trans. K. Forster and D. Ghirardo, *Oppositions*, no. 25, pp. 21–51 (see especially p. 38).
14. CWGC Archives WG 1406, and WG 1406/6 contain examples.
15. Sentiments of this sort appear in almost every war memorial committee's appeals for funds.
16. P. Gibbs, *Realities of War*, London, William Heinemann, 1920.
17. An ex-servicemen wrote to the press to defend the memorial against critics, saying that in fact the position represented was one of readiness, not of actual attack (*Yorkshire Observer*, 6 July 1922).

18. *Bradford Daily Telegraph*, 3 July 1922.
19. R. M. Bracco, *Merchants of Hope: British Middlebrow Writers and the First World War, 1919–1939*, Oxford, Berg, 1993, p. 153.
20. Hackney Record Office, SN/W/1/25, untitled newspaper cutting, 15 Oct. 1920.
21. *Daily Herald*, 2 Aug. 1932.
22. J. C. Lerner, 'Changes in Attitudes Toward Death: The Widow in Great Britain in the Early Twentieth Century', in B. Schoenberg et al. *Bereavement: Its Psychosocial Aspects*, New York, Columbia University Press, 1975, pp. 91–115.
23. *Durham County Advertiser*, 10 June 1921.
24. *Daily Herald*, 11 Nov. 1920.
25. *War Memorials*, London Brighton and South Coast Railway, undated pamphlet, in PRO/RAIL 258/447.
26. *Daily Mail*, 11 Nov. 1935.
27. An article to this effect by Philip Gibbs is in Cumbria Record Office, Carlisle, Ca/C10/12/1 (unidentified press cutting); see also *Carlisle Journal*, 13 and 27 May 1919.
28. *Islington Daily Gazette*, 30 Aug. 1918.
29. *Islington Daily Gazette*, 1 Apr. 1919.
30. Hackney Archives Department, SN/W1/1-25.
31. *Enfield Gazette*, 5–26 Dec. 1919.
32. A. Gregory, *The Silence of Memory: Armistice Day 1919–1946*, Oxford, Berg, 1994, is the definitive account of the origin and development of Armistice Day. Gregory's discussion of the movement in 1925 and 1926, in which Revd Dick Sheppard played a large part, to increase the solemnity of Armistice Day is especially interesting. By suppressing the hedonistic element of celebration, he argues, distinctions of wealth and consequently distinctions in the capacity for pleasure, were made less conspicuous. A greater stress on the sanctity of Armistice Day thus increased the social unity of the occasion (pp. 65–80).
33. *Journal of the Royal Institute of British Architects*, series 3, vol. 28, 25 June 1921, p. 474.
34. *Daily Herald*, 12 Nov. 1924, 11 Nov. 1933; *Manchester Guardian*, 11 Nov. 1930; Gregory, *The Silence of Memory*, p. 125.
35. *Times Literary Supplement*, 6 Jan. 1921, p. 6.
36. *Yorkshire Observer*, 3 July 1922.
37. *Bradford Daily Telegraph*, 31 July 1922.
38. *Bradford Daily Telegraph*, 7 July 1922.
39. *Manchester Guardian*, 11 Nov. 1920; *Birmingham Post*, 6 July 1925.

40. For example, *Daily Herald*, 12 Nov. 1924.
41. Not all collective acts showing reverence for memorials contributed to harmonious social relations. War memorials were used as meeting places for strikers in the 1923 agricultural workers' dispute, emphasizing the fact that many strikers had fought in the war, whereas employers and strike-breakers were sometimes accused of avoiding service. See A. Howkins, *Poor Labouring Men: Rural Radicalism in Norfolk, 1872–1923*, London, Routledge & Kegan Paul, 1985, pp. 167–8. I am grateful to Nick Mansfield for this reference. See also N. Mansfield, 'Class conflict and Village War Memorials, 1914–1924', *Rural History* 6 (1995), pp. 67–87.

–8–

Commemorating 1916, Celebrating Difference: Parading and painting in Belfast

Neil Jarman

The importance that historical events play in the politics of contemporary Ireland is frequently noted. The Irish, and in particular those in the north of the island, are often viewed as a people trapped in the past, forever reliving the religious conflicts that dominated early modern Europe, unable to free themselves from the shackles of history and move into the late twentieth century. The Irish past is not just facts to be retrieved from history books, but something that people are actively aware of, something that is still being used and manipulated. It is true that some historical events do have an unusual prominence in contemporary political life, but little attention has been paid either to the fact that very few events are treated in this way, or to the means in which these past events are remembered, and through which they retain their prominence for contemporary communities. The remembered history of Ireland, of war, rebellion and sectarian conflict, is but one of any number of possible readings of the past, but these other pasts are not celebrated or commemorated in any collective manner. The power of the past, of a collective memory, to influence the present and the future relies heavily on the process, or practice, of commemoration, and the selectivity of memory and of forgetting.

In this chapter I want to explore how beliefs and memories of the past persist, by focusing on the prominent means that are used to generate and sustain a social memory and consider how groups use their memories to guide, rationalize and justify their beliefs and activities. It is important to emphasize the social or collective nature of these memories because, as Maurice Halbwachs argued, memories of past events are primarily maintained and structured within membership of a social group rather than by individuals. Halbwachs asserted that social memory

> can only be stimulated in indirect ways through reading or listening or in commemoration and festive occasions when people gather together to remember in common the deeds and accomplishments of long-departed members of the group.[1]

Paul Connerton[2] has developed this line of thought to argue that commemorative occasions are specific types of ritual events that are particularly suited to generating a collective memory. This is achieved because the commemoration acts as a physical re-presentation of the primal or historical event through which the participants bodily re-enact their history and in so doing create a conjuncture of past and present in which a sense of time passing, or change occurring, is denied. The commemorative act is repetitive and formalized, like all ritual events, but its power is further enhanced because the re-enactment takes place on the anniversary day itself, at the calendrical conjuncture of past and present, which thereby reaffirms the unchanging state of their belief and identity. Each actor and each generation that participates in these rituals relives the trials and tribulations of his or her forbearers in the 'rhetoric of re-enactment'. They consolidate their collective identity in the present, at the same time as they reaffirm their collective unity with their past.

However Connerton's argument does tend to fossilize the commemorative process. It consigns the participants to always, and only, re-enact the past as the original act, it tends to anchor the actors to their history rather than to draw history into the present. There is little or no scope for social dynamics, for changes of meaning, or for multiple interpretations of the ritual event. He sees rituals as events that are controlled from the centre rather than as dynamic interactions in which the power of the event emerges from the process of the total performance. This is because his focus is on the importance of the form of the proceedings rather than the content of the event, and on what they do, rather than on what they say. The argument for emphasizing the role of performative power, of active participation in sustaining collective faith, as a strong element of the mnemonic process, is important, but it is not sufficient in itself. The meaning of the event, what is being said, or claimed, or asserted, is also important and contributes to its social power. The problem here is that the meanings that are generated in ritual are always difficult to control. Unlike bodily movements, which can be quite regimented and formalized, and therefore readily repeated over the years, meaning is often more elusive and diverse. Paradoxically, it is this elusiveness that enhances the appeal of ritual as a collective process, people can participate in a common practice while giving their actions quite different meanings.

Nevertheless organizers of ritual or commemorative events aspire to control the meaning as much as the performance, and symbols, icons and other images or artefacts are used to focus meaning. This aspect illustrates another theoretical approach, traceable to Cicero and other classical thinkers, which has emphasized the way in which memory as a dynamic process, is generated through the use of images.[3] In the classical model, the emphasis is on the individual mnemonic process, and the images are mental constructs that are situated in clearly defined places. Recalling a memory involves the individual making a physical, or mental, journey around familiar sites and recounting the mental images that are encountered *en route*. The images themselves do not function as literal representations but serve as codes or triggers, they are symbolic, rather than iconic, devices. The classical tradition emphasized the use of mental images, but recent work has drawn attention to the importance of material images in the creation of a collective memory, which can operate in conjunction with, or instead of, textual or verbal expression.[4] Ernst Gombrich[5] has argued that because images are always open to multiple points of focus and interpretation, if they are to be useful as mnemonic devices they must be simplified and schematized, stripped of much of the extraneous information and detail. Images are most memorable when they are reduced to a childlike simplicity, with the subject centred, enlarged and, where appropriate, depicted in bright colours. Such simplified images carry no obvious, or 'natural' meaning, nor does the schematization deny the natural polysemy of images; rather, as with any image, their specific meaning is constructed and 'anchored' through their social context and physical placement. This tends to reinforce the contingency, flexibility and creativity of the act of remembering.

Formalized physical enactment and symbolic displays, which are relatively fluid in their exact meaning, therefore provide two key elements for the collective mnemonic process. One offers the suggestion of solidity, stability, structure and organization; the other allows for flexibility, variability and personal interpretations. Of course in practice, they are not so polarized: performances always vary and meanings are never unrestricted, but coalesce around generalized norms.

In Northern Ireland highly formalized rituals and elaborate visual displays form the basis of the popular commemorative process. Each year the two dominant communities, Protestant/unionist and Catholic/nationalist, hold in the region of 3,000 parades to celebrate their culture and commemorate their history.[6] This essay draws together some of the seemingly divergent strands that go to make up the commemorative process in Northern Ireland and explores how the long-established customs of parading with music and decorative banners, and painting elaborate wall murals, are combined to maintain an extensive social, as opposed to an official or historical, memory – a popular memory in contrast to a state-sanctioned memory.[7] I will also compare and contrast the form and content of nationalist and unionist practices, to do this I want to focus on commemorations that are held in Belfast to mark the events of 1916.

Of all the commemorations in Northern Ireland, those of 1916 are arguably the most important, although unionists would dispute this and point to the commemorations of the battle of the Boyne in 1690, held on 12 July, as the most significant event of their entire calendar.[8] However both communities draw much of their ideological sustenance from two key events of 1916: nationalists commemorate the Easter Rising in Dublin in April, while unionists focus on the Battle of the Somme, which began in northern France on 1 July. Neither of these replaced earlier historical events as the bedrock of social and political identity but were added on to it, reinforcing some existing attitudes while refocusing others. Both events helped to consolidate contrasting notions of collective identity in a period of political upheaval, and served to emphasize the divergent paths that the two cultural traditions were pursuing.

The Demand for Home Rule

Demands to dismantle the colonial relationship between Britain and Ireland dominated the Irish political agenda for some fifty years following the formation of the Home Government Association in 1870 (relaunched as the Home Rule League in 1873). Having established itself as an integral part of the Imperial industrial regime, the northern Protestant community vigorously opposed plans for change. Faced with a community increasingly defining its national identity in terms of its Roman Catholic and Gaelic-Irish heritage,[9] the Protestants began to redefine themselves as British and Ulstermen rather than as Irishmen and, politically, as Unionists rather than conservatives or liberals.[10] In January 1913 the Ulster Unionist Council began to raise a paramilitary Volunteer Force of 100,000 men, which would be used to reinforce political opposition to Home Rule. In April 1914 the Ulster Volunteer Force (UVF) landed some 25,000 rifles and 3 million rounds of ammunition, bought in Germany, at Larne and Bangor.[11] In spite of this opposition, the third Home Rule Bill appeared certain to be successful, even when the start of the First World War, in August 1914, meant that there was a pause in the proceedings.

Although constitutional nationalists supported the proposals for Home Rule, more radical nationalists advocated complete independence from

Britain and the formation of an Irish Republic. On Easter Monday, 24 April 1916, they occupied numerous key buildings in Dublin and read a Proclamation of Independence of the Irish Republic, from the steps of the General Post Office. However the Rising failed to attract mass support in Dublin or elsewhere, and the city was severely bombarded by British forces for nearly a week before the rebels surrendered. The widespread destruction only served to harden public opinion against the rebels. Although they had sustained a more determined resistance than previous attempts to oust the British in 1798, 1803, 1848 and 1867, the rebellion appeared to have achieved no more success. The British Government then made a supreme error when it decided to make an example of the leaders and execute them. The prolonged cycle of executions, between 3 May and 12 May, transformed public reaction to the Rising. The killings generated immense sympathy for the rebels and anger at the British government. The dead leaders were rapidly adopted into the pantheon of heroes who had been martyred to the cause of Ireland, and who offered inspiration for future rebels. In 1918 at the first post-war General Election Sinn Féin, who had previously been an insignificant political force, won 73 of 105 Irish seats, while the constitutional Irish Party was virtually wiped out.

The outbreak of war, in the summer of 1914, had brought the Ulster Unionists back from the brink of armed rebellion against the British government. In August the Unionist leaders, Sir Edward Carson and James Craig, volunteered the membership of the UVF for the British army, and Lord Kitchener agreed to keep them together in an Ulster division. On 1 July, just two months after the Rising had been defeated, the Battle of the Somme began in northern France. At the heart of the British offensive was the 36th (Ulster) Division, which included many members of the Ulster Volunteer Force. On the first day of the battle some 5,500 members of the Ulster Division were killed or wounded. It is popularly recounted that scarcely a Protestant family in Belfast was untouched by this disaster. Although many tens of thousands of Irishmen, of both faiths, were to die during the remainder of the war, it was the decimation of the Ulster Division that was to be retained in popular memory in the north of Ireland. It became *the* single event that illustrated that the Ulster Protestants were as British as they claimed.

The two events of 1916 confirmed the divergent ideologies of the two communities. Both had offered their blood for their collective national identities. In 1921 the British government acceded to the nationalist demands for Home Rule, but only for 26 of the 32 Irish counties. The island was partitioned, divided between two states. The sacrifice on the

Somme ensured that the six of the counties of Ulster with the largest proportions of Protestants, remained apart, and a part of the United Kingdom.

Commemoration

In the decade after the war had ended, memorials were erected in most towns and villages in the north of Ireland. These became the focus of state-organized commemorations on Armistice Day, 11 November. A small number were also erected in the rest of Ireland.[12] The Somme was also immediately drawn into, and was used to extend, the existing structure of popular public expressions of Orange/unionist identity that centred on the Twelfth of July commemorations of the battle of the Boyne. In July 1917 references had been made on public decorations in Belfast to those who had died at the Somme, and a parade to commemorate the battle had been held in East Belfast. At the first Twelfth parade held after the war, in July 1919, the sacrifice on the Somme was incorporated into the broadening unionist iconography: at least one new banner included a depiction of the battle on the reverse of a painting of King William at the Boyne, thereby linking the two key events in Ulster Protestant history. The first mural to the Somme dead was unveiled the same year, and similar images continued to be painted throughout the 1920s and into the 1930s.

The Rising in its turn was widely commemorated both in the newly established Free State,[13] and in the north, where small commemorations were held within nationalist communities. However wide-scale public displays of support for Irish nationalism were not welcome in the newly established Northern Ireland. The Special Powers Act and (from 1954) the Flags and Emblems Act were used to constrain nationalist displays, but while commemorations were banned this was often ignored, and instead parades were restricted to strongly nationalist towns like Newry or Lurgan or held on the Falls Road in Belfast, where the Irish tricolour could fly more freely.[14]

In 1966 extensive celebrations were planned for the 50th anniversary of the Rising. This was also a time when liberalizing concessions and gestures were being made by the O'Neill government, although these were under attack from a rising populist orator, the Revd Ian Paisley. The combined influence of republican celebrations and the apparent softening of the unionist position in the north encouraged a small group of Shankill Road loyalists to resurrect the name of the long disbanded Ulster Volunteer Force. In what was to be a prologue to the troubles, the UVF carried out

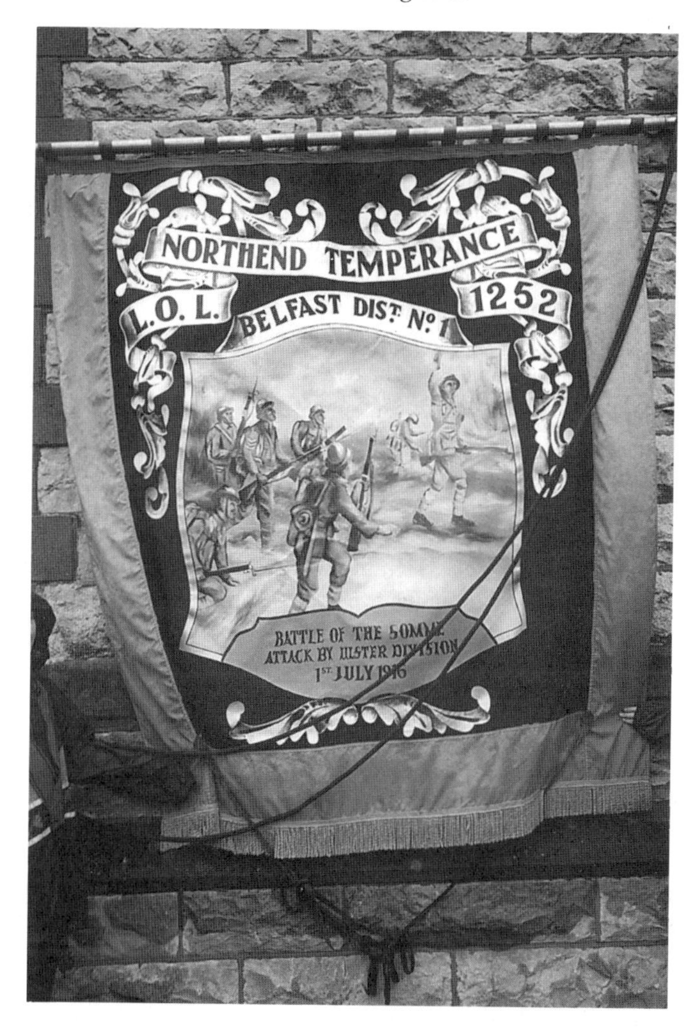

Figure 26 Orange Order banner depicting the start of the Battle of the Somme. Based on the painting *Charge of the 36th (Ulster) Division, Somme, 1st July 1916* by J. Prinsep Beadle.

a series of gun and bomb attacks through the spring of 1966. These climaxed in the murder of a young Catholic, just days before the anniversary of the Somme. The leaders of the UVF were soon arrested and sentenced to prison, but this period of conflicting commemorations helped to reconfirm the political polarity of the north.[15]

Since the Troubles began in 1969, the Rising and the Somme have become an increasingly important feature of the visual and performative rhetoric of the two conflicting communities in the north. The displays and parades held to commemorate the two events hold them prominently in the public eye. They help to locate the Rising and the Somme as a link between the traditional facets of communal identity and those contemporary events that are continually redefining them. Although they are a continuation of earlier practices, both anniversaries have been changed as a result of the Troubles. The Somme has been brought more to the fore in Orange and loyalist celebrations, whereas the Rising has become more closely identified with Sinn Féin and the IRA, as less militant groups have abandoned public displays on the anniversary.

Remembering the Somme

There is a formal wreath-laying ceremony at the Cenotaph, beside Belfast City Hall on 1 July, but more significant are the Orange parades held in east and south Belfast later in the evening. Although these parades have been established for some years, in the past few years Orangemen in many other districts have begun to hold small parades or unfurl new banners at this time,[16] as 1 July has become an increasingly popular counterpoint to the Twelfth. Both parades are local events, in which the Orangemen, wearing their regalia and carrying their banners, march to the sound of flute and drum on a circuitous route of some 3 miles through their home areas. Along the route crowds line the streets to watch the parade and listen to the bands. Wreaths are laid at local war memorials at some point. These parades are complex events that work on many levels. Although they are principally held to commemorate the sacrifice of the Somme, the parades also consolidate local identities within strict geographical parameters; they ground the memory more clearly in the home localities of those who fought and died than does the central commemoration, held earlier at the Cenotaph. While Armistice Day commemorates all the war dead, and the ceremony at City Hall remembers those who died at the Somme, these parades recall those who lived locally: they incorporate the memory of the Somme onto the streets of Belfast.

The parade honours the dead in an act of mimesis: the Orangemen march in military manner, each lodge identified by its regalia and, accompanied by a military-style band, they present a display of local strength and unity. By mirroring the form of the military parade, the Orangemen re-enact the departure of the Ulster Volunteers to the First World War, a performance that emphasizes a sense of continuity between those who fought in 1916 and the men currently prepared to defend the cause of Ulster. The parade itself is a very male, or at least masculine, affair, women are largely consigned to the margins, waving and cheering from the roadside. The few girls who perform in some of the bands do so by adopting the male role: dressing in the same uniform as the bandsmen and replicating the military step. But while they are excluded from the parades, the women remain an important part of the commemorative process: as witness to their men's resolve, they cheer and encourage them on their departure and welcome them on their return. While affirming traditional gender roles this extends the unity and solidity of the community, as the male declaration of loyalty is publicly witnessed by family and friends. Although the event is ostensibly an act of mourning for those who fell in battle, the atmosphere of the parade recreates the hopeful mood of the departure rather than reflecting on the horrors of the conflict or the sadness of the return. While acknowledging the loss, the tone of the parade simultaneously affirms the validity of the cause for which the men died, and confirms the declared willingness of the present generation to fight again if necessary.

The Somme is the only anniversary besides the Williamite events that is commemorated by the Orange Order. These parades therefore also serve as a preparatory event for the Boyne commemorations on 12 July. The similarities of form between these two events helps to emphasize the parallels, but the connection is primarily affirmed visually. Although the Somme remains a relatively minor theme within the central iconography of Orangeism, some form of visual representations of the battle are a feature of all Orange parades. The Somme is recalled visually in two distinct forms: on Orange banners and on regalia carried by the bands. Williamite themes and religious images dominate the imagery of Orange banners at all parades and emphasize the values of the Protestant ascendancy.[17] But the Somme has been readily incorporated into the Orange canon, although without disrupting or dominating traditional expressions of faith. Instead it adds to this tradition by drawing analogies between the recent sacrifices and the long-distant past. Rather than offering a lineal narrative, the presentation of banner images is a jumbled display that emphasizes the seeming cyclical repetition of history.

The most widely used image, based on a painting in Belfast City Hall, depicts the men of the Ulster Division leaving their trenches to begin their assault on the German lines. As shells explode around them one figure falls to the ground, but beside him another soldier stands, arm aloft, encouraging the Ulstermen to continue their attack. Variations show members of the 36th (Ulster) Division attacking a German trench and inflicting heavy casualties on the enemy. In many cases the motto '*Lest we forget*' is displayed prominently. The emphasis seems to focus on the heroic bravery and determination of the Ulstermen rather than the severity of the casualties, which is usually stressed in written history. Other banners portray individual soldiers in uniform. In these cases the dead man is less clearly identified with the Somme in particular, than with the war in general, and while they appear to maintain the memory of specific individuals this detail is often lost on those carrying the images. I have often asked Orangemen who the various paintings represented or why a particular man was being commemorated, but few of them knew any specific details of the individuals recalled on their banners, beyond the fact that 'he was killed at the Somme' or 'he died in the war'. But this was very often only stating the obvious. Where the Williamite campaign is commemorated through its heroic leaders, the social memory of the Somme dissolves individuality into the single identity of the Ulster Division, while all battles are condensed in the memory of the Somme. Just as the First World War was supposedly the 'war to end all wars', so the Somme has come to signify all the battles fought by Ulstermen in recent wars. All deaths in these wars are remembered as acts of equally heroic sacrifice in which each death is a brick in the wall dividing Ireland, each memory reaffirming Ulster's British identity.

The Somme parades are organized by the Orange Order, but they also offer an opportunity for other voices within the unionist community to be heard. The period of the Troubles has seen major changes in the relationship between the marching bands and the Order, especially in the urban areas. Increasingly the bands have established themselves as independent bodies and have developed their own styles of costume and regalia.[18] Contemporary bands are younger, brasher, louder, more colourful and less sophisticated than those of the previous generation. While the Orange Order has come to stand for the voice of the conservative, unionist establishment, the 'blood and thunder' bands represent a rejection of these values. This rejection is drawn from urban, working-class roots and personal experiences of the Troubles. For a large number of these bands the Ulster Volunteer Force, the Ulster Division and the Somme have been adopted as the inspiration for their collective, public image. The public prominence of these events has been dramatically increased by the visual rhetoric of the bands, their uniforms and regalia, as they accompany the Orangemen on parade.

The bands parade in brightly coloured, or military-style uniforms, and follow a colour-party who carry an array of flags and banners. Most carry the Union flag and the Ulster cross and have a bannerette with their name

Figure 27 Ulster Volunteer Force bannerette of Monkstown YCV Flute Band, listing the campaigns fought by the 36th (Ulster) Division during the First World War.

and emblem, usually based on an heraldic design incorporating the Red Hand of Ulster and a Crown, some of these emblems include reference to the Ulster Division or the Somme. A large number of bands also carry UVF or Young Citizen Volunteers (the youth wing of the UVF) flags. These are yellow, purple or white in colour and depict the emblem of the UVF, a Red Hand in an oval surrounded by the words 'for God and Ulster', or the shamrock emblem of the YCV, and a list of the campaigns fought in World War One. While the Orange banners make it clear that they are commemorating the 36th (Ulster) Division, however, the band regalia generally commemorate the Ulster Volunteer Force, which is not the same thing. The emphasis shifts from a commemoration of the heroic sacrifice in battle to a celebration of the indigenous tradition of paramilitarism. While the Ulster Division was a regular part of the British army, the UVF, under the authority of local politicians, Carson and Craig, was prepared to defy and challenge the British government. The bands appear to be commemorating a local tradition, but it is clear that it is not the same tradition valorized by the Orange Order. Furthermore, the logo and motto that the bands display is the one used by the contemporary UVF paramilitary group. This division, between bandsmen and Orangemen, over the meaning of the UVF is further emphasized by the regular appearance of the regalia of other loyalist paramilitary groups, the Ulster Defence Association and the Red Hand Commando within the broader band culture.

In the performance of the parade there is a unified adherence to the military ideal, bands and lodges march in formation and in step to a common tune. However it is less clear what this military ideal means in practice. While the Orange Order has guidelines and rules concerning the regalia that can be carried on parades, the bandsmen regularly ignore these, and have thereby extended the loyalist repertoire to include a place for the contemporary, illegal, paramilitary bodies in public displays. The Orange banners contextualize the relevance of the historic UVF through its transformation into the Ulster Division and, although banners recall events from the rebellious years before the war, such as the signing of the Ulster Covenant in 1912, or politicians such as Carson and Saunderson, these can readily be recontextualized within a democratic and constitutional framework. The UVF itself, past or present, is not recalled on the Orange banners. In contrast, the bandsmen display no coyness in remembering their own paramilitary tradition, and its role in making Ulster distinctively British.

This widespread use of visual displays extends the act of remembrance into all other parades held throughout the marching season. The increasing number of loyalist parades, which have grown from under 1,900 in 1987 to over 2,400 in 1996, means that these images are seen by ever larger numbers of people in more and more locations. All loyalist parades therefore make some acknowledgement to the Somme and its historical era, even if the banners offer different interpretations of its meaning. While this divergence of meaning clearly exists, however, the structuring framework of the Orange parades largely serves to limit the interpretative potential of the Somme, and contain it within the broader ideals of Orangeism. Although the bandsmen offer alternative understandings of its worth, at the Orange parades the Somme remains largely anchored within Williamite tradition of constitutional unionism.

However, the popular commemorative process is more extensive than just the parades. I have already noted how the parades spatialize the memory of the Somme within the working-class loyalist areas of Belfast, the many references to the Somme on mural paintings extends this aspect of the commemorative process still further. Images painted on the walls of working-class Belfast now confront the residents throughout the year, and here its meaning is freed from the constraining ideals of the Orange parades. Murals can be likened to the numerous war memorials, in so far as they are (relatively) permanent reminders to the dead. Whereas the self-effacing, grey, stone memorials are discreet, often to the point of invisibility, however, the murals are bright explosions of colour on the gable walls.[19] What was once just a part of Orange street decorations has now been adopted by the supporters of the paramilitary groups and expanded in its range of images. Murals have often been likened to territorial markers, defining the boundaries between loyalist and nationalist areas, but they are more readily understood as part of an internal debate, within the community, and are used to rephrase traditional symbols and icons to changing circumstances. In the same way as band parades have stepped outside Orange constraints, the wall paintings have become a medium in which the paramilitary groups redefine the loyalist tradition to suit there own claims.

Numerous murals in Belfast commemorate the Somme, some more directly than others. Some follow the pattern of band regalia by displaying the regimental colours of the Ulster Division, or they include the emblems or make other references to the historic UVF, in this way a clear connection is made between the activities of recent years and those of two generations earlier. Other murals extend this connection and equate the memory of sacrifice at the Somme with the memory of paramilitary members who have been recently killed. One long-established Somme mural on Donegall Pass depicts three silhouetted figures standing with heads bowed and arms resting on their rifles. This image of mourning gunmen, has subsequently been adopted by each of the paramilitary groups in the commemoration of their own dead: at Roden Street a memorial to former UDA leader John McMichael is flanked by a pair of similar figures; in Woodvale a mural to UVF member Brian Robinson has a single figure mourning his death; another memorial mural, to Red Hand Commando Stevie McCrea, contains the words

For he shall not grow old
as we that are left grow old
age shall not weary him
nor the years condemn
at the going down of the sun
and in the morning
we shall remember him.

which are based on Laurence Binyon's poem 'For the Fallen', written in the first weeks of the war and since adopted as part of the formal state ritual of remembrance.[20] These paramilitary murals help complete the connection made by the band regalia: they equate the activities of contemporary paramilitary groups with the events at the Somme rather than just with the pre-war UVF. But they can only heroicize these figures by ignoring, or forgetting, the circumstances of the various individuals' deaths. McMichael was rumoured to have been betrayed by his own organization; Robinson was killed by the RUC while lying wounded on the ground; McCrea had spent 16 of his 35 years in prison before he was shot, in front of another Somme mural, on the Shankill. These men are remembered not for the manner of their deaths but for the cause for which they fought, and in this they are proclaimed as the equals of the members of the Ulster Division. Murals commemorating the Somme emphasize the act of emulation and claim continuity with the current political situation. The sacrifice of 1916 ensured that Ulster would remain British and these murals re-assert the performative rhetoric of the parades, that such sacrifices will readily be made again.

Commemorating Easter

Mural painting is also an important part of the commemorative process among the republican community,[21] and a number of murals were painted in nationalist areas of Belfast to mark the 75th anniversary of the Rising in 1991. Although murals are more readily used by Sinn Féin as part of its political campaigns, these memorial paintings make no direct reference to the contemporary political or military campaigns of Sinn Féin and the IRA, but instead they situate the Rising historically, within a range of nationalist symbols. Foremost amongst these is the Easter lily, whose white petals, orange stamen and green leaves replicate the colours of the Irish tricolour. The flower was widely used to decorate churches at Easter time and was adopted as a commemorative emblem by the republican women's movement, Cumann na mBan, in the 1920s, thereby mirroring the use of the red poppy as a symbol of Britain's war dead.[22] Apart from the lily the most important symbols of the Rising are the leaders themselves. One painting in Unity Flats depicted a lily besides the portraits of Padraig Pearse and James Connolly, while the memorial in the Ardoyne surrounds the lily with the portraits of each of the seven signatories to the Proclamation of Independence. The most elaborate of these murals, on Whiterock Road, situates the leader of the Rising among a range of symbols that more clearly embrace the history of the Irish rebel tradition. Connolly, Pearse and Tom Clarke (the socialist, the romantic nationalist and the Fenian revolutionary respectively) are the dominant portraits. Behind them the date '1916' appears in huge flaming red and yellow figures, while the GPO burns in the corner. Within the apex of the gable are a sunburst, a starry plough and a phoenix rising from the flames, symbols that link the Rising with the 19th century Fenians, with the nationalist heroes of the 18th century: Wolf Tone and the United Irishmen, and even the earlier Volunteer movement. The Fenian phoenix, rising from the ashes of defeat, has in turn come to symbolize the historical inevitability of the current IRA campaign, as successor to the partial victory won at Easter 1916.

Although armed IRA volunteers are depicted on a large number of murals, it is rare for them to be portrayed in conjunction with a reference to events of 1916. The importance of that year must be understood through the heroes of the past. The paintings lionize the founding fathers of the modern Irish republic so that memory of the Rising exists as an idealized memory of heroism, but the connection with the contemporary violence is always left implicit. As the formative event in the emergence of the Irish state, however, the partial success of the Rising serves to legitimize the use of violence in the pursuit of political ends, while emphasizing the noble ideals behind the contemporary campaign. The focus on the murals is less on the achievement, the effects, or the events of Easter, than its aspirations; on its symbolic, rather than empirical, qualities. The signatories to the declaration are recalled not as individuals but as the embodiment of an ideal, as representatives of the martyred dead of Ireland. This process continues through the figure of Bobby Sands, who since his death in the 1981 hunger strikes, has been admitted to the broad pantheon of republican heroes. He now appears on the walls as a contemporary representative of the wider tradition of voluntary sacrifice, as a symbol, rather than simply as an iconic representation of himself. Sacrificed to the ideal of Irish independence these men signify the 'dead generations' who fought and died for Ireland, and in whose name the IRA have claimed their right to take up arms.

Figure 28 Mural to the 1916 Easter Rising, painted for the 75th anniversary, Whiterock Road, West Belfast. The figures are the seven signatories to the Proclamation of Independence plus (second from right) Countess Markievicz, Sinn Féin member and first woman elected as an MP to Westminster, in 1918.

The murals may act as a reminder to the people of west Belfast throughout the year, but the anniversary of the event is the occasion for a more explicit and extensive commemoration across nationalist Ireland.[23] Each year many parades are held throughout Ireland over the Easter weekend, with one of the largest being held in Belfast. Nationalist parades have never been as numerous as Orange parades in Northern Ireland, they have never been welcomed by the state and have been largely restricted to areas defined as nationalist.[24] The main Belfast commemoration, organized by the republican movement, is held on the Falls Road on Easter Sunday. Supporters assemble at Beechmount Avenue for the parade to Milltown cemetery, following the route they have used for some 50 years. Green, white and orange bunting decorates the area, but the main visual impact is made by a large mural depicting a manacled hand clenching an Easter lily over a map of Ireland, above it a phoenix rises from a flaming GPO, while in the corners are the heraldic shields of the four provinces of Ireland. A small plaque commemorates local IRA volunteers who have died in the troubles while on the wall to the back yard of the house are the (unacknowledged) words that Padraig Pearse spoke at the funeral of O'Donovan Rossa in Dublin in 1915:

> The fools, the fools,
> they have left us our Fenian dead,
> and while Ireland holds these graves,
> Ireland unfree shall never be at peace.

The parade itself, involves a walk of about a mile to the republican plot at Milltown. The colour party carries a range of flags: the Irish tricolour is followed by Connolly's Starry Plough, the sunburst flag of the Fianna, the republican youth wing, and a blue flag with a gold trim bearing the words *Oglaigh na hÉireann* (the Irish name of the IRA) and finally the flags of the four provinces. No other flags or banners are carried on the parade. The colour party are followed by a band and a number of others march within the body of the procession.[25] In the cemetery a small platform is erected, for the speakers, in front of the County Antrim Memorial, which lists IRA and Sinn Féin members who have been killed since 1916. It also remembers those killed in the United Irishman rebellion of 1798, in Robert Emmett's rising of 1803, and the Fenians of 1867. The commemoration begins with a reading Proclamation of Independence, and a decade of the Rosary, wreaths are then laid on behalf of Sinn Féin, the IRA, republican prisoners, the Gaelic Athletic Association and the National Graves Association. Just as the Rising was an explicitly political act, however, so the commemoration is used as a platform for political rhetoric. In recent years Sinn Féin leaders have used the platform to reiterate their desire for peace, while each year the IRA convey their message that they are ready, and willing, to continue the armed struggle. The commemoration comes to a close as all flags are lowered to half-mast while a single piper plays a lament. In the same way as the Somme parades are used to remember all those who have fought and died for Ulster, so the Easter commemoration honours all those who have fought and died for Ireland.

As the Sinn Féin supporters drift home, supporters of the Workers Party make their way along the Falls Road for their own commemoration in Milltown. Despite numerous moves to distance themselves from their origins, in the IRA schism of 1969, the Workers Party still claim their right to the inheritance of 1916 and hold a similar style of parade to their plot in the cemetery. (The smaller republican groupings, Republican Sinn Féin and the Irish Republican Socialist Party, usually gather at the cemetery earlier in the day, but do not parade.) Although their parade is a much smaller affair, the Workers Party follow the same array of flags as Sinn Féin, lacking only the *Oglaigh na hÉireann* flag, and their ceremony includes a similar mixture of acts of remembrance and political rhetoric. While the Orange Order has managed to retain the diverse loyalist groupings within a single commemorative event, the nationalist movement has tended to fragment. As one section of the republican movement votes to compromise and work within a political framework, another group has always been ready to claim the inheritance of the armed struggle and the right to transform the system through violence. As can be seen with the Workers Party, however, it has proved more difficult to reject the symbolism of Irish nationalism than the tactics, and consequently even conservative groups must still acknowledge the powerful presence of the armed struggle in Irish history.

Neither of the conservative, constitutional nationalist parading bodies, the Ancient Order of Hibernians and the Irish National Foresters (INF) publicly commemorate the Easter Rising. Until the late 1960s the INF paraded alongside the Gaelic Athletic Association, the Trades Council, trade union groups and numerous nationalist clubs at Easter, but by the early 1970s they had abandoned the day to the supporters of the Provisional and the Official IRA. However, there are still references to the event on the banners that they carry on St Patrick's Day and other occasions. One Hibernian banner shows Daniel O'Connell presenting the maid of Erin with a document labelled 'Catholic Emancipation' while he is overseen from the four corners by Pearse, Connolly, Clarke and McDonagh, and the Foresters still parade banners featuring Padraig Pearse and Roger Casement. Amidst the portraits of saints, Popes, early Irish heroes and nineteenth-century constitutional politicians, the Rising retains a foothold for the military tradition within all fractions of the nationalist movement.

Parading Difference

Orange and Green show a broad similarity in their use of public parades for commemorative events, but there is a substantial difference between the structure and form of the parade in each community. In contrast to the military-style presentation of unionist events, and the rigid separation of participants and spectators and the division of participants into distinct, independent groups, republican parades are much more open affairs. There is little formality, no structured dress code and no separation by gender or age. Anyone can participate in a republican parade, people walk as individuals, as supporters of a common ideal, rather than as part of a formal group. Although both commemorations include brash military-style bands, republican parades do not move with the same militarized step as the loyalists, they have a more relaxed, informal air about them. The crowd that follows the colour party includes large numbers of women and girls (and even babies in prams), who are excluded from participating in Orange parades. While Orange parades are essentially triumphal expressions of a collective determination, a celebration of strength in unity and brotherhood, republicans commemorate the continued resolve in defeat, the determination to carry on the fight. The followers mourn the dead, draw strength from their sacrifice and assert that their heroes have not died in vain. This suggests something of the two historical traditions that are being drawn on in the contemporary commemorative practices: the optimistic march to war, and the more solemn funeral parade.

The loyalist style of parading, and those of the Hibernians and Foresters, can be traced to the paramilitary traditions of the eighteenth century Volunteer movement, customs that were formalized and redefined, in the combative sectarian politics of the nineteenth century, to emphasize the power and unity of the community. Republican commemorations draw heavily on the tradition of the funeral procession, which dates from the same era – Ribbonmen and Freemasons paraded in large numbers to funerals in the early nineteenth century – but this practice has a less readily documented history.[26] Funerals and memorials to well-known political figures have often been turned into major public events and have mobilized the Catholic population more readily than simple commemorative parades. The return of the body of the exiled Young Irelander T. B. McManus, in 1861, provoked a mass demonstration of patriotism, in stark contrast to the lack of support for their attempted rebellion in 1848; half a century later the political mobilization of nationalists for the funeral of O'Donovan Rossa, in August 1915, enabled Pearse and the Irish Volunteers to lay public claim to the inheritance of the Fenian tradition. In the aftermath of the Rising, the funerals of hunger strikers Thomas Ashe and Terence MacSwiney provoked major displays of support for the republican cause. Over 30,000 people followed Ashe's coffin through Dublin.[27] This tradition has subsequently been extended to IRA funerals. Bobby Sands' funeral procession, in 1981, was probably the biggest demonstration of support and sympathy for republicanism in recent times. Honouring the fallen hero has been the most consistent means of mobilizing public support. It is this practice that underlies the Easter commemorations in Belfast. In contrast to the celebratory commemoration of a military victory that structures loyalist parades, the republican movement mourns its dead: of Easter, of Bloody Sunday and of the hunger strikes.

While drawing on entwined traditions of commemorative ritual, current practices serve to emphasize two opposing senses of communal identity and destiny, which are grounded in an essentialism, exclusiveness and sense of difference, that is ultimately based on religion. The Somme commemorations assert that Ulster is both Protestant and British: Catholics are excluded from the process, as Catholics, as the loyal orders remain exclusively Protestant. While the Easter parades are theoretically open to anyone, in practice they are scarcely less exclusive than Somme parades. In a society where every aspect of life is potentially indicative of one or the other community, the structure and form of the Easter commemorations indicate a distinctly Catholic activity. The location and timing as well as the more obvious religious symbols of the commemoration (lily, rosary) enhance the identification with a religious anniversary. The religious sense of Easter is also connoted in the name – not rebellion, revolution nor even uprising, simply 'The Rising'. Its timing coincides annually with Christ's death and resurrection, since the event is commemorated as part of the Christian calendar, rather than on 24 April, as part of the secular calendar. This conjunction substantiates the performative rhetoric of the commemorations by drawing on long-standing and deeply felt religious codes for legitimacy.

Easter is commemorated through the individuals who signed the Proclamation of Independence, who were executed as martyrs to the cause of Ireland and who today are honoured as vainly concealed, secularized modern-day saints. Republican murals devoted to the hunger strikes drew quite clearly on religious iconography, and in particular Pieta-type imagery when depicting the plight of the men in the H Blocks. The personal suffering and sacrifice of these individuals gives them the moral authority and the leadership of the community of followers. In contrast, the loyalist commemoration of the Somme is enacted through remembering and honouring the community of individuals involved. Although occasional references are made to the Ulster Protestant soldiers who received the Victoria Cross during the First World War, essentially the event is viewed as a collective sacrifice. Immediately after the war some Protestant leaders were celebrated above others – Carson is still widely lionized – but other figures of this era receive scant recognition nowadays. Individuals who fought and died may be remembered locally on lodge banners, but, as with the numerous Orange worthies, they are no more than first amongst equals. Protestant authority remains invested in the community of the faithful, collectively.

Forgetting 1916

I have been trying to draw out something of the similarities and differences between the two commemorative practices. These are rooted both in a common ground and in two distinct pasts. A shared history is used and reworked to enhance the identity of each community, but also to mark it as emphatically different from the other; they mirror each other and gain internal strength from their mutual opposition. The broad view of these commemorative practices can be used to emphasize the similarity of such features as the parades, music and visual displays, whereas many of the details serve to stress the distinctiveness of two identities rooted in opposing religious and political ideals.

The events of 1916 are commemorated in a way that builds on, and strengthens, existing concepts of Protestant/unionist and Catholic/nationalist identities. No less an important aspect of public commemorations are those inconvenient features of the past that do not substantiate the preferred reading, those events and details that contradict widely held assumptions or at least provoke awkward questions, and thereby, rub against the grain of both official, and popular, understanding and memory. These are the events, or facts, of history that are written out of the dominant literature, erased from public commemorations and forgotten by popular memory. Ireland is no different from other countries in this manner. The importance in stressing the Catholic nationalism of Ireland or the loyal Protestantism of Ulster, is to maintain an entrenched resolve behind the barricades of an essential identity. This has meant that more emphasis has been placed on the apparent differences between the two communities rather than exploring what exists of a shared past.

The Rising and the Somme are important in so far as they emphasize the irreconcilably different aspirations of Protestants and Catholics. However when one considers some of the ignored facts about the war years the simple symmetry of the polarization is difficult to sustain. On

20 September 1914, just two days after the Home Rule Bill had become an Act of Parliament, John Redmond, leader of the Irish Party and the nationalist Irish Volunteers, encouraged his organization's 170,000 members to support the war effort. The 10th and 16th Divisions were recruited from the nationalist population and sent to England for training. Ulster Catholics volunteered in proportionately equal numbers to Protestants in 1915, and by the autumn of that year, over 80,000 Irishmen had volunteered for the British Army. Some 27,000 were members of the Ulster Volunteers and a similar number were members of the Irish Volunteers. Only a minority of the membership of either the Ulster Volunteers or the Irish Volunteers ever joined up, but altogether over 200,000 Irishmen enlisted in the British forces during the war. Among them seventeen Catholic Irishmen won Victoria Crosses in the first fifteen months of the war.[28]

However in Ireland the war is largely regarded as a unionist commemoration. Some memorials were erected in the south but not with the public prominence they received in the north,[29] and only with the distance of time has official recognition been more easily given.[30] The events of Easter 1916 have eclipsed the nationalist and Catholic contribution to the Great War. Their remembrance would undermine the unity drawn around the independent Irish state and obscure the clarity of the sense of distinction between Britain and Ireland. In contrast, the sanctity of the memory of Easter 1916 is such that Charles Haughey's Government provoked outrage among republicans when the official seventy fifth Anniversary commemorations of the Rising were reduced to a minimal level. This reaction ignores the fact that support for the republican cause only became substantial after the defeat of the Rising; and in the north, republicans were largely unimpressed with Dublin's plans for their role in the Rising and did nothing. After the war Catholic Belfast still remained supporters of the constitutional nationalist position.[31]

But the nationalist contribution to the war is no less an inconvenience for the loyalists, who would ideally include all Catholics within the rebel camp, and portray themselves as the paragons of loyalty. This position, which emphasizes their sacrifices of 1916, allows them to forget or ignore the uncomfortable facts of 1914. To forget that in the weeks preceding the war, while the Irish Party was working through Parliament for Home Rule, loyalists had been on the verge of an armed rebellion against the Government; that they were unwilling to accept the will of the democratic majority in Parliament; that they had imported arms from Germany to support their effort; and that they had provoked a mutiny amongst the British army officers in Ireland in support of their cause. The Protestant tradition of opposing locally unpopular, Government decisions by the threat of armed rebellion is scarcely less extensive than that of the nationalist community, but their opposition has always been clouded by fervent expressions of loyalty.

Social memories do not draw on some unquestioned mass of empirical facts, rather are the product of a sifting through the confusion of the past for evidence that serves to substantiate existing beliefs. Public commemorations help convert those selective details into unquestionable history. In Ireland, popular memory, sustained and extended by annual parades and extensive visual *aides-memoire*, forgets these awkward, grey areas that point towards the common ground, and mutually sustains the social truth of irreconcilable difference and antagonism between Protestant and Catholic.

Notes

1. L. Coser, 'Introduction' to M. Halbwachs, *On Collective Memory*, Chicago, University of Chicago Press, 1992, p. 24.
2. P. Connerton, *How Societies Remember*, Cambridge, Cambridge University Press, 1989.
3. F. Yates, *The Art of Memory*, London, Routledge & Kegan Paul, 1966.
4. M. Carruthers, *The Book of Memory: a Study of Memory in Medieval Culture*, Cambridge, Cambridge University Press, 1990; S. Küchler and Melion, W. (eds), *Images of Memory: On Remembering and Representation*, Washington, Smithsonian Institute Press, 1991; N. Jarman, *Material Conflicts: Parades and Visual Displays in Northern Ireland*, Oxford, Berg, 1997.
5. E. Gombrich, *Art and Illusion: a Study in the Psychology of Pictorial Representation*, Oxford, Phaidon, 1980.
6. N. Jarman and D. Bryan, *Parade and Protest: a Discussion of Parading Disputes in Northern Ireland*, Coleraine, Centre for the Study of Conflict, 1996.
7. Jarman, *Material Conflicts*.
8. D. Bryan, 'Ritual, "Tradition" and Control: the Politics of Orange Parades in Northern Ireland', PhD. thesis, University of Ulster, Coleraine, 1996.
9. J. Sheehy, *The Rediscovery of Ireland's Past*, London, Thames & Hudson, 1980.

10. T. Hennessey, 'Ulster Unionist Territorial and National Identities 1886–1893: Province, Island, Kingdom and Empire', *Irish Political Studies* 8 (1993), pp. 21–36; A. Jackson, 'Irish Unionist Imagery, 1850–1920', in E. Patten (ed.), *Returning to Ourselves: the Second Volume of Papers from the John Hewitt International Summer School*, Belfast, Lagan Press, 1995.
11. J. Bardon, *A History of Ulster*, Belfast, Blackstaff Press, 1992.
12. B. Bushaway, 'Name Upon Name: the Great War and Remembrance', in R. Porter (ed.), *Myths of the English*, Cambridge, Polity Press, 1992; K. Jeffrey, 'The Great War in Modern Irish Memory', in T. G. F. Fraser and K. Jeffrey (eds), *Men, Women and War*, Dublin, Lilliput Press, 1993; J. Leonard, '"Lest We Forget": Irish War Memorials', in D. Fitzpatrick (ed.), *Ireland and the First World War*, Dublin, Lilliput Press and Trinity History Workshop, 1988.
13. R. Ryan et al., 'Commemorating 1916', *Retrospect* (1984), pp. 59–62.
14. N. Jarman and D. Bryan, 'Green Parades in an Orange State: Nationalist Parades in Northern Ireland', in T. G. F. Fraser (ed.), *We'll Follow the Drum: the Irish Parading Tradition*, Basingstoke, Macmillan, in press.
15. D. Boulton, *The UVF, 1966–73: an Anatomy of Loyalist Rebellion*, Dublin, Torc Books, 1983.
16. N. Jarman, 'Material of Culture, Fabric of Identity', in D. Miller (ed.), *Why Some Things Matter*, London, UCL Press, 1997.
17. N. Jarman, 'Troubled Images: the Iconography of Loyalism', *Critique of Anthropology* 12 (1992), pp. 133–65; Jarman, *Material Conflicts*; Jarman, 'Material of Culture'.
18. D. Bell, *Acts of Union: Youth Culture and Sectarianism in Northern Ireland*, London, Macmillan, 1990.
19. B. Rolston, *Drawing Support: Murals in the North of Ireland*, Belfast, Beyond the Pale Publications, 1992; Rolston, *Drawing Support 2: Murals of War and Peace*, Belfast, Beyond the Pale Publications, 1995; Jarman, *Material Conflicts*.
20. Bushaway, 'Name upon Name'.
21. Rolston, *Drawing Support*; Rolston, *Drawing Support 2*; Jarman, *Material Conflicts*.
22. B. Loftus, *Mirrors: Orange and Green*, Dundrum, Picture Press, 1994, p. 86.
23. Jarman, *Material Conflicts*.
24. N. Jarman 'Intersecting Belfast', in B. Bender (ed.), *Landscape, Politics and Perspectives*, Oxford, Berg, 1993; N. Jarman and D.

Bryan, *From Riots to Rights: Nationalist Parades in the North of Ireland*, Coleraine, Centre for the Study of Conflict, 1998.

25. C. de Rosa, 'Playing Nationalism', in A. D. Buckley, *Symbols in Northern Ireland*, Belfast, Institute of Irish Studies, 1998.
26. T. Garvin, *The Evolution of Irish Nationalist Politics*, Dublin, Gill and Macmillan, 1981, p. 42; Jarman, *Material Conflicts*.
27. R. Kee, *The Green Flag*, vols. 1–3, Harmondsworth, Penguin Books, 1989.
28. A. Morgan, *Labour and Partition: the Belfast Working Class 1905–1923*, London, Pluto Press, 1991.
29. Jeffrey 'The Great War in Modern Irish Memory'.
30. Leonard, '"Lest We Forget"'.
31. Morgan, *Labour and Partition.*

Bibliography

Abramson, D., 'Maya Lin and the 1960s: Monuments, Time Lines, and Minimalism', *Critical Inquiry* 22 (1996), pp. 679–709

Agulhon, M., 'La "Statuomanie" et l'histoire', *Ethnologie Française* 8 (1978), pp. 145–72.

Allemagne, H-R. d', *Les cartes à jouer du XIVe au XXe siècle*, vol. 1, Paris, Librairie Hachette, 1906.

American Institute of Graphic Arts, 'Who Owns Cultural Images: The Property Issue', *Journal of Graphic Design* 14 (1995).

Ankermann, B., *Volkerkundliche Aufzeichnungen im Grassland von Kamerun 1907–1909*, eds H. Baumann and L. Vajda, Baesseler Archiv, NF. Bd. VII/2., Basle, 1959.

Aristotle, *De Memoria et Reminiscentia*, 450b11, trans. R. Sorabji, *Aristotle on Memory*, London, Duckworth, 1972.

Argenti, N., 'The Material Culture of Power in Oku: North West Province, Cameroon', PhD. thesis, University of London, 1996.

Armanski, G., *'Und wenn wir sterben müssen': Die politische Ästhetik von Kriegerdenkmälern*, Hamburg, VSA-Verlag, 1988.

Assmann, A., and D. Harth (eds), *Kultur als Lebeswelt und Monument*, Frankfurt am Main, Fischer Taschenbuch Verlag, 1991.

Assmann, A., and D. Harth (eds), *Mnemosyne: Formen und Funktionen der kulturellen Errinnerung*, Frankfurt am Main, Fischer Taschenbuch Verlag, 1993.

Babadzan, A., *Les dépouilles des dieux: Essai sur la religion tahitienne à l'époque de la découverte*, Paris, Editions de la maison des sciences de l'homme, 1993.

Bach, M., *Studien zur Geschichte des deutschen Kriegerdenkmals in Westfalen und Lippe*, Frankfurt-am-Main, Lang, 1985.

Bachelard, G., *The Poetics of Space*, transl. M. Jolas, Boston, Beacon Press, 1969.

Bah, N. J., 'Marriage in Oku', Baesseler Archiv, Basle, in press.

Bardon, J., *A History of Ulster*, Belfast, Blackstaff Press, 1992.

Barth, F., 'The Guru and the Conjurer: Transactions in Knowledge and the Shaping of Culture in Southeast Asia and Melanesia', *Man*, (n.s) 25 (1990), pp. 640–53.

Battaglia, D., *On the Bones of the Serpent*, Chicago, University of Chicago Press, 1990.

Beckford, W., *Travel Diaries of William Beckford of Fonthill*, ed. G. Chapman, Cambridge, Constable/Houghton, 1928.

Bell, D., *Acts of Union: Youth Culture and Sectarianism in Northern Ireland*, London, Macmillan, 1990.

Belley, J-B., *Le Bout d'Oreille des Colons, ou le Système de l'Hotel de Massiac, mis au jour par Gouli*, n.d.

Benjamin, W., *Illuminations*, ed. H. Arendt, trans. H. Zohn, New York, Schocken Books, 1969.

Bénot, Y., 'Comment la Convention a t-elle voté l'abolition de l'esclavage en l'an II?', *Annales historiques de la Révolution française* 34 (1993), pp 349–62.

Berger, J., 'Ways of Remembering', *Camerawork* 10 (1978); reprinted in J. Evans (ed.) *The Camerawork Essays*, London, Rivers Oram Press, 1997.

Bergson, H., *Matter and Memory*, New York, Doubleday, 1959.

Beyer, A., '"Apparitio Operis": Vom vorübergehenden Erscheinen des Kunstwerks', in M. Diers (ed.), *Mo(nu)mente, Formen und Funktion ephemerer Denkmale*, Berlin, Akademie Verlag, 1993.

Bievre, E. de, 'The Urban Subconscious: the Art of Delft and Leiden', *Art History* 18 (1995), pp.222–52.

Bindman, D., and M. Baker, *Roubiliac and the Eighteenth Century Monument: Sculpture as Theatre*, New Haven and London, Yale University Press, 1995.

Black, J., *The British Abroad: the Grand Tour in the Eighteenth Century*, Stroud, Sutton Publishing, 1992.

Blier, S. P., *The Anatomy of Architecture: Ontology and Metaphor in Battammaliba Architectural Expression*, New York, Cambridge University Press, 1987.

Bloch, M., *Prey into Hunter: the politics of religious experience*, Cambridge, Cambridge University Press, 1992.

——, and J. Parry, *Death and the Regeneration of Life*, Cambridge, Cambridge University Press, 1982.

Bodnar, J., *Remaking America: Public Memory, Commemoration, and Patriotism in the Twentieth Century*, Princeton, Princeton University Press, 1992.

Bogue, R., *Deleuze and Guattari*, London, Routledge, 1990.

Boulton, D., *The UVF, 1966–73: an Anatomy of Loyalist Rebellion*, Dublin, Torc Books, 1983.

Bourdieu, P., *Outline of a Theory of Practice*, Cambridge, Cambridge

University Press, 1977.
——, *Distinction: A Social Critique of the Judgement of Taste*, London, Routledge, 1984 (1979).
Bracco, R. M., *Merchants of Hope: British Middlebrow Writers and the First World War, 1919–1939*, Oxford, Berg, 1993.
Bredekamp, H., 'Der simalierte Benjamin: Mittelalterliche Bemerkungen zu seiner Aktualität', in A. Berndt, P. Kaiser, A. Rosenberg, and D. Trinkner (eds), *Frankfurter Schule und Kunstgeschichte*, Berlin, Dietrich Reiner Verlag, 1992.
Brilliant, R., *Portraiture*, London, Reaktion Books, 1991.
Broughton, Rt. Hon Lord [J. C. Hobhouse], *Italy, remarks made in several visits from the Year 1816–1852*, London, John Murray, 1859.
Brown, S., 'Girodet: a Contradictory Career', PhD. thesis, University of London, 1980.
Brownell, M., *Alexander Pope and the Arts of Georgian England*, Oxford, Clarendon Press, 1978.
Bryan, D., 'Ritual, "Tradition" and Control: the Politics of Orange Parades in Northern Ireland', PhD. thesis, University of Ulster, Coleraine, 1996.
Burkert, W., *Homo Necans: the Anthropology of Ancient Greek Sacrificial Ritual and Myth*, Berkeley, University of California Press, 1983.
Bushaway, B., 'Name Upon Name: the Great War and Remembrance', in R. Porter (ed.), *Myths of the English*, Cambridge, Polity Press, 1992.
Carmichael, D., J. Hubert, B. Reeves, and A. Schanche, *Sacred Sites, Sacred Places*, London, Routledge, 1994.
Carruthers, M., *The Book of Memory: a Study of Memory in Medieval Culture*, Cambridge, Cambridge University Press, 1990.
Casey, E. S., *Remembering: a Phenomenological Study*, Bloomington and Indianapolis, Indiana University Press, 1987.
Certeau, M. de, *The Practice of Everyday Life*, trans. S. Rendall, Berkeley, University of California Press, 1984.
Chateaubriand, F. R. de, *Génie du Christianisme,* ed. M. Regard, Paris, Bibliothèque de la Pléiade, 1978.
Chaussard, P., *Exposition des ouvrages de peinture, scupture, architecture, gravure, dans les Salles du Muséum, premier Thermidor, an VI par Chaussard,* Collection Deloynes, XX.
Comay, R., 'Memory Block: Rachel Whiteread's Proposal for a Holocaust Memorial in Vienna', *Art and Design Profile* 55 (1997), pp. 64–75.
Connerton, P., *How Societies Remember*, Cambridge, Cambridge University Press, 1989.
Coser, L., 'Introduction' in M. Halbwachs, *On Collective Memory*, Chicago, University of Chicago Press, 1992.

Coupin, P.-A., *Oeuvres posthumes de Girodet-Trioson, peintre d'Histoire, suivies de sa correspondance, précédées d'une notice historique et mises en ordre par P.-A. Coupin*, vol. 1, Paris, Jules Renouard Librairie, 1829.

Cousins, M., 'Inside, Outside', *Tate Magazine* (Winter 1996), pp. 36–41.

Craske, M., 'The London Sculpture Trade and the Development of the Imagery of the Family in Funerary Monuments of the Period 1720–60', PhD. thesis, University of London, 1992.

Crow, T., *Emulation: Making Artists for Revolutionary France*, New Haven and London, Yale University Press, 1995.

Danto, A., 'The Vietnam Veterans Memorial', *The Nation*, 31 Aug. 1986, pp. 151–4.

Davis, S. G., *Parades and Power: Street Theatre in Nineteenth-Century Philadelphia*, Berkeley and London, University of California Press, 1988.

Debien, G., *Les colons de Saint-Domingue et la Révolution: Essai sur le Club Massiac (août 1789–août 1792)*, Paris, 1953.

Deleuze, G., *Difference and Repetition*, Paris, PUF, 1968.

——, *The Logic of Sense*, New York, Columbia University Press, 1990.

——, and F. Guattari, *A Thousand Plateaux: Capitalism and Schizophrenia*, London, Athlone Press, 1992.

Diduk, S., 'Twins, Ancestors and Socio-Economic Change in Kedjom Society', *Man* (n.s.) 28 (1993), pp. 551–71.

Diers, M. (ed.), *Mo(nu)mente, Formen und Funktion ephemerer Denkmale*, Berlin, Akademie Verlag, 1993.

Drewal, J. H., 'Performing the Other: Mami Wata worship in West Africa', *Drama Review*, 32 (1988), pp. 160–85.

Eustace, J. C., and R. C. Hoare, *A Classical Tour through Italy and Sicily*, London, Mawman, 1819.

Fardon, R., *Between God, the Dead and the Wild: Chamba Intepretations of Religion and Ritual*, Edinburgh, Edinburgh University Press, 1990.

Farington, J., *The Diary of Joseph Farington*, ed. K. Garlick and A. Macintyre, Vol. II, New Haven and London, Yale University Press, 1978.

Feeley-Harnik, G., 'Finding Memories in Madagascar', in S. Küchler and W. Melion (eds), *Images of Memory: On Remembering and Representation*, Washington D.C., Smithsonian Institution Press, 1991.

Ferretti, F., *Afo-A-Kom: Sacred Art of the Cameroon*, New York, Third Press, 1975.

Forster, K. W., 'Monument/Memory and the Mortality of Architecture', *Oppositions* 25 (1982), pp. 2–19.

Forsyth, J., *On Antiquities, Arts and Letters in Italy*, London, John Murray, 1835.

Freud, S, 'Mourning and Melancholia' in *Standard Edition*, vol. 14, London, Hogarth Press, 1957.

——, *Case Histories*: 'Lucy R.', in *Standard Edition*, trans. J. Strachey, vol. 2, London, Hogarth Press, 1960.

——, *The Psychopathology of Everyday Life*, in *Standard Edition*, vol 6, London, Hogarth Press, 1960.

——, *Civilization and Its Discontents*, trans. J. Riviere, London, Hogarth Press, 1969.

——, *The Interpretation of Dreams*, Harmondsworth, Penguin Books, 1976.

Frossard, B. S., *La Cause des esclaves nègres et des habitans de la Guinée, portée au Tribunal de la Justice, de la Religion, de la Politique*, Geneva, Slatkine Reprints, re-impression of edition de Lyon, 1789.

Garvin, T., *The Evolution of Irish Nationalist Politics*, Dublin, Gill & Macmillan, 1981.

Gauthier, F., *Triomphe et Mort du Droit Naturel en Révolution*, Paris, Presses Universitaires de France, 1992.

Geary, C., *Things of the Palace*, Paideuma: Studien zur Kulturkunde 60, trans. Kathleen Holan, Wiesbaden, Franz Steiner Verlag, 1983.

Gebauer, P., 'Architecture of Cameroon', *African Arts* 5 (1971), pp. 41–9.

Gell, A., *Metamorphosis of the Cassowaries: Umeda Society, Language and Ritual*, University of London Monographs on Social Anthropology, London, Athlone Press, 1975.

——, 'Technology and Magic', *Anthropology Today*, 4 (1988), pp. 6–9.

——, 'The Technology of Enchantment and the Enchantment of Technology', in J. Coot and A. Shelton (eds), *Anthropology, Art and Aesthetics*, Oxford, Clarendon Press, 1992.

——, 'Vogels Net: Traps as Artworks and Artworks as Traps', *Journal of Material Culture* 1 (1996) pp. 5–11.

Gibbs, P., *Realities of War*, London, William Heinemann, 1920.

Gillis, J. R. (ed.), *Commemorations: the Politics of National Identity*, Princeton, Princeton University Press, 1994.

Ginzburg, C., 'Repräsentation: das Wort, die Vorstellung, der Gegenstand', *Freibeuter* 22 (1991), pp. 3–23.

Girard, R., *Violence and the Sacred*, Baltimore, Johns Hopkins University Press, 1977.

Giroud, J., *Les monuments aux morts dans le Vaucluse*, L'Isle sur Sorgue, Editions Scriba, 1991.

Goethe, J. W. von, *The Italian Journey*, trans. R. Heiter, Princeton, Princeton University Press, 1994.

Goldsmith, O., *A Citizen of the World*, London, 1761.

Gombrich, E., *Art and Illusion: a Study in the Psychology of Pictorial Representaion*, Oxford, Phaidon, 1980.

Greenfield, V., 'Making Do or Making Art? A Cognitive- Behavioral Study of Recyclers, Material Transformations, and the Creative Process', PhD. thesis, University of California, Los Angeles, 1984.

Gregory, A., *The Silence of Memory: Armistice Day 1919–1946*, Oxford, Berg, 1994.

Griswold, C. L., 'The Vietnam Veterans memorial and the Washington Mall: Political Thoughts on Political Iconography', *Critical Inquiry* 12 (1986), pp. 688–719.

Guidieri, R., and F. Pellizi, 'Nineteen Tableaux on the Cult of the Dead in Malekula, Eastern Melanesia', *Res* 2 (1981), pp. 1–86.

Halliday, A. S., 'French Portraiture under the Directory and the Consulat', PhD. thesis, University of London, 1996.

Handbook for travellers in Central Italy, Murray, 1843

Hare, A., *Walks in Rome*, London, Strahan, 1871.

Harrison, S., *Stealing People's Names: History and Politics in Sepik River Cosmology*, Cambridge Studies in Social and Cultural Anthropolgy 71, Cambridge and New York, Cambridge University Press, 1990.

——, 'Intellectual Property and Ritual Culture', *Man* (n.s.) 21 (1991), pp. 435–56.

——, 'The Commerce of Cultures in Melanesia', *Man* (n.s.) 28 (1993), pp. 139–58.

——, 'Anthropological Perspectives on the Management of Knowledge', *Anthropology Today* 11 (1995), pp. 10–14.

Hazlitt, W., *The Complete Works of William Hazlitt: Notes on a Journey through France and Italy*, ed. P. P. Howe, London, Dent & Sons, 1932.

Heidegger, M., *Being and Time*, trans. J. Macquarrie and E. Robinson, New York, Harper & Row, 1962.

——, 'The Question Concerning Technology', in Heidegger, *The Question Concerning Technology and Other Essays*, New York, Harper & Row, 1977.

Hennessey, T., 'Ulster Unionist Territorial and National Identities 1886–1893: Province, Island, Kingdom and Empire', *Irish Political Studies* 8 (1993), pp. 21–36.

Hervey, J., *Meditations Among the Tombs*, London, 1796.

Heusch, L. de, *The Drunken King: or the Origin of the State*, Bloomington, Indiana University Press, 1982.

——, *Sacrifice in Africa*, Cambridge, Cambridge University Press, 1986.

Honour, H., *The Image of the Black in Western Art, 4: From the American Revolution to World War 1,* Part 1, Cambridge MA., Harvard University Press, 1989.

Howkins, A., *Poor Labouring Men: Rural Radicalism in Norfolk, 1872–1923*, London, Routledge & Kegan Paul, 1985.

Hubert, H. and M. Mauss, *Sacrifice: Its Nature and Function*, London, Cohen & West, 1964.

Hubert, N., 'Musées de Malmaison et de Bois-Préau. Nouvelles Acquisitions: Peintures, Miniatures, Gravures', *La Revue du Louvre et des Musées de France* 3 (1986), pp. 210–15.

Jackson, A., 'Irish Unionist Imagery, 1850–1920', in E. Patten (ed.), *Returning to Ourselves: the Second Volume of Papers from the John Hewitt International Summer School*, Belfast, Lagan Press, 1995.

Jarman, N., 'Troubled Images: the Iconography of Loyalism', *Critique of Anthropology* 12 (1992), pp. 133–65.

——, 'Intersecting Belfast', in B. Bender (ed.), *Landscape, Politics and Perspectives*, Oxford, Berg, 1993.

——, *Material Conflicts: Parades and Visual Displays in Northern Ireland*, Oxford, Berg, 1997.

——, 'Material of Culture, Fabric of Identity', in D. Miller (ed.), *Why Some Things Matter*, London, UCL Press, 1997.

——, and Bryan, D., *Parade and Protest: a Discussion of Parading Disputes in Northern Ireland*, Coleraine, Centre for the Study of Conflict, 1996.

——, and Bryan, D., 'Parading Culture, Protesting Triumphalism: Social Policy and Anthropology', in H. Donnan and G. Macfarlane (eds), *Culture and Policy in Northern Ireland*, Belfast, Institute of Irish Studies, 1997.

——, and Bryan, D., *From Riots to Rights: Nationalist Parades in the North of Ireland*, Coleraine, Centre for the Study of Conflict, 1998.

——, and Bryan, D.,'Green Parades in an Orange State: Nationalist Parades in Northern Ireland', in T. G. F. Fraser (ed.), *We'll Follow the Drum: the Irish Parading Tradition*, Basingstoke, Macmillan, in press.

Jeffrey, K., 'The Great War in Modern Irish Memory', in T. G. F. Fraser and K. Jeffrey (eds), *Men, Women and War*, Dublin, Lilliput Press, 1993.

Jeffreys, M. D. W., 'Snake Stones', *Journal of the Royal African Society* (Oct. 1942), p. 250.

——, 'Serpents=Kings', *Nigerian Field* 12 (1947), pp. 35–41.

Jolly, W. P., *Lord Leverhulme*, London, Constable, 1976.

Judenplatz Wien 1996. Competition Monument and Memorial Site dedicated to the Jewish victims of the Nazi Regime in Austria 1938–1945, Vienna, Folio, Stadt Wien, Kunsthalle Wien, 1996.

Kantorowicz, E. H., *The King's Two Bodies, A Study in Mediaeval Political Theology*, Princeton, Princeton University Press, 1957.

Kapferer, B., *Legends of People, Myths of State*, Washington D.C., Smithsonian Institution Press, 1988.

Kee, R., *The Most Distressful Country: the Green Flag*, vol. 1, Harmondsworth, Penguin Books, 1989.

——, *The Bold Fenian Men: the Green Flag*, vol. 2, Harmondsworth, Penguin Books, 1989.

——, *Ourselves Alone: the Green Flag*, vol. 3, Harmondsworth, Penguin Books, 1989.

King, A., 'Acts and Monuments: National Celebrations in Britain from the Napoleonic to the Great War', in A. O'Day (ed.), *Government and Institutions in the Post-1832 United Kingdom*, Lewiston and Lampeter, Mellen, 1995.

Kooijman, S., *Art, Art Objects and Ritual in the Mimika Culture*, Mededelingen van het Rijksmuseum voor Volkenkunde, Leiden, 24, Leiden, E. J. Brill, 1984.

Koos, M., (ed), *Begleitmaterial zur Ausstellung 'Mnemosyne'*, Hamburg, Doling und Galitz Verlag Gmbh, 1992.

Koselleck, R., 'Kriegerdenkmäle als Identitätsstiftung der Überlebenden', in O. Marquard and K. Stierle (eds), *Identität*, Munich, Fink, 1979.

Kramer, F., *The Red Fez*, London, Verso, 1993.

Kratz, C. A., 'Rethinking Recyclia', *African Arts* 1 (1995), pp. 7–12.

Krauss, R., *The Originality of the Avant Garde*, Cambridge MA., MIT Press, 1986.

Küchler, S., 'Malangan: Art and Memory in a Melanesian Society', *Man* (n.s.) 22 (1987), pp. 238–55.

——, 'Malangan: Objects, Sacrifice and the Production of Memory', *American Ethnologist* 15 (1988), pp. 625–37.

——, 'Landscape as Memory: the Mapping of Process and its Representation in Melanesian Society', in B. Bender (ed.), *Landscape: Politics and Perspectives*, Oxford, Berg, 1993.

——, 'Sacrificial Economy and its Objects: Ethnographic Collection Reconsidered', *Journal of Material Culture* 2 (1997), pp. 39–60.

——, and Melion, W. (eds), *Images of Memory: On Remembering and Representation*, Washington D.C., Smithsonian Institute Press, 1991.

Kundera, M., *The Book of Laughter and Forgetting*, trans. A. Asher, New York, Harper Perennial, 1996.

Kuscinski, A., *Les Députés au Corps législatif, Conseil des Cinq-Cents, Conseil des Anciens de l'an V à l'an VI*, Paris, Au Siège de la Société, 1905.

Laqueur, T., 'Memory and Naming in the Great War', in J. R. Gillis (ed.), *Commemorations: The Politics of National Identity*, Princeton, Princeton University Press, 1994.

——, 'The Past's Past', *London Review of Books,* vol. 18, no. 18 (1996), pp. 3–7.

Lebeuf, J.-P., *L'Habitation des Fali*, Paris, Librairie Hachette, 1961.

Lemprun, J., *Literature or Life*, London, Viking, 1998.

Leonard, J. '"Lest We Forget": Irish War Memorials', in D. Fitzpatrick (ed.), *Ireland and the First World War*, Dublin, Lilliput Press and Trinity History Workshop, 1988.

——, 'The Twinge of Memory: Armistice day and Remembrance Sunday in Dublin Since 1919', in R. English and G. Walker (eds), *Unionism in Modern Ireland: New Perspectives on Politics and Culture*, Basingstoke, Macmillan, 1996.

Lerner, J. C., 'Changes in Attitudes Toward Death: The Widow in Great Britain in the Early Twentieth Century', in B. Schoenberg, I. Gerber, A. Wiener, A. H. Kutscher, D. Peretz and A. C. Carr (eds), *Bereavement: Its Psychosocial Aspects*, New York, Columbia University Press, 1975.

Levesque, C., *Journey through Landscape in Seventeenth-Century Holland: the Haarlem Print Series and Dutch Identity*, University Park PA, Pennsylvania State University Press, 1994.

Lewis, M., 'What is to be Done', in A. and M. Kroker (eds.), *Ideology and Power in the Age of Lenin in Ruins*, New York, St Martins Press, 1991.

——, and Mulvey, L. (directors) *Disgraced Monuments*, 1992. Script published in *Pix* 2 (1997), pp. 102–11.

Libeskind, D., lecture at the Bartlett, University College London, Feb. 1998.

Lipp, W. (ed.), *Denkmal-Werte-Gesellschaft: Zur Pluralität des Denkmalbegriffs*, Frankfurt am Main and New York, Campus Verlag, 1993.

Loftus, B., *Mirrors: Orange and Green*, Dundrum, Picture Press, 1994.

Lowenthal, D., 'Memory and Oblivion', *Museum Management and Curatorship* 12 (1993), pp. 171–82.

——, *The Heritage Crusade and the Spoils of History*, London, Viking, 1997.

Luria, A. R., *The Mind of a Mnemonist*, Cambridge MA, Harvard University Press, 1987.

MacDonald, R. R., *The Burial-Places of Memory: Epic Underworlds in Virgil, Dante and Milton*, Amherst, University of Massachusetts Press, 1987.

Mai, E., and G. Schmirber (eds), *Denkmal-Zeichen-Monument: Skulptur und Öffentlicher Raum heute*, München, Prestel Verlag, 1989.

Maier, C. S., *The Unmasterable Past: History, Holocaust and German National Identity*, Cambridge MA, Harvard University Press, 1988.

Mansfield, N., 'Class conflict and Village War Memorials, 1914–1924', *Rural History* 6 (1995), pp. 67–87.

Mathieu-Meusnier, A., *Archives de l'Art Français*, 2e série, I. (1861).

Michel, R., *Aux Armes et Aux Arts! Les Arts de la Révolution 1789 – 1799*, Paris, Editions Adam Biro, 1988.

Miller, Lady A., *Letters from Italy describing the Manners, Customs and Antiquities &c of the Country in the Years MDCCLXX and MDCCLXXI*, vol.III, London, Edward & Charles Dilly, 1776.

Morgan, A., *Labour and Partition: the Belfast Working Class 1905–1923*, London, Pluto Press, 1991.

Moriarty, C., 'The Absent Dead and Figurative First World War Memorials', *Transactions of the Ancient Monument Society* 39 (1995), pp. 7–40.

Mortier, R., *La poétique des ruines en France: ses origines, ses variations, de la Renaissance à Victor Hugo*, Histoire des Idées et Critique Littéraire 144, Genève, Droz, 1974.

Mosse, G. L., *Fallen Soldiers: Reshaping the Memory of the First World War*, Oxford, Oxford University Press, 1990.

Napier, D., *Masks: Transformation and Paradox*, Berkeley, University of California Press, 1986.

Neisser, U., *Cognition and Reality*, San Francisco, Freeman, 1976.

Nonis, M., and M. Epstein, 'Piranesi's "Thoughts on Architecture"', *Oppositions* 26 (1984), pp. 6–25.

Oakeshott, M., *Rationalism in Politics*, London, Methuen, 1962

Okri, B., *Astonishing the Gods*, London, Phoenix House, 1995.

Pausanius, *Guide to Greece*, vol. 1, trans. P. Levi, Harmondsworth, Penguin Books, 1971.

Penny, N., *Church Monuments in Romantic England*, London, Yale University Press, 1978.

Perec, G., *Species of Spaces and Other Pieces*, trans. J. Sturrock, London, Penguin Books, 1997.

Petit, P., 'Les Charmes du Roi Sont les Esprits des Morts: Les Fondements Religieux de la Royauté Sacrée Chez les Luba du Zaïre', *Africa* 66 (1996), pp. 349–66.

Piranesi, G. B.: *Giovani Battista Piranesi: Drawings and Etchings at Columbia University*, New York, Columbia University, 1972.

Potts, A., Review of D. Bindman and M. Baker, *Roubiliac and the Eighteenth Century Monument: Sculpture as Theatre*, in *Burlington Magazine* 139 (1997), pp. 879–81.

Prévost, M., and Roman d'Amat, C., *Dictionnaire de biographie française*, vol. V, Paris, Letouzey et Ané, 1951.

Proust, M., *Swann's Way*, trans. C. P. Scott-Moncrieff, London, Chatto & Windus, 1922.

Raynal, G.-T., *Histoire philosophique et politique des établissments et du commerce des Européens dans les deux Indes*, vol. IV, The Hague, Gosse fils, 1774.

Riegl, A., 'The Modern Cult of Monuments: Its Character and Its Origin', trans. K. Forster and D. Ghirardo, *Oppositions* 25 (1982), pp. 21–51.

Robert, A., E. Bourloton, and G. Cougny, *Dictionnaire des parlementaires français*, vol. I, Paris, Bourloton, 1891.

Rogers, S., *The Italian Journey of Samuel Rogers*, ed. J. R. Hale, Faber & Faber, London, 1956.

Rolston, B., *Drawing Support: Murals in the North of Ireland*, Belfast, Beyond the Pale Publications, 1992.

——, *Drawing Support 2: Murals of War and Peace*, Belfast, Beyond the Pale Publications, 1995.

Rosa, C. de, 'Playing Nationalism', in A. D. Buckley, *Symbols in Northern Ireland*, Belfast, Institute of Irish Studies, 1998.

Rossi, A., *The Architecture of the City*, trans. D. Ghirardo and J. Ockman, Cambridge MA and London, MIT Press, 1982.

Roth, M., 'Dying of the Past: Medical Studies of Nostalgia in Nineteenth Century France', *History and Memory* 3 (1991), pp. 5–29.

Rowlands, M., 'The Creolization of West-African Culture', *Museums Journal* 91 (1991).

Ryan, R., 'Commemorating 1916', *Retrospect* (1984), pp. 59–62.

Schieffelin, E., 'Performance and the Cultural Construction of Reality', *American Ethnologist* 12 (1985), pp. 707–24.

Schneider, S., 'Rumpelstiltskin's Bargain', in A. Weiner and S. Schneider (eds), *Cloth and Human Experience*, Washington, Smithsonian Institution Press, 1989.

Schoelcher, V., *Vie de Toussaint Louverture*, Paris, Ollendorf, 1889.

Séguin, J.-P., *Le Jeu de cartes*, Paris, Bibliothèque Nationale, 1966.

Shanklin, E., 'The Path to Laikom: Kom Royal Court Architecture', *Paideuma: Mitteilungen zur Kulturkunde* 31 (1985), pp. 111–50.

Sheehy, J., *The Rediscovery of Ireland's Past*, London, Thames & Hudson, 1980.

Sheriff, S., *Recycled Reseen: Folk Art from the Local Scrap Heap*, New York, Harry N. Abrams/Museum of New Mexico, 1996.

Sherman, D., 'Art, Commerce and the production of Memory in France after World War I', in J. R. Gillis (ed.), *Commemorations: The Politics of National Identity*, Princeton, Princeton University Press, 1994.

Springer, P., 'Paradoxie des Ephemeren: Ephemere komponenten in zeitgenössischen Monumenten', in M. Diers (ed.), *Mo(nu)mente, Formen und Funktion ephemerer Denkmale*, Berlin, Akademie Verlag, 1993.

Starke, M., *Travels in Europe for the use of travellers on the Continent*, London, John Murray, 1833.

Steinhauser, M., 'Works of Memory: On Jochen Gerz's Memorials', *Daidalos* 49 (1993), pp. 104–13.

Stone, L., and J. C. Fawtier Stone, *An Open Elite? England 1540–1880*, Oxford, Oxford University Press, 1986.

Strathern, M., 'Artefacts of History: Events and the Interpretation of Images', in J. Siikala (ed.), *Culture and History in the Pacific*, Suomen Antropolisen Seuran toimituksia 27, Helsinki, Finnish Anthropological Society, 1990.

Tardits, C., *Le royaume bamoum*, Paris, Librairie Armand Colin, 1980.

Theuws, J. A., 'Naître et mourir dans le rituel Luba', *Zaïre* 14 (1960), pp. 115–73.

Thompson, M., *Rubbish Theory: the Creation and Destruction of Value*, Oxford and New York, Oxford University Press, 1979. Forward by E. C. Zeeman.

Tilley, C., *A Phenomenology of Landscape: Places, Paths and Monuments*, Oxford, Berg, 1994.

Turner, V., *The Forest of Symbols: Aspects of Ndembu Ritual*, Ithaca and London, Cornell University Press, 1967.

La Vérité en riant ou les tableaux traités comme ils le méritent, en vaudeville, Collection Deloynes, no. 1, Paris, an VI, XIX.

Vinograd, R. E., 'Private Art and Public Knowledge in Later Chinese Painting', in S. Küchler and W. Melion (eds), *Images of Memory: On Remembering and Representation*, Washington D.C., Smithsonian Institution Press, 1991.

Warnier, J.-P., 'Trade Guns in the Grassfields of Cameroon', *Paideuma: Mitteilungen zur Kulturkunde* 26 (1980), pp. 79–92.

Warnier, J.-P., *L'esprit de l'entreprise au Cameroun*, Paris, Karthala, 1993.

Weston, H., 'Representing the Right to Represent: the Portrait of Citizen Belley, Ex-representative of the Colonies by A.-L. Girodet,' *Res* 26

(1994), pp. 83–99.

Whitehouse, H., 'Memorable Religions: Transmission, Codification and Change in Divergent Melanesian Contexts', *Man* (n.s.) 27 (1992), pp. 777–97.

Winter, J. M., *Sites of Memory, Sites of Mourning: The Great War in European Cultural History*, Cambridge, Cambridge University Press, 1995.

Wittkower, R., 'Piranesi 's "Parere Su Archittetura"', *Journal of the Warburg Institute* II (1939), pp. 147–58.

Wolin, S. S., *The Presence of the Past*, Johns Hopkins University Press, Baltimore, 1989.

Yampolsky, M., 'In the Shadow of Monuments', in N. Condee (ed.), *Soviet Hieroglyphics*, London, British Film Institute, 1995.

Yates, F., *The Art of Memory*, London, Routledge & Kegan Paul, 1966.

Young, J. E., *The Art of Memory: Holocaust Memorials in History*, New York, The Jewish Museum/Presto, 1994.

——, *The Texture of Memory: Holocaust memorials and meaning in Europe, Israel and America*, New Haven, Yale University Press, 1993.

Index

abolition of slavery *see* decree of 4 February 1794
Abramson, Daniel, 143
Addison, Joseph, 93, 95–6
'age-value', 4, 15, 114, 122
Agulhon, M., 147
Alexander VII, Pope, 121
All Quiet on the Western Front, 152
ambiguity, 22, 35, 159, 164
Ancient Order of Hibernians, 188
Ankermann, B., 37
Antichità Romane, 111, 115–121
architecture, 24–30
  see also memory, architecture and
    Armistice Day, 155, 161–2, 164, 176
Ashe, Thomas, 190
Assman, Aleida, 59
A Young Child looking at Images in a Book, 82

Bachelard, Gaston, 15–16
banners, 176–182
Beadle, J. Prinsep, 177
Beckford, William, of Fonthill, 112, 114–5, 118–9, 122
Bella, Stefano della, 117
Bellay, Jean-Baptiste Mars, 75–88
Benjamin, Walter, 16, 61
Bianchini, Francesco, 119–20
Binyon, Laurence, 184
Birmingham Post, 163
Bishop of London, 156
Bloch, Maurice, 134
Blomfield, Sir Reginald, 161
'blood and thunder' bands, 180–3
Bodnar, John, 149
Boltanski, Christian, 6
Bonaparte, Napoleon, 78, 80, 85
Bonneville, François, 76
Boyne, Battle of, 174, 176, 179
Brilliant, Richard, 85
Buonamici, Antonio, 120

Camera Sepolcrali, 119
Canaletto, Antonio, 109–10
Capitoline Satyr, 85
Carson, Sir Edward, 175, 182, 191
Casement, Roger, 188
Castoriadis, Cornelius, 137
Certeau, Michel de, 7, 59, 63–4, 68
Charge of the 36th (Ulster) Division, Somme, 1st July 1916, 177, 179
Charity, 97–9
Chateaubriand, François-René de, 85
Chaussard, Pierre-Jean-Baptiste, 75, 81, 84, 86
Chilver, S., 37
Christ the Savour church, Moscow, 10
Cicero, 173
cicerone, 109, 117–18, 122
city, 15, 107–123 *passim*
Clarke, Tom, 185, 188
Club Massiac see Société Correspondante des Colons Français de Sainte-Domingue
collections, 37–8, 55
Commonwealth War Graves Commission, 151, 161
Condorcet, Marquis de, 79
Connerton, Paul, 2, 74, 110, 117, 172
Connolly, James, 185, 188
Cousins, Mark, 130–1
Craig, James, 175, 182
Cumann na Mbhan, 184

Daily Herald, 158
Daily Mail, 158
David, Jacques-Louis, 77, 87
Danto, Arthur, 130
Davis, Susan G.,150
decay, 27, 31, 57, 60, 123
  see also 'age-value'

decree of 4 February 1794, 75–81, 85, 87
Deleuze, Gilles, 132, 143
Della Magnificenza ed Architettura de Romani, 112
Descrizione e Disegno dell' Emissario del Lago Albano, 116
destruction of objects, 61
Disgraced Monuments, 10–11
Duchamp, M., 62
Durkheim, Emile, 2, 134
duty *see* obligation

Easter Rising, 174–5, 178, 184–192 *passim*
Égalité des Couleurs, 83–4
Emmett, Robert, 187
Endymion, 77
epitaphs, 102–3
equality, 81–5
Eustace, J.C., 120
Exposition de l'Elysée, 1797, 77, 80

Falls Road, Belfast, 176
fame, 93–7
Farington, Joseph, 113
fates, 99
figures *see cicerone*
Flags and Emblems Act, 176
Flaxman, John, 113
Folkes, Martin, 99
forgetting, 110, 119, 122, 191–3
  death and *see* mourning
  objects and 1–16 *passim*
    destroying, 1, 9–12, 53, 58
    making, 1, 9–10
  necessity of, 1, 7–8
  processes of,
    separation, 8–9
    exclusion, 9–10
    'burial', 58–62
  will-to-forget, 86–88
  see also memory
'For the Fallen', 184
Forsyth, Joseph, 113–14
Foundations of Castel S. Angelo, 117
Frauenkirche, Dresden, 9–10
Freemasons, 189
Freud, Sigmund, 107, 130, 132, 136, 143
  see also memory, Freudian model; mourning

Gadie, Alderman, 163
Gaelic Athletic Association, 187–8
Galbaud, General, 78
Geary, C., 29
Geertz, Clifford, 147, 149
Gell, Alfred, 34
Gellée, Claude, 109
gender, 179
Gerz, Jochen, 6–7
Gibbs, Philip, 152
Gillis, , J.R., 64
Ginzberg, Carlo, 54
Girodet, 75–88
'God of the market', 38–41
Goethe, J.W. von, 108, 111, 114, 118–9
Goldsmith, Oliver, 97, 104
Gombrich, Ernst, 173
gratitude *see* obligation
Grégoire, Abbé, 79
grief, 94, 97–103 *passim*, 130, 139, 157–8
  see also mourning
guidebooks, 109–10, 112–13
Griswold, C.L., 141

Haarlem, 110
Halbwachs, Maurice, 171
Halliday, Anthony, 82
Hare, Augustus, 107
Harrison, Simon, 62–3
Haughey, Charles, 192
Hazlitt, William, 114
Hédouville, General, 80
heritage, 53, 60
herms, 85–6
Hervey, James, 93–4, 103
'historical value', 115, 122
history paintings, 81–2, 84, 88
Hobhouse, J.C., 113
Hollar, Wencelaus, 109
Holocaust *see* memory, Holocaust and; monuments, Holocaust memorials
Home Government Association, 174
Home Rule Bill, 174, 192
Home Rule League, 174
Hope Fredrick William, 112
Hubert, H., 134

iconoclasm *see* forgetting and objects, destroying; monuments, destruction

inheritance, 94, 101–2, 104
Imperial War Graves Commission *see* Commonwealth War Graves Commission
insurrections *see* Sainte-Domingue insurrections
intellectual property, 62–8 *passim*
interpretation, 148–150, 158, 162, 164, 183
interregnum, 8, 20–68 *passim*
IRA, 185, 187–8, 190
Irish National Foresters, 188–9
Irish Party, 192
Irish Republican Socialist Party, 188
Irish Volunteers, 189, 192

Jewish Museum extension to Berlin Museum, 16
Johns, Jasper, 2
Journey's End, 154

Kantorowicz, Ernst, 8, 54–5, 59, 65
Kapferer, Bruce, 133–4
Kitchener, Lord, 175
Klee, Paul, 62
Krauss, Rosalind, 139
Kundera, Milan, 11

Leclerc, General, 80
Le Déménagement du Sallon ou le Portrait de Gilles, 82
L'Egalité accordée aux Noirs, 82
Lemprun, Jorge, 6
Letters from Italy, 112
Lewis, Mark, 10
Libeskind, Daniel, 16
Lin, Maya, 137, 139, 142
Luria, Alexander, 1
Lurgan, 176
Lutyens, Sir Edward, 161

McCrea, Stevie, 183–4
McManus, T.B., 189
McMichael, John, 183–4
MacSwiney, Terence, 190
malangann, 5, 55–9, 64–8
Manchester Guardian, 163
Markievicz, Countess, 186
masquerade, 22, 41–5
Mauss, M., 134
meaning of death, 151, 156–8, 164
mementoes *see* souvenirs
memorials *see* monuments; war memorials
memory, 1–16 *passim*, 20–1, 53–68 *passim*, 93, 110, 114
  alterity and, 63–4
  animatorical, 60, 63
  architecture and, 14–16
  Aristotlean model, 2–4, 15, 54
  bodily 24, 41–5
    see also habit memory
  cognitive, 2
  collective, 2 , 15, 54, 109–110, 122, 133
    see also memory, social
  commemoration, 147–164 *passim*, 171–193 *passim*
  computers and, 54, 61
  eschatological, 59–60
  familiar, 108
  Freudian model, 5–6, 59
  habit, 23–4, 41–5
  Holocaust and, 6–7, 12–13, 16
    see also monuments, Holocaust memorials
  images and, 173
  'incorporated', 117–19, 122
  'inscribed', 110, 118–19
  location and, 7, 53–72 *passim*
  memoria, 53–4, 59, 61
  mneme, 54
  objects and, 2
  performative *see* habit
  social, 171–2, 180, 193
    see also memory, collective
  see also fame; forgetting; monuments; war memorials
'Memory Piece (Frank O'Hara)', 2–3
metamorphosis, 22–3, 32–4, 38, 42–3
Michel, Régis, 85
Miller, Lady Anne, 112, 117
Misiano, Viktor, 10
monuments, 4, 6–13, 53–5, 93–104 *passim*
  County Antrim Memorial, 187
  destruction of, 10–12. 53, 58
  dialogical space of, 55, 62
  ephemeral monuments, 4–5, 20–68 *passim*, 151

Hamburg memorial against fascism, 6
Lincoln memorial, 138–9, 141, 143
Holocaust memorials, 129, 142–3
Memorial to Austrian Jews for Judenplatz, Vienna, 12–13, 129, 132
Saarbrucken, 7
see also memory, Holocaust and
funerary effigies and sculptures, 8–9, 30–2, 54–5
Bishop Beckington at Wells, 8
Bishop John Hough at Worcester Cathedral, 102–3
Duke of Argyll at Westminster Abbey, 9
Duke and Duchess of Montagu at Warkton Church, Northants, 97–101, 103
Field Marshall George Wade at Westminster Abbey, 9, 95–7
French kings at St Denis, 8
George Lynn at Southwick, Northants, 101, 103
Hargrave at Westminster Abbey, 96–7, 103
Mary Myddelton at Wrexham, 103
memorials and, 130–1, 144
maintenance, 150–1
see also war memorials
mourning, 129–137 *passim*, 143, 147, 158, 179, 189
see also grief
murals, 183–7
Ardoyne, 185
Donegal pass, 183
Roden Street, 183
Unity Flats, 185
Whiterock Road, 185–6
Woodvale, 183
Mulvey, Laura, 10

names, 65–7, 93, 101, 138–144 *passim*
see also fame; inheritance
nation, 133–141 *passim*
National Graves Association, 187
New Ireland, 5, 55–9, 64–8
Newry, 176
New York Times, 7–8
Northern Ireland, 8, 171–193 *passim*
Northampton, Lord, 160

obligation, 94, 100, 102, 151, 156, 158
see also inheritance
O'Connell, Daniel, 188
Oku, Cameroon, 20–68
O'Neill government, 176
Orange Order, 176–183, 187, 189
Owen, Wilfred, 162

Paisley, Revd Ian, 176
Panini, Paolo, 114
parades, 150, 173–193 *passim*
Parere su Architettura, 115
Peace Pledge Union, 161
Pearse, Padraig, 185–9
photographs, 1, 62
Picasso, Pablo, 62
Piozzi, Hester Lynch, 120
Piramide de C. Cestio, 121–2
Piranesi, Giovanni Battista, 60, 74, 107–123
politics, 148–9, 157–8, 160, 165, 187–8
Portrait of Citizen Belley, Ex-Representative of the Colonies, 75–88 *passim*
Pothos (Desire), 85
power, 24, 26, 38, 41–5, 150, 160, 164–5, 171–2
Prima Parte di Architettura e Prospettive, 111
Proclamation of Independence, 175, 185–7
Proust, Marcel, 16, 54
Pyramid of Cestius, 117, 119–121
see also Vedute del Sepolcro di Cajo Cestio, Piramide de C. Cestio

Raynal, Abbé Guillaume-Thomas, 79–87 *passim*
recyclia *see* rubbish
Red Hand Commando, 182–3
Redmond, John, 192
regicide, 29–30
Remarque, Erich Maria, 152
Renan, Ernest, 7
repetition, 132
Republican Sinn Féin, 188
Ribbonmen, 189

Riegl, Alois, 4, 15, 62, 115, 117, 122
rite de passage, 85–6
Robespierre, Maximilien, 78, 80, 87–8
Robinson, Brian, 183–4
Robson, James, 111
Rome, 107–123
Rosa, Salvator, 117
Rossa, O'Donovan, 187, 189
Rossi, Aldo, 15
Rossi, Girolami, 119–120
Roth, Michael, 60
Roubiliac, Louis Francois, 8, 93–104 *passim*
rubbish, 61–2
Ruisdale, Jacob van, 109

sacrifice, 54–8 *passim*, 131–137 *passim*, 141–4, 151, 157, 176, 182, 184–5, 189–191
Sainte-Domingue insurrections, 78, 80, 83, 86
Salon of 1796, 76
Salon of 1798, 76, 78, 81
Sands, Bobby, 185, 190
Schieffelin, Edward L., 23
Scopas, 85
Shankill Road, 176
Sherriff, R.C., 154
silence, 161–2, 164
Sinn Féin, 175, 184, 186–8
Siphnos, 85
Société des Amis des Noirs, 79
Société Correspondante des Colons Français de Sainte-Domingue, 79
society, 150
Somme, Battle of, 174–184, 188, 190–1
souvenirs, 62, 67, 110
Staatsgalerie, Stuttgart, 14
state, 149–150
Stirling, James, 14
Stone, Lawrence, 101
surprise, 22, 31, 36, 40–1, 44

The Death of Marat, 87
The Special Powers Act, 176
'The Troubles', 178, 180
Time, 96–7
tombs *see* monuments, war memorials
Tomb of L. Arrunzio, 117–9
Tomb of the Household of Augustus, 119
topography, 109–112
Toussaint-Louverture, 80
Trades Council, 188
Turner, Victor, 34–5
'twins', 32–5, 40

Ulster Covenant, 182
Ulster Defence Association, 182–3
Ulster Division, 175, 180–4
Ulster Unionist Council, 174
Ulster Volunteer Force, 174–184 *passim*
United Irishmen, 185, 187

Vasi, Giuseppe, 111
Vedute del Sepolcro di Cajo Cestio, 121
Vedute di Roma, 108, 111–12, 121
Veldte, Essias van de, 110
Versailles, 77, 81
Victoria Crosses, 192
'View of the Bridge and Castello Sant'Angelo', 107–8
Vinograd, R., 60–1
Visscher, Claes Janz, 110

Wales, Prince of, 157
Warburg, Aby, 54
Warkton Church, Northants, 97–9
war memorials, 9, 55, 127–195 *passim*
  Anzac memorial, Sydney, 133–5, 143
  First World War memorials, 129, 147–165 *passim*, 176
    Bradford war memorial, 152, 155, 162–3
    Brancepeth war memorial, 158
    Islington memorial, 159–160
    London Brighton and South Coast Railway's memorial, 158
    London memorial, Mansion House, 152–3
    memorial to the missing of the Somme, Thiepval, 157
    Port Sunlight memorial, 152, 154
    Stoke Newington memorial, 156, 160
    The Cenotaph, Belfast City Hall, 178
    The Cenotaph, Whitehall, 161–2
    The Unknown Warrior, Westminster Abbey, 163
  morality and, 152, 154–6, 162–3

Vietnam Veterans Memorial, Washington, 129–131, 137–144
victims of genocide in Cambodia, 129
violence and, 152
war of independence in Zimbabwe, 129
see also monuments; murals
Westminster Abbey, 9, 93–6, 163
Whiteread, Rachel, 12–13, 129–130, 132
Wilford, Michael, 14
Wilson, Richard, 109
Winckelmann, Joachim, 112
Wolfe, Tom, 138, 141
Wolf Tone, 185
Women's Co-operative Guild, 161
Workers Party, 188

Yampolsky, Mikhail, 11
Yates, Frances, 53
Young, James, 6, 62, 129
Young Citizen Volunteers, 181